Tom Beardsley

Our Little Army in the Field

OUR LITTLE ARMY IN THE FIELD

The Canadians In South Africa
1899-1902

Brian A.Reid

Vanwell Publishing Limited

St. Catharines, Ontario

Vanwell Publishing Limited
1 Northrup Crescent, Box 2131
St. Catharines, Ontario L2M 6P5

First edition 1996
Printed in Canada
99 98 97 96   1 2 3 4 5

Design Susan Nicholson

Canadian Cataloguing in Publication Data

Reid, Brian A.
Our Little Army in the Field : The Canadians in South Africa, 1899-1902

Includes bibliographical references and index.
ISBN 1-55125-024-1

1. South African War, 1899-1902 - Participation,
Canadian. 2. South African War, 1899-1902 - Campaigns.
3. Canada. Canadian Army - History - South African
War, 1899-1902. I. Title

DT1913.C3R45 1996   968.04'84   C95-932651-0

Table of Contents

Introduction

IN CONVENTIONAL wisdom, the Boer war of 1899-1902 remains the nadir of military achievement. If South Africa provided an unwelcome dose of reality to the British, the experience was much more positive for Canadians. Canada emerged from the war with a well-earned military reputation, albeit one earned as a bit player. It was more than chauvinism that prompted the chief staff officer in Ottawa to write on 31 May 1900, "We will be getting conceited about our little army in the field." That is not to say that Canadian performance was beyond reproach. Their story is a mosaic of inspiration and incompetence, of advantages seized and opportunities missed, of brilliance, and of blunders. Still, on balance Canadians showed that they could hold their own against a competent, agile enemy.

At the time the concept of Canadian, separate from British citizenship, was very much undeveloped. I believe that any attempt to define these men by age, occupation, or birthplace misses the point. Whatever their social station, they had all volunteered to fight. Melded by danger and discipline into cohesive fighting units, native born and immigrant alike were Canadian in their approach and attitude. As for their motivation, some were no doubt patriots while others sought adventure, glory, or even escape. As in any volunteer force, most were driven by a combination of motives. A number were, to paraphrase a comment about the men who fought in Korea half a century later, soldiers of fortune and not the type "we want in the regular army." Like most Canadians of the time they considered anyone who was not a white, male citizen of the British Empire as an inferior being and that probably was among their more progressive opinions. Before dismissing them as politically incorrect Neanderthals, remember that most obeyed the Ten Commandments for the most part, except that looting for other than personal profit was not really theft, regardless of what the Queen's Regulations said.

I am neither a trained historian nor an accomplished author. I could only bring to the task professional insight gained from more than three decades in Canadian uniform and a fascination with the subject. I have deliberately avoided political issues, except as seen by the soldier in the field. If my criticism of the Liberal party seems harsh, I doubt that the Conservative party of the time would have done things very much differently.

I relied as much as possible on primary sources such as unit diaries, letters, and private diaries, as well as contemporary personal accounts and histories. The war generated a flood of books of varying quality. The best overview of the Canadian experience is Evans's *Canadian Contingents*. The reader is cautioned to approach popular works such as *Canada's Sons on Kopje and Veldt* or Sir Arthur Conan Doyle's history carefully. The best works by Canadians who served in the field are Hart-McHarg's *From Quebec to Pretoria with the Royal Canadian Regiment* and Morrison's *With the Guns in South Africa*. A cut below, but still useful are Hubly's *G Company* and Brown's *With the Royal Canadians*. Both *The Times History* and the German General Staff history proved invaluable in placing events in perspective. Most recent works are useful and Carman Miller's *Painting the Map Red* is required reading for anyone interested in Canada's part in the war.

I owe a great deal to a large number of people. The volunteers of the Kemptville Public Library were able to track down some valuable references via the interlibrary loan system. The

National Defence Headquarters reference library has a staggering amount of information in its collection; my thanks to its staff for allowing me to retain a number of volumes for longer than the regulation period. The staff at the Canadian War Museum, the National Library of Canada, and especially the National Archives of Canada were, as always, most helpful and professional throughout. Valuable assistance was provided by the Royal Canadian Dragoons, Lord Strathcona's Horse (Royal Canadians), the Royal Regiment of Canadian Artillery, and The Royal Canadian Regiment. Special thanks go to R. Guy Carrington Smith of Brockville for providing me copies of the correspondence of Captain Herbert Carrington Smith. Ron Haycock provided helpful insights into Sam Hughes, although I am sure he would not agree with my harsh assessment of that most remarkable Canadian. Both Carman Miller and Tony Kellett provided useful assistance and encouragement. This work owes much to the advice and counsel of Mike McNorgan and Bob Caldwell who read and commented on chapters, often many times. I owe an immense amount to Vanwell Publishing for taking a chance on an inexperienced author. Thanks to my editor, Harold Otto, who seems to have fostered no hard feelings for his experiences as a subaltern in Halifax's First Field Artillery Regiment when I was Chief Instructor in Gunnery at the Artillery School in Gagetown. The other members of the "Kemptville Express" provided a long-suffering audience for my Boer War anecdotes during commutes to and from Ottawa. Last, my deepest appreciation to my wife, Tish, who endured the endless clatter of my keyboard, and Champ, our Yellow Lab, who was ever ready to safeguard my files by sleeping on them.

Although I am reasonably confident that conclusions and interpretations can be supported by the available data, I make no claim of infallibility. Responsibility for any errors in interpretation is mine alone. I hope you enjoy reading this work at least as much as I enjoyed writing it.

Chapter

1 Background To The War

SOUTH AFRICA was made up of two British colonies, Cape Colony and Natal, and two Boer republics, the Orange Free State (OFS) and the Transvaal. A number of contemporary works described the background to the war in detail. Most, with the exception of *The Transvaal Outlook*, were pro-British or at best, barely neutral. A number took extreme positions and one went so far as to suggest, in pseudo-Darwinism, that the Boers were regressing into apes. A confrontation probably was inevitable.

From the time the British gained a foothold in southern Africa during the Napoleonic Wars, the relationship between Britons and Afrikanders was one of mutual dislike and distrust interspersed with periodic clashes of arms and wills. The presence of powerful, warlike black nations on the frontiers forced somewhat reluctant cooperation between the two self-righteous, nationalistic white tribes. The defeat of the Zulus by the British in 1879, however, removed the main threat to the predominantly Boer Orange Free State and Transvaal (ZAR) and war broke out in 1880. The British lost a number of minor battles, including the debacle of Majuba Hill on 27 February 1881. While humiliating, these defeats were not decisive; nevertheless, the Gladstone government capitulated with indecent haste. The Boers drew conclusions that would prove fatal to their aspirations two decades later.

The Transvaal soon prospered from the exploitation of the vast gold deposits discovered in 1886. The mines attracted adventurers and merchants from around the world—the "Uitlanders." While the Boers were quite happy to exploit the fruits of the Uitlanders' labour by heavy taxation, they were not prepared to grant a universal franchise, especially as many Uitlanders openly advocated annexation by Britain. The strains were compounded by the Uitlanders' perception that the administration of the Transvaal was incompetent, corrupt, and arrogant. All of this provoked demands for Britain to annex the Transvaal, which in turn hardened the intransigence of the burghers.

The Jameson raid mounted on 27 December 1895 from British territory aimed to overthrow the Transvaal government. The ill-advised and ill-fated operation soon collapsed with the surrender of Jameson and his men at Doornkop southwest of Johannesburg on 2 January 1896. The blatant violation of the Transvaal's sovereignty not only hardened attitudes on both sides, but also alienated many Boers living in the Cape Colony and Natal.

Despite claims to the contrary, there is evidence that annexation is precisely what British policy aimed at. The distinction between the legitimate exercise of British policy and the imperial and commercial aspirations of Cecil Rhodes and his cronies became blurred. It seemed inevitable that some kind of South African political union would be forged sooner or later. From the British point of view, the ideal solution was peaceful union under the Crown. If union could not be achieved peacefully, it had to be accomplished by force.[1]

The British people were proud of their empire and confident of their place at the centre of the world. Even those who deplored the exploitation of lesser nations could find little attractive in the actions of the Boer republics. Tolerance is very fine up to a point, but when a collection of ignorant farmers persecuted British citizens and belittled British institutions, enough was enough. While this position was not universally held, the majority of the British press and public accepted the premise that concern for the welfare of the Uitlanders was the reason for the growing conflict with the OFS and ZAR. Those who pondered strategic considerations must have realized that Britain's interests would best be served by compliant Boer states, especially if under British rule. By the close of the 1890s the atmosphere had dissolved into mistrust and dislike.

A characteristic of democracies, often misinterpreted as weakness, is the resolution of disputes by noisy debate. The insular Boers may have misread the British will because of the diverse views expounded publicly. That is not to say that the Boers were not willing to fight, but their faith in their own position was reinforced by the belief that the British lacked the will to see the affair through to the end. Many Boer leaders had convinced themselves that one or more European powers would intervene on their side, just as had happened in the American Revolution.

Natal and the Cape Colony were not united against the Boer position. In the months preceding the war, large quantities of rifle ammunition were openly shipped up the western railway line with the knowledge of the Cape government. In the last weeks of peace, prominent Cape politicians were openly advocating neutrality. As large areas of the Cape and Natal were openly sympathetic to the Boer cause, the outbreak of war could have led to rebellion and the emergence of a third Boer republic.

The British garrisons in South Africa were pitifully small, two and a half infantry battalions in the Cape Colony and two cavalry regiments, four artillery batteries and three infantry battalions in Natal facing potentially 40 000 to 60 000 Boers. On the eve of war a further 10 000 troops from India and two other battalions arrived in Natal, just in the nick of time. As well, several thousand troops had been raised locally although these would be of limited use for some time to come.

The British army planned to despatch an army corps to the front. This was easier said than done. The only force of any size that had fought since the Indian Mutiny was Wolseley's at Tel-el-Kebir, a small infantry corps and a cavalry division. More recently, only two British and four Egyptian and Sudanese brigades had fought at Omdurman. The corps was finally mobilized on 7 October 1899, after arguments between the army and the treasury over whether it could be reduced by the reinforcements already sent. By recalling reservists to the colours and scraping together troops from the corners of the Empire, a corps of 50 000 men was formed. As it was, the corps would not be complete and ready for action in South Africa until four to five months had passed. From their perspective on the veldt, the Boers detected ominous signs of British preparations for war. The moderate and sympathetic British commander-in-chief was replaced. British reinforcements were ordered from India and Malta, and Natal was reinforced from the Cape. The British, faced with the unpalatable course of invading two small white countries, delayed action as long as possible. If the British could not be provoked into aggression, then the Transvaal must choose the time to strike. The Orange Free State was less enthusiastic, but would support its fellow republic. It became a matter of striking before the British could build up overwhelming forces while waiting until the southern spring covered the veldt with grass to feed the Boer ponies. On 9 October the Transvaal presented an ultimatum couched in very undiplomatic language. If a satisfactory reply was not received by 5:00 p.m. on Wednesday, 11 October 1899, the Transvaal warned: "it will, with great regret, be compelled to regard the action of Her Majesty's Government as a formal declaration of war." The British rejected the ultimatum.[2]

Access to and from the Boer republics was limited by mountain passes, rivers and plains to a few approaches along the railway lines. From west to east from Cape Town these were the western line from Cape Town to Bulawayo in Rhodesia (now Zimbabwe); the central line from Port Elizabeth and South London joining in the southern OFS and running northeast through Bloemfontein and Kroonstad to Pretoria and on to Pietersburg in the northern Transvaal; the Natal railway running northwest from Durban to Johannesburg; and the Delagoa Bay line running east from Pretoria to the seaport of Lourenço Marques in Portuguese East Africa (now Mozambique). The Boers were in a strong position with a secure eastern frontier. The frontier with Bechuanaland (now Botswana) and Rhodesia could be screened by light forces, although it was some time before the Boers appreciated that the British could not mount a major offensive from that direction. This left the three main approaches along the western, central, and Natal railway lines.

Strategic options were sacrificed by the pledge of the president of the Orange Free State to not invade the Cape Colony. The two approaches into Natal, one from the Transvaal and the other from the OFS, were both east of Basutoland through the formidable barrier of the Drakensberg Range. The Transvaal approach followed the railway through Laing's Nek to Dundee, Ladysmith, and on to the sea at Durban. The OFS approach ran east via Van Reenan's Pass to join the other approach at Ladysmith. The Boers knew that the British garrison in Natal was weak and that reinforcements were en route from India and other places. Some pushed for an advance to the coast at Durban. If Durban fell, the British would have been faced with immense political and military difficulties. Most of the troops so hastily rushed from India and other colonies would be dead or prisoners, while the army corps could not be complete for several weeks. British forces in the Cape Midlands and along the Orange River would be out on a very long limb, threatened by overwhelming forces and disheartened by the example of Natal. Such a course was beyond the comprehension of the Boers, who opted for a more limited objective. This sacrificed any chance of victory and made the re-annexation of the Boer republics inevitable.

The British recognized that war with the Transvaal was a near certainty, but were less sure of the motives and actions of the OFS. This had resulted in a decision to concentrate forces in Natal to absorb the expected attack from the Transvaal and then advance along the railway to the Transvaal capital of Pretoria. Lighter forces would screen the frontier with the OFS and the Transvaal in the Cape Midlands, where the central line crossed the Orange River, and along the western line. Later when the build-up of forces was complete, the British planned to pressure the OFS to either declare war or to guarantee its neutrality (which probably included agreeing to some sort of British occupation). The British Cabinet, before the outbreak of war, had directed the army to plan an advance up the central line through the OFS capital of Bloemfontein to Pretoria.

Any British optimism concerning the possible neutrality of the OFS was dispelled when both republics invaded Natal during the night of 11 October 1899. Unfortunately, political pressure led to a decision to surrender as little territory as possible, while General White chose to defend Ladysmith rather than carry the war to the enemy in strength. Divided objectives and unclear aims usually lead to disaster. Natal was not to prove the exception to the rule. Ladysmith, at the junction of two railway lines and blessed with abundant water, was a valuable forward base for an offensive into enemy territory, and thus it had strategic importance for both sides. However, Ladysmith was a poor defensive position, dominated by a ring of surrounding hills. Once it was besieged, the relief of White's force there would be a dominant feature of the war in Natal for months.

The Boers were forced to deal with British forces on their northern and western flanks in Bechuanaland and Rhodesia as well in the Far North Cape. The Boers, aided by Cape rebels, quickly dominated a large area from Kenhardt and Upington near German South West Africa (now Namibia), east along the Orange River basin, and north along the railway to Bechuanaland and Rhodesia, where the British were forced back from the Limpopo River. Only tiny Mafeking and the diamond mining centre of Kimberley still held out.

The Cape Midlands were left alone for the time being, but on 1 November Boers captured the police posts at the Orange River bridges and advanced cautiously into British territory, splitting the British forces and jeopardizing the strategy of a thrust along the central line. Once again the lack of a killer instinct worked against the republics. The Boers probably could have driven to Naauwpoort and then west to De Aar, isolating the British on the Orange River.

In the meantime, the first troops of the army corps were beginning to arrive under the command of General Sir Redvers Buller, VC.

British senior officers were divided into two groups, the "Wolseley Gang" and the "Roberts Gang," named for the two distinguished soldiers. Wolseley's reputation was earned in Africa, while Roberts had served in India. In 1899 Wolseley was the professional head of the British army while Roberts was commanding the British forces in Ireland, putting in time until he retired. Buller was a member of the "Wolseley Gang" who had served in the Red River expedition where he had impressed the Canadians by packing 200- and 300-pound loads across portages. It would have been inconceivable for Wolseley to appoint a Roberts man to command the corps. It would have been just as impossible for Roberts, who superseded Buller, not to blame Buller, and by extension, Wolseley, for the British defeats and disasters. While most historians followed the lead of *The Times History*, in condemning Buller, his reputation has been restored somewhat in recent years.[3]

Chapter

2   **The Players**

THE FIGHTING BOERS

THE ARMIES OF THE TWO Boer republics were, with some exceptions, "non-active militia," loosely organized into units called "commandos." Military affairs were managed by a commandant general assisted by five assistant commandant generals, all elected for a term of up to ten years. Each of the districts provided a commando under an elected commandant. Commandos, which ranged in size from less than 300 to nearly 3000 were divided into two or more field cornetcies of 150 to 200 men, which were subdivided into corporalships of 25 men. In practice the size of field cornetcies and corporalships was flexible. A burgher was free to decide which officer he would serve with and could even choose his own commando. In all the Boer forces probably numbered between 40 000 and 45 000 at the start of the war on 11 October 1899.[1]

Developed in response to the threat posed to the Voertrekkers by the black tribes, the commandos could be mobilized quickly and effectively. With some exceptions based on occupation, all able-bodied burghers between 16 and 60 were liable for military service, although there was fairly widespread evasion of service. Individuals mustered locally and were required to report with a rifle and ammunition (provided by the government at a nominal cost), a horse, saddle and bridle, and food for eight days. There were no uniforms, the men trusting to their own judgement and personal preference. To the modern eye, the Boers appear to have been a cruel caricature of an army dressed in rumpled jackets, collars, and ties. Closer inspection reveals determined men with clean, modern rifles, full bandoliers, and well-cared-for horses. The Boers were excellent horsemen, good shots and well able to live on the featureless veldt.[2]

Besides the citizen soldiers of the commandos, there were foreign volunteers and even a few regulars in the Boer forces. The Boers' cause was popular outside of the British Empire. The image of two plucky little republics facing the might of the Empire attracted an eclectic collection of anglophobes, adventurers, and idealists. The Boer attitude to the foreign contingents was, at best, ambivalent. There was little encouragement and assistance for volunteers, and relatively few were able to make their way to South Africa. The total, including Uitlanders, that took to the field probably did not exceed a few thousand. Those who went fought bravely with a casualty rate on occasion much higher than the Boers. The image begat reality, and, to borrow a marketing term, the sizzle of the foreign contingents was more important than the steak of their limited numbers.[3]

The only regular forces were the two state artilleries and the Transvaal Police, the "ZARPs." The latter, from the initials for South African Republic Police in the Boer language, were tough young Boers who earned an enviable reputation as "slim" fighters. However, the number that actually took to the field, roughly 1400, was not significant. The contribution of the state artilleries was a different matter. Equipped with modern guns and trained by foreign professionals, they proved to be a potent force. The two artilleries combined numbered only about 60 modern guns. Consequently the Boers were outgunned in most of their battles, although they learned to compensate for the imbalance by dispersing and concealing their guns during the early stages of the engagement. The Boer gunners were respected and, an indication of their ability, credited with feats beyond their potential.[4]

Aimed rifle fire by skilled marksmen was the backbone of Boer tactics, although there was no effort to direct and control the fire of individual burghers. The method of fighting was unmethodical and haphazard, and the Boers rarely maintained a reserve. Given the want of military training, leadership, and organization as well as the almost total lack of discipline, Boer commanders dared not attempt too much. The future of the people depended upon the safe return of the males, and therefore the Boer saw no virtue in dying for his country. War was to be won at the lowest possible cost. What had started as a spirited defence might deteriorate into a rush for the horses, and the last men could be in for an unpleasant surprise. Two captured American volunteers complained, "When ... it is time to get out, he [the Boer] takes the first horse he can catch, if his own is not handy; ... [W]hen we ... looked round for our horses, we found they had taken them, and of course we couldn't get away."[5]

The scruffy, psalm-singing Boers must have appeared hopelessly archaic and comical to the British regulars. On the surface, there were some valid reasons to underestimate the Boers. First, they were puritanical and believed implicitly that they were resisting the enemies of the Almighty. Second, they were unschooled in the military art and their tactics flowed from instinct, rarely the best of teachers. Third, they were a mounted rabble in an era when "real" armies were based on well drilled-infantry.[6]

The commando system allowed the Boers to mobilize quickly and gain the initiative in the early weeks of the war. By ignoring opportunities to win at this time, the Boers allowed the initiative to pass to the British. The Boers could, however, rapidly exploit a tactical advantage and defeat an overextended force. This frustrates the foe and reinforces the image of highly capable mobile forces, but rarely wins wars against determined commanders and courageous troops. This was more a case of circumstance than of military genius, but, by any criteria, the Boer was a first-class enemy and an excellent fighter. Unfortunately, the Boers must join the ranks of soldiers whose military accomplishments were undermined by the remorseless military maxim that God is on the side of the big battalions.

THE BRITISH ARMY

British soldiers had fought in one dangerous corner of the world or another during every year of Queen Victoria's reign. Most campaigns were small affairs involving no more than a few thousand British troops supplemented by locally raised levies. Even so, a battalion might see considerable action on overseas service, especially if posted to India or Egypt. However, for every battalion that saw active service, two or three paraded and polished at home or in outposts like Jamaica, Malta, or Hong Kong. Some battalions had not fought in four decades. Still, regiments garrisoned the Empire from Bermuda and Halifax to the Khyber Pass and China. Table 2.1 shows the distribution of British Army units in 1898-9.

Table 2.1 Distribution Of Units Of The British Army 1898-9

Location	Infantry Battalions	Cavalry Regiments	Field Artillery Batteries	Garrison Artillery Companies	Engineer Companies
Home	78	19	68	46	45
Abroad	79	12	66	64	16
Total	**157**	**31**	**134**	**110**	**61**

In round numbers the army numbered a quarter of a million regulars supplemented by half a million reservists, militia, yeomanry, and volunteers. The reservists were ex-regulars who were required to report to their old regiment on mobilization. Militia, yeomanry, and volunteers were part-time soldiers formed into units of varying degrees of efficiency.[7]

Table 2.2 traces the chain of command and organizations with the rank that filled the appointments at the time.[8]

Table 2.2 Chain of Command of the British Army in the Boer War

Theatre or Army
(Field Marshall or General)
⇩
Corps
(General or Lieutenant General)
⇩
Division
(Lieutenant General)
⇩
Brigade
(Major General, Brigadier General or Colonel)
⇩
Battalion, Regiment or Brigade Division (Artillery)
(Lieutenant Colonel)
⇩
Company, Squadron or Battery
(Major or Captain)
⇩
Troop, Artillery Section or Half Company
(Lieutenant or Second Lieutenant)
⇩
Cavalry or Infantry Section or Artillery Sub Section
(Sergeant with one or more Corporals)
⇩
Private, Trooper, Gunner or Driver
(referred to collectively as "men")

Besides the field army there was another organization that reported to the commander-in-chief, the Lines of Communications. This organization which could be fully as large as the field army, existed to support the army in the field and to administer occupied territory. It included organizations to run the ports and to despatch troops and materiel forward to the front, hospitals and recuperation camps to care for the sick and wounded, a remount department to resupply the army with horses and mules, depots to stockpile supplies, workshops to repair damaged equipment, finance offices to pay the bills, a railway network, military prisons, and prisoner-of-war camps.

The British army, on paper, should have easily crushed the Boer forces. That it did not is as least as much due to British tactical sclerosis as to Boer aptitude. J.F.C. Fuller's observation that the British had spent 84 years preparing for another Waterloo is not too great an overstatement. Furthermore, the studied amateurism of the officer class coupled with the docile obedience of the men in the ranks combined to produce an army both unprepared for war against an elusive enemy on the veldt and incapable of easy adjustment to changing conditions.[9]

BRITISH ARMY TACTICS

The infantry battalion commanded by a lieutenant colonel was the basic fighting element of the army. A battalion was made up of a small headquarters and eight companies each commanded by a captain or major with two lieutenants or second lieutenants. Each company was divided into four sections of about 20 men commanded by a sergeant. A full-strength battalion was authorized 29 officers including a doctor, one warrant officer, 51 senior NCOs, and 929 rank and file. Units were rarely at full strength. In February 1900 the 29 British battalions in Lord Roberts' army averaged 22 officers and 811 men or 82% of their war establishment.[10]

The cavalry was the social elite of the army. A cavalry regiment commanded by a lieutenant colonel fielded three or four squadrons divided into four troops, each under a lieutenant or second lieutenant. A three-squadron regiment numbered 25 officers and 506 men. As was the case with the infantry, cavalry regiments were often understrength.

Conditions in South Africa were particularly hard on horses. Nowhere was this more evident than in the regular cavalry, which was notorious for abysmal horse care and conservation. In an effort to conserve horses, exceptional efforts were taken to lighten the loads carried and units would often dismount and walk their horses for every other hour. One successful mounted commander remarked that this was deliberately hard on the men and easy on the horses as a soldier could "go sick" or raise objections, while a horse could not.[11]

The British had developed mounted infantry (MI) in response to the long distances to be covered in earlier campaigns in Africa. Every home-based battalion trained a number of men as mounted infantrymen to be grouped into MI battalions in war. To complicate matters, an MI company operated on a different establishment from either marching infantry or cavalry. A company, commanded by a major or captain, had five officers and 137 men. MI rode into battle, but fought on foot. It did not take the British long to realize that mounted men were the key to coping with the Boers, and they embarked on a scheme of raising several MI battalions. Every regular battalion in South Africa gave up a company to be trained as MI. The army also organized a number of irregular mounted units, distinguished by their unusual dress and discipline, and described by a certain Major Douglas Haig as "scallywag corps." Another general described one unit as full of men he would not care to have bivouac on his estate. The quality of mounted troops varied from excellent to poor because of variations in the time and care taken in their training. The story of the mounted infantryman who ended up in the saddle facing the rear of his horse is not apocryphal.

Most units had a small section of one or two machine guns. These weapons were of two types, the Maxim and the air-cooled Colt. While the Maxim had a higher rate of fire, 600 rounds a minute compared with 480 for the Colt, most mounted units preferred the Colt. This was primarily because of the superior mobility of the Colt, which was mounted on a light "Dundonald" carriage drawn by a single horse.[12] A variation of the machine gun was the pom-pom, named for the noise it made when fired. The pom-pom was a British manufactured automatic cannon that fired a one-pound shell. The pom-pom was originally used by the Boers, but not the British, who hurriedly followed their example. While it was unnerving to be on the receiving end of a burst of pom-pom fire, troops soon learned that its bark was much worse than its bite.[13]

In war, battalions and regiments were formed into brigades. An infantry brigade normally consisted of four battalions, although some fought with three, while a cavalry brigade had two or three cavalry regiments. Two brigades with supporting troops made up a division. Besides the brigades, a division included an MI battalion, an engineer company, and medical and transport units. However, the most visible supporting element was the field artillery. Horse artillery, a variation of field artillery, supported the cavalry.

The British field gun was the 15-pounder, which resembled its predecessor the 12-pounder, which was still in use by the horse artillery and the Canadians. The main field artillery weapon was the shrapnel round, a hollow shell filled with metal balls packed on an expelling charge, which was initiated by a fuse set to a predetermined time. When the charge functioned, the balls were pushed out the front of the shell and dispersed by the centrifugal force of the spinning shell in a cone about 10 to 15 degrees wide. While the shrapnel round was deadly at shorter ranges, at longer ranges the drag of air on the shell had so reduced its velocity that the expelled balls often did not have sufficient energy to inflict a serious wound.

A gun, technically a sub-section, consisted of the gun and limber (a two-wheeled trailer loaded with gun stores and ammunition) drawn by a six-horse team and an ammunition wagon and limber drawn by another six-horse team. Two sub-sections made up a section, commanded by a lieutenant. The field artillery's fighting unit was the battery of six guns, although the three sections could operate independently. Each battery was commanded by a major, with a captain as second in command. In war, field artillery was grouped into brigade divisions of three batteries and an ammunition column. A brigade division was normally allotted to an infantry divison. The ammunition column supplied all units in the division, not just the artillery. In addition to the field artillery, both the garrison artillery (a separate branch of the service), and the navy manned heavy guns drawn by long teams of oxen.

Later in the war divisions and brigades were replaced by combinations of all arms. For example, an officer might be allotted two infantry battalions, a mounted infantry company and a section of field guns to defend a stretch of railway. To mount a foray, a "flying column" of two or three cavalry or mounted infantry units, a battery, and a battalion or two might take to the field. By the end of the war most of the infantry held the blockhouse lines that penned the Boers into smaller and smaller areas. The rest of the army, all mounted, pursued the Boers across the veldt.

To fight, an army uses tactical doctrine, a common set of procedures and formations, based on its and the enemy's organization and weapons, to manoeuvre its forces to gain the advantage over the enemy. As the enemy usually refuses to sit still while this is going on, officers generally keep a quarter to a third of their force uncommitted to allow for the unforeseen. This is all much easier said than done. The British army, while equipped with modern weapons, had not adapted its tactics to suit. Tactics and parade square drill were indivisible. Mastery of drill meant that an infantry battalion or cavalry regiment could deploy into battle formation in response to standardized orders.[14]

Even on the open veldt, it was far too easy to blunder into an ambush. To prevent this, advancing forces would throw out an advance guard of perhaps a quarter of the total force. The advance guard, made up of cavalry or mounted infantry with some guns, normally preceded the main body by a few thousand yards. The main body followed out of the range of enemy artillery, but still near enough to reinforce the advance guard within an hour. Lighter forces guarded the flanks, while a relatively strong force guarded the rear to keep the enemy out of artilery range of the main body.

When the enemy was located and his position fixed, it was time for an attack by the infantry who deployed in three lines. The first, the firing line, advanced driving in the enemy's skirmishers until it was within 500 yards of the main position, where it paused. The supports, the next line, made up of the majority of the battalion, advanced in line to within a few hundred yards of the firing line. If resistance was light the supports advanced, picking up the firing line, and charged. If resistance was heavy the troops moved by alternate sections doubling forward covered by their comrades. Eventually the firing line was reached and reinforced by the supports. This combined force tried to move closer by short rushes and crawling, while engaging the enemy with volleys of rifle fire. Meanwhile the reserves, perhaps two or more companies, kept a few hundred yards behind the supports. The aim was to get close enough to charge with fixed bayonets. No attempt was made to suppress enemy fire before the charge. This may have worked when the enemy used spears or muskets, but it failed dismally when faced by Boers with magazine Mausers. The British soon learned to space their troops five, ten, and even fifteen paces apart in line. This, of course, greatly increased a company's frontage and the difficulties of control. The number of lines was increased, in some cases battalions attacking in eight successive lines, each a company strong. To the Boers, long lines of khaki figures stretching across the veldt and resolutely advancing created an impression of invincibility that closed ranks never managed to achieve.[15]

The cavalry or mounted infantry would be trying to work around the enemy's flanks. When ordered to attack, mounted infantry would gallop forward and dismount. While one man in four took his section's horses to cover, his comrades fought on foot with their rifles, the same weapon used by marching infantry. Able to move like cavalry and fight on the ground like infantry, mounted infantry brought the shock action that the other arms were unable to achieve to the battlefield. It had one disadvantage. MI could not charge into the enemy because they lacked any weapon they could use while mounted.[16]

The cavalry was a force of great potential. Like the infantry it was magnificently drilled and geared to shock action. The aim of every cavalryman from Lieutenant General Sir John French to the most humble trooper was to charge with lance and sword and cut the enemy down. In practice, the cavalry charge was rarely used. Instead, cavalry scouted and screened and sometimes fought dismounted. Because of the inadequacies of their weapons (lances, sabres and carbines) for anything but close combat, they were at a disadvantage compared with the other arms and Boers alike.[17]

There are some other tasks for mounted troops that should be mentioned. Security, or protection from surprise attack or ambush, was absolutely vital. Infantry would normally provide close-in security, sometimes holding key features with a section or even a company. Infantry provided outposts in all weather and especially at night. Mounted troops covered wider areas, often by the use of cossack posts of four men that provided early warning but could not hold ground. Their other task was escorting artillery. A field or horse artillery battery was vulnerable to attack while on the move and even in action. Unlike today, the only firearms in a battery were carried by the officers and drivers. Most artillerymen carried nothing more lethal than a sword bayonet. A company or squadron would be detailed to escort the guns. The escort was expected to stay close to the guns to protect them from being overrun by a sudden charge. In South Africa, where the enemy attempted to silence the guns by fire, this merely increased the size of the target. In time the escorts learned that the guns could be protected without clustering near the gun line.

The British army was not ready for war against a modern army. Deficient in doctrine, organization and training, far too many brave officers and men paid the ultimate price for the tactical sins of their superiors.

THE CANADIAN MILITIA

Canadians based their defence policy on patronage, parsimony, and the dogma that Canadian settlers, not British regulars, had won the War of 1812. As a result the first line of defence was the militia. Militia officers, who included many prominent politicians, perpetuated the legend to their own benefit. The result was a highly politicized defence structure. The minister of militia and defence was a coveted cabinet post because of the patronage he controlled. The defence budget, however, was so tiny that the department could not match the excesses of public works and the post office. None of this really mattered. There was no real threat. To paraphrase one prime minister, Canada's first line of defence was provided by the Royal Navy and the Monroe Doctrine. As a result, the main role of the army was internal security.[18]

The Militia Act of 1868 had provided for a large militia, but no permanent military establishment. The Canadian government relied upon British regulars to train the militia. In 1871 the British withdrew their Canadian garrisons except for the one at Halifax. Reluctantly, the Canadian government established two permanent artillery batteries at Kingston and Quebec to train the militia, followed by infantry and cavalry schools in 1883. By the 1890s the regular army of about 1000 officers and men had small garrisons from Winnipeg to Fredericton. The series of British generals seconded as the general officer commanding the Canadian militia periodically tried to raise standards. One of the steps had been to organize the permanent force on a regimental basis, which did a great deal to foster a military ethic in the permanent force. Despite periodic reaffirmations by the Canadian government that the only role of the regulars was to train the reserves, the militia considered any attempt to improve the lot of the permanent force as a threat to the militia's ascendancy. Any general with spark and drive soon found himself at odds with both the party in power and the militia establishment, usually the result of his hopelessly naive belief that the defence budget was for defence, not patronage. Table 2.3 shows the distribution of forces in Canada in 1899.[19]

Table 2.3 The Canadian Militia, October 1899, regular and (reserve) units

District	HQ	Cavalry		Field Artillery		Garrison Artillery		Infantry	
1	London	0	(1)	0	(2)	Nil		1	(10)
2	Toronto	1	(2)	0	(1)	Nil		1	(17)
3	Kingston	0	(2)	2	(1)	0	(1)	0	(9)
4	Ottawa	0	(1)	0	(2)	Nil		0	(6)
5	Montreal	0	(2)	0	(1)	0	(1)	0	(9)
6	St-Jean, Que.	0	(1)	0	(1)	0	(1)	1	(5)
7	Quebec	0	(1)	0	(1)	1	(1)	1	(7)
8	Saint John, N.B.	0	(1)	0	(2)	0	(1)	1	(5)
9	Halifax	0	(1)	Nil		0	(1)	0	(8)
10	Winnipeg	1	(1)	0	(1)	Nil		0	(3)
11	Victoria	Nil		Nil		0	(1)	0	(4)
12	Charlottetown	0	(1)	Nil		0	(1)	0	(1)
Totals		2	14	2	12	1	8	5	84

While the majority of the reserve units were battalion size, say 1000 men on paper, the regular units were much smaller. There also were a number of reserve independent rifle companies in centres such as Brandon, Manitoba; Rossland, British Columbia; and Sault Ste-Marie, Ontario.

After the North-West Rebellion in 1885 there were only a few occasions when an opportunity for active service, other than in aid of the civil power, arose. In 1894 there had been an abortive proposal that the permanent force garrison Hong Kong. Four years later the regular army moved a quarter of its strength to the Yukon to reinforce Canadian sovereignty without incident. Fortunately, most were back east before the outbreak of war in South Africa.[20]

Besides the permanent and non-permanent active militia, there was another military force, the North West Mounted Police. The NWMP, especially in its early days, had both police and military roles. By 1899 25 years of police service should have displaced the military tradition, but it had not. The Mounted Police continued to train as mounted infantry and considered itself more than the equal of the tiny permanent cavalry. In 1896 the commissioner had suggested to Prime Minister Laurier that a contingent should be sent to the Sudan. While the suggestion (and the NWMP) went nowhere, within four years the chance would come. In December 1899 the commissioner submitted an application to raise "three companies of mounted rifles made up of picked police, ex-police and cowboys." While this offer was overtaken by events, 245 members served in the Canadian contingents, and 42 joined the South African Constabulary. The granting of the title "Royal" to the North West Mounted Police and the battle honour "South Africa 1899-1902" on the RCMP guidon commemorates its first overseas service.[21]

Chapter

3   **Mobilizing The First Contingent**

ON 3 JULY 1899 Joseph Chamberlain, the colonial secretary, asked the governor general if Canada would provide a contingent in the event of war. The Earl of Minto, governor general since 12 November 1898, replied that, while Canada as a whole was enthusiastic, Prime Minister Laurier would be hesitant because of the lack of any support for war in his French Canadian power base. Furthermore, Laurier would disguise the divisions by citing the costs involved as his reason for inaction. There was, however, wide support for the British cause in English Canada. The government had passed a resolution of support for the Transvaal "Uitlanders" on 31 July but that was as far as Laurier was prepared to go. Parliament adjourned in early August and was not scheduled to sit again for a number of months. Laurier firmly discouraged Canadian participation in the war: "I do not favour at all the scheme for sending an armed force to Africa. We have too much to do in this country to go into military expenditures," he firmly told his minister of militia and defence, Dr Frederick Borden.[1]

Despite all the efforts of Laurier, the imperialist tidal wave was building. The general officer commanding (GOC), Major General Edward Hutton, and his chief staff officer, Colonel Hubert Foster, were drawing up plans for a Canadian overseas contingent of 1209 officers and men, 314 horses, and six guns. The GOC, who was actively advocating Canadian participation in the war, was certain that, while the prime minister was opposed, public opinion would eventually force Laurier to act. Political calculations always produced the same result. While Laurier shared the aversion of his Quebec base to imperial adventures, there was wide support for the war in English Canada and among its MPs of all parties.[2]

Sam Hughes was a staunchly Protestant, energetic Conservative member of Parliament, firm Canadian nationalist, rabid partisan publisher of the *Victoria Warder*, and enthusiastic militia colonel. Hughes burst upon the scene like a libidinous bull in Hutton's china shop. Never one to underestimate himself, Sam offered to raise and command a battalion or even a brigade for active service. To ensure that his offer would not pass unnoticed or be pigeonholed by some fumbling clerk, he forwarded it to Hutton as a soldier, Laurier as a politician, and Chamberlain as a "citizen of the Empire." Laurier saw it as a godsend. Imperial aspirations could be satisfied and the zealots sent off to the front without undermining the support of his power base. It took a great deal of persuasion by Hutton to convince Laurier that it would be advisable to decline Hughes' scheme. Hutton must have been sorely tried, faced, on the one hand, with a reluctant prime minister and, on the other, an energetic egomaniac. Relations between Hutton and Hughes degenerated into mutual distrust and abuse.[3]

On 3 October the *Canadian Military Gazette* published details of the Hutton plan with a report that began, "If war should be commenced in the Transvaal—which seems most probable—the offer of a force from the Canadian militia will be made by the Canadian Government." Immediately upon the appearance of the story, Laurier described it as "pure invention" in an interview published in the pro-Liberal Toronto *Globe*.[4]

On the same day that the story appeared in the *Military Gazette*, a telegram was sent from the colonial secretary thanking Canada for its offer of a contingent. The telegram is similar to those sent to South Australia, New South Wales, Queensland, Victoria, and New Zealand. The wire was based on a War Office letter dated 2 October which stated that: "From Canada no definite offer has, as yet, reached Lord Lansdowne [the secretary of state for war] but he understands that 1,200 men are anxious to volunteer." The British were aware of the widely publicized offers of volunteers and one of the other recipients, South Australia, as well as Western Australia and Tasmania, had yet to offer troops, while New Zealand had made its formal offer on 28 September. The complete text of the telegram follows:

> Secretary of State for War and Commander-in-Chief desire to express high appreciation of signal exhibition of *patriotic spirit of people of Canada shown by offers to serve in South Africa,* and to furnish following information to assist organization of force offered into units suitable for military requirements. Firstly, units should consist of about 125 men; secondly, may be infantry, mounted infantry, or cavalry; in view of numbers already available infantry most, cavalry least, serviceable; thirdly, all should be armed with .303 rifles or carbines, which can be supplied by Imperial Government if necessary; fourthly, all must provide own equipment and mounted troops own horses; fifthly, not more than one captain and three subalterns each unit. Whole force may be commanded by officer not higher than major. In considering numbers which can be employed, Secretary of State for War guided by nature of offers, by desire that each colony should be fairly represented, and limits necessary if force is to be fully utilized by available staff as integral portion of Imperial forces; would gladly accept four units. Conditions as follows: *Troops to be disembarked at port of landing South Africa fully equipped at cost of Colonial Government or volunteers.* From date of disembarkation Imperial Government will provide pay at Imperial rates, supplies and ammunition, and will defray expenses of transport back to Canada, and pay wound pensions and compassionate allowances at Imperial rates. Troops to embark not later than October 31, proceeding direct to Cape Town for orders. *Inform accordingly all who offered to raise volunteers.*
> [My emphasis]

Chamberlain later advised Minto that the British government had no intention of accepting privately raised volunteers in place of official contingents. This was an attempt to force action from recalcitrant colonies rather than any admission of error by the Colonial Office.[5]

Laurier believed that the *Globe* interview had put paid to both the *Gazette* story and the Colonial Office telegram. With that he departed on an official visit to Chicago on 7 October. Despite the logic of his position, English Canada would have none of it. The outbreak of war on 11 October 1899 unleashed another wave of enthusiasm. Laurier cut short his visit to Chicago to hurry back to Ottawa and a hastily convened Cabinet meeting on 12 October. The

Chamberlain telegram provided Laurier a way out in light of his earlier stated concerns. After two days' deliberation by the cabinet, he announced that Canada would send a contingent of 1000 men (or twice the number suggested) to fight with the Imperial forces in South Africa. On the same day Minto wired the colonial secretary, "my Government offers 1,000 infantry on organization proposed in your telegram of October 3."

Some hurdles needed to be overcome before a contingent could be despatched, including the lack of any provision for overseas service in the Militia Act. The government appeared to carefully skirt the legalities, in part because of British willingness to pay most of the bills. The attestation form included the following:

> I am willing to serve wherever Her Majesty The Queen may direct in the *Canadian Contingent for Active Service* under the provision of the Militia Act of Canada so far as it applies, under the Queen's Regulations and Orders for the Army and the Army Act, for a term of six months, or one year if required, or until sooner lawfully discharged or dismissed, at the rate of pay fixed for the Permanent Corps of Canada, *until landed in South Africa, and after disembarkation to serve in Her Majesty's Regular Forces* at the rates of pay fixed by Royal Warrant for the pay of the British Army. [My emphasis][6]

It was decided to create new permanent force units and to man them with a regular cadre and volunteers enlisted for a fixed period of full-time service. In this way, wide militia representation could be assured while, since The Royal Canadian Regiment of Infantry already existed, there was a convenient source of unit tradition and pride and a place to perpetuate any honours accruing from service in South Africa. On 14 October the government announced that eight independent companies, each of 125 men, would be recruited. Recruiting instructions had been sent to the 12 military districts to recruit the non-commissioned members of the companies. Recruiting was centred in the cities shown in Table 3.1, although the company designations did not come until 20 October:

Table 3.1 Recruiting centres for First Contingent

Company	Province	Centre(s)
A	British Columbia	Victoria, Vancouver
	Manitoba	Winnipeg
B	Ontario	London
C	Ontario	Toronto
D	Ontario	Kingston, Ottawa
E	Quebec	Montreal
F	Quebec	Quebec
G	New Brunswick	Saint John
	Prince Edward Island	Charlottetown
H	Nova Scotia	Halifax

Lieutenant Colonel W.D. Otter, who was to have commanded the contingent in the Hutton plan, was offered command on the terms of the Colonial Office cable by letter on 17 October, that is, he would go as a major, but he was told that this could change. Otter accepted on 18 October (the postal service was quicker in those days) and soon was hard at work.

Fifty-six-year-old Canadian-born William Dillon Otter was an erect, autocratic product of impoverished English minor gentry. He enlisted in the Queen's Own Rifles in the early 1860s, and his approach to discipline and training was coloured by the debacle at Ridgeway in 1866. A member of the permanent force since 1883, he had commanded the Battleford Column in the North West Rebellion. Otter had authored a popular guide for militia officers, which covered in minute detail virtually every aspect of the organization and administration of unit life. His penchant for strict discipline and "no frills" soldiering would bring him in direct conflict with the free-and-easy militia approach to military life. Once in South Africa he gained the confidence of his British superiors and was no more prone to stupid decisions than his Imperial contemporaries. Whatever his real or perceived failings, his bravery and willingness to expose himself to fire were never in question. Otter rose against obstacles of poverty, intrigue and lack of opportunity to end his life as Canada's first general.[7]

On 18 October the Canadian government requested, via the usual route of the governor general to the colonial secretary: "After further consideration my Ministers have decided to offer a regiment of infantry 1,000 strong, under command of Lieutenant-Colonel Otter. My Ministers hope the Canadian contingent will be kept together as much as possible, but realize that this must be left to discretion of War Office and Commander-in-Chief."

An infantry battalion created a requirement for further numbers over and above the companies. There was, of course, the commanding officer (CO), a lieutenant colonel, who bore responsibility for every success and failure of the unit. If the unit did well, the CO could expect to be showered with praise, promotion and decoration. If it did poorly, he could expect censure. While he had some latitude in shifting blame, ("shit flows downhill," as soldiers say), the consequences of failure in battle and the responsibility of command bore heavily.

Infantry battalions consisted of eight companies, usually organized into right and left half battalions of four companies each. To command the right and left halves there were two majors, one of whom was also the second in command of the battalion (the 2ic), who understudied the CO and filled in for him in his absence. These appointments went to two regulars. Lawrence Buchan, an infantry officer and professional rival of Otter, was appointed 2ic, while a gunner and son of the speaker of the Senate, Oscar Pelletier, received the second majority. There were other officer appointments to fill: adjutant, quartermaster, machine-gun officer, and medical officer for example. There also were a number of staff noncommissioned officers including the regimental sergeant major, regimental quartermaster sergeant, chief clerk and armourer. Dr Miller's claim, that the militia department had structured the battalion in such a way that the Hutton plan could be resurrected does not stand up. For example, a large number of artillerymen enlisted, but they were mainly garrison artillery who had no training as field artillery.

A rifle company was commanded by a captain with three lieutenants or second lieutenants and a colour sergeant to assist him. The companies for South Africa were authorized four sergeants, five corporals, two buglers, and 109 privates. A company was divided into four sections each commanded by a sergeant assisted by a corporal and a lance corporal or two. Given the need for men for the machine-gun, transport, and signals sections, officers' servants and grooms, stretcher bearers, storemen, and cooks as well as the drain of disease and injury, companies could field no more than 80 private soldiers before suffering any battle casualties.[8]

Companies were equipped with new ten-shot Lee Enfield rifles purchased at the time of the Venezuela boundary dispute. The Magazine Lee Enfield Mark One was a bolt-operated, magazine-fed weapon that fired a .303 calibre moderate-velocity round. Officers were armed with Colt revolvers and swords and wore uniforms of better cut and material than the standard issue. The lessons of active service soon sunk in though, and officers campaigned in issue uniforms with subdued badges of rank. Swords certainly, and revolvers probably, were left in stores, and officers, dressed in issue uniforms and carrying rifles, were indistinguishable from the rank and file.

The selection of officers was complicated by the contemporary Canadian habit of the political tail wagging the military dog. General Hutton, quite properly, wished to reserve for himself selection and appointment of the officers. Here, for not the first or last time in his short and stormy tour in Canada, he found himself faced with a government, in the form of the minister of militia and defence, convinced that political considerations were as important as qualifications and ability. The delays were of much concern to Otter, both because of the extra work for the few actually appointed and the uncertainty concerning his slate of officers. The officers eventually selected were a representative cross-section of the officer corps. Otter certainly believed the officers were the weakest element of the battalion. The final slate included 12 extra officers: two in battalion headquarters, a machine-gun officer, an extra medical officer and one lieutenant per company (as authorized for the 125-man units in the Colonial Office telegram of 3 October 1899). There also were four officers attached for instructional purposes; Captain F.J. Dixon, editor of *The Canadian Military Gazette*, as historical recorder; Catholic, Anglican, and Presbyterian chaplains; and a third medical officer and four nurses. A number of officers either accepted reduction in rank to serve as lieutenants or captains or resigned their commissions to serve in the ranks.

After the turmoil of the previous few months it would have taken a plague that wiped out all the other senior officers in the Canadian militia before Hutton would have allowed a place to go to Sam Hughes, and Otter probably would have been delighted to see Hughes standing on the pier as the troop-ship steamed away to war. However, Dr Borden had gone so far as to propose Sam for a command in the contingent on a number of occasions; perhaps as much to get him out of the country as for his military talent. Sam was always tenacious and persuasive. He cajoled, he appealed, he begged, and he wept until he wore down Hutton's resistance sufficiently to obtain authority to accompany the contingent on the troop-ship, with the proviso repeated in Otter's written instructions, "This officer does not proceed in any military capacity whatever, and will, accordingly, not wear uniform on board ship." Hutton also advised the commander-in-chief in South Africa that "I am not prepared to recommend his [Hughes'] appointment in any military capacity in South Africa."[9]

The tiny permanent force provided about 15 percent of the first contingent. Not the least of its contributions were the majority of the staff non-commissioned officers and the colour sergeant in each company, and 13 of the battalion's 41 officers (another officer was a member of the British army, Captain A.C. Bell, an aide de camp to the GOC). Regulars were distributed through the ranks in the companies with the greatest number in F Company, which had been plagued by slow recruiting, where the regulars totaled almost one in four.[10]

Conventional wisdom has it that the unit was drawn from militia regiments across Canada. Certainly there was wide representation from militia units. In Military District One in southwestern Ontario, nearly half of B Company came from three militia units, with 20 men from the 7th Fusiliers, 18 from the 21st Essex Fusiliers, and 22 from the 26th Middlesex Light Infantry. The remainder of the company was made up of 18 regulars (10 gunners and 8 infantrymen) and single-digit numbers from 12 other militia units, all infantry except for six cavalrymen from the 1st Hussars and four gunners from the 6th Field Battery. The "Toronto" company included men from militia units ranging from Sault Ste Marie to Niagara. This pattern generally held in the various military districts, with urban units providing the majority of the recruits. The response to the call for volunteers was strong except in eastern Quebec. Any shortfall was easily made up by allotting vacancies to other districts, for example, 40 percent of F Company was made up of men enlisted in Montreal and the Maritimes. Across Canada the majority were affiliated with militia units, although others listed affiliations such as civilian, various police forces, and "late 6th U.S. Infantry." Some affiliations resulted from no more than walking through the armoury door. Otter estimated that a third of the battalion were without prior military service and that fully half were no more than recruits. Only half of the men came from the ranks of the militia, and even many of the militiamen had very little experience. Despite claims that the battalion represented all of Canada, there were no volunteers from Moosomin to the Crow's Nest and from Ungava to the Klondike.[11]

Almost overnight Canada was to raise and equip 1000 men and send them off to war. Except for weapons and Canadian Oliver equipment, the cupboard was bare. The magnitude of the task was staggering. Take uniforms: 2000 khaki frocks and the same number in serge; 2740 khaki trousers and 2000 serge; 976 greatcoats; 2000 woolen shirts; 3000 grey flannel shirts; 3000 pairs of socks; and 3000 ankle boots. The cloth had not even been woven, let alone cut and sewn. The list goes on: axes, pick, helved, 78; brushes—blacking, cloth, hair, polishing, and shaving,—1000 of each; braces, pairs, 1000; all the way through the convoluted prose of the storemen to syringes, hypodermic, 2; tents, circular, complete, 80; and valises, blanket, 120. Hardly a fraction was in the warehouses and all of it had to be dockside by the end of October.[12]

The Allan Line cattle boat SS *Sardinian* was selected and outfitted in about two weeks. The official report methodically details all that was done: a galley and bake house on the spar deck; accommodation in hammocks and bunks for the men on the main deck and in steerage; cabins for the officers and senior non-commissioned officers; stables for the seven horses; two miniature rifle ranges and two revolver ranges; kit room, baggage room, guard room and prison; rifle racks, awnings, air scoops, and windsails; and the ship painted inside and out.

Table 3.2 demonstrates that, for cramming men into space, the *Sardinian* was in a class by herself.[13]

Table 3.2 - Troopships for First and Second Contingents

Name/ Year Built	Unit(s) Carried	Tonnage	Length/ Beam in ft.	Passengers Carried	Horse Losses
Sardinian 1875	2 RCR	4376	400 x 42	63 offrs 1001 men 7 horses	nil
Laurentian 1872	D & E Btys	4522	400 x 42	2 offrs 343 men 263 horses	26
Pomeranian 1882	2 CMR	4365	381 x 43	18 offrs 304 men 295 horses	9
Milwaukee 1897	1 CMR C Bty Tp 2 CMR	7317	470 x 56	28 offrs 605 men 614 horses	38
Monterey 1897	SH Rft RCR	5478	445 x 52	34 offrs 613 men 599 horses	173

On 23 October 1899, the day that authority to provide a battalion instead of eight independent companies was received, orders were issued to move the companies to Quebec, the point of concentration. Several days would be required at Quebec to clothe and equip the troops before sailing for South Africa. Time was very short, especially for the British Columbians of A Company, who entrained the same day and did not arrive in Quebec until the early morning hours of 29 October. As travel arrangements were finalized, companies mustered and marched through cheering crowds to the stations. The troops were still dressed in the uniforms of their parent units, and some were in civilian clothes or a combination of military and mufti. Except for A Company, the companies were no more than an overnight trip from Quebec. The Nova Scotians left Halifax at 3:00 p.m. on the 25th and arrived at Levis at 12.30 the following afternoon, while B Company departed London shortly after 2:00 p.m. on the same day in one baggage and two pullman cars and pulled into Quebec City 23 hours later.[14]

Over 1000 men were kitted and medically examined in four days, in itself no small accomplishment. A number of men failed the medical examinations but boarded the ship anyway. There, of course, was no time for training, even if there had been lecture rooms, rifle ranges, or training areas available. Finally, on 27 October the battalion, which was designated 2 (Special Service) Battalion, Royal Canadian Regiment of Infantry, was formed and the officers gazetted. The battalion was no more than a collection of individuals and capable of not much more than forming ranks and marching without getting out of step too often.

By Sunday the 29th, a cold, wet day like the 28th, the battalion was complete in Quebec. That evening, on the eve of departure, the governor general entertained the officers and the usual collection of dignitaries at dinner. The occasion was graced, besides the usual speeches, by a drunken altercation between Dr Borden and a local militia officer that nearly degenerated into a fist fight. It must have been an edifying spectacle for Minto and Hutton.

On the 30th, another wet day with rain and hail, the battalion, incongruously resplendent in new rifle green serge uniforms, paraded on the Esplanade prior to sailing. The usual collection of addresses by dignitaries was followed by an inspection of the battalion. The import of the moment and the messages of the speakers were probably lost on the troops, who, wearing full packs and equipment, stood at attention in the wet and cold for three hours. Then came the march through the streets past cheering crowds and onto the *Sardinian*. Embarkation was completed by 4:00 p.m. and the ship edged away from the dock at 4:35 and steamed downstream, accompanied by yachts loaded with enthusiastic spectators, towards the Gulf of Saint Lawrence, the open seas and South Africa. It seemed a good omen that the sun, which had been hidden behind clouds for several days, appeared and bathed the scene in the glory of a northern sunset.

The first night afloat was a shambles. Preparations had been so hurried, time so short, and Canadian experience with sea travel so limited that consideration of important details of shipboard routine fell between the cracks. It is true that quarters had been allotted to companies, shipboard routine scheduled, and plans made for a training program. However, there is much more to trooping than boarding and bedding, just as there is more to soldiering than uniforms and parades. Otter wrote that "we are all getting a good experience in troop ship duties and have lots to learn." The fault was not that of the battalion alone. The Sardinian was a cattle ship; there was little in the recent experience of her crew that could prepare them for the task of sustaining 1000 men for a month. Despite this, little fault was found with the efforts of the crew to provide for the welfare of the battalion during the voyage.[15]

The *Sardinian*, soon nicknamed the "Sardine," was a long, low ship with a single tall funnel amidships and a forest of masts and cranes. She was, of course, coal fired and driven by a single screw. She seems to have been a lively ship that rolled easily, especially as the voyage progressed, and she rode higher and higher as coal was burned. Since she lacked the means to convert enough salt water to fresh, water had to be rationed. Thirty days on the "Sardine" was a very long time.

The ship sailed with seven horses and 1144 souls on board: 1039 Royal Canadians, eight officers attached for instructional and other purposes, a YMCA representative, three chaplains, four nurses, four war correspondents, two officers "attached for passage," and 80 crew. The count included 20 men who had failed their medicals but by one means or another found their way on board. An embarrassed Otter reported this to Ottawa, noting that he had no idea what had happened. The total also included three stowaways from The Royal Canadian Regiment of Infantry who successfully gambled that once the ship was out of Canadian waters, the battalion would make the best of their unexpected appearance and take them on strength.

One of the officers on board was Sam Hughes, who, despite the instructions to travel in civilian clothes, soon appeared in uniform. With little to occupy himself with he began to pen letters to British and Canadian politicians. By the time he went ashore, Hughes must have prepared quite a collection of unsolicited advice, pleas for succour, and attacks on his enemies, including a litany of assaults on Hutton. In a particularly odious example of ambition overriding principle, he went so far as to suggest to Laurier that, if he were appointed to a high-ranking command in the force, he might be able to see some merit in the Liberal point of view.

The other officer attached for passage was Captain Todd, Royal Dublin Fusiliers, who did not indulge in self-aggrandizement and intrigue. Instead, he was made responsible for details of shipboard administration and, in the opinion of Otter and the men, did an excellent job.[16]

The voyage would take a month at an average speed of about 11 miles per hour. Despite the cramped conditions and the lack of amenities much could be accomplished in a month, if the weather cooperated. It was not a good start to run into heavy going in the Gulf of St Lawrence, after which from 6 November, in Otter's words, "The passage, as far as weather was concerned, was a most delightful one." But first tragedy struck. Private Ted Deslauriers of D Company died shortly after reveille on 3 November. He was said to have been disoriented, hallucinatory and even suicidal on the 2nd. At 4:30 p.m. on the 3rd a quiet party gathered round a flag-draped body, and the ship slowed on the grey, cold waves of the southeast end of the Grand Banks. A short service was held, followed by the "wham" of Lee Enfields, clatter of bolts, and "ping" of warm brass on cold deck; then a splash and swirl, the renewed throb of the engine, and men left engrossed in individual thoughts.[17]

The first week was occupied by finding sea legs in rough weather and little other than vaccinations were attempted. By 6 November, as the ship steamed steadily into more temperate climes, the job of training a battalion on a crowded ship began in earnest. The morning began with a run around the deck by companies. After the run the troops made for the forecastle, stripped and showered under the spray of a salt-water hose, followed by a brisk towelling and breakfast. The officers and senior NCOs were quartered in cabins which, although crowded, provided a certain amount of privacy. Their meals were taken seated at proper tables in dining-rooms. The rank and file ate at long tables running down the centre of the compartments. The dreary monotony of institutional meals was not relieved by the work of amateurish cooks (potatoes were not peeled before cooking and rotten spuds added a certain something to the hash) or its presentation in large pots that had been lugged and sloshed along decks and companionways.

After breakfast there were drill and exercises, and for a company at a time, rifle practice; then lunch and a short rest, followed by more drill and exercise until supper. The Maxim machine-gun squad was organized and drilled separately. For the officers there were daily lectures and much badly needed experience in the never-ending responsibilities that accompany the privileges of rank. The evenings brought concerts and other entertainment, and religious services were regularly held and well attended. Some, perhaps the majority, felt the battalion devoted too much time to drill and not enough to marksmanship. It is difficult to see any other choices. One of Otter's memories was the spectacle, 33 years past, of ill-trained militiamen routed by confusion, not the enemy. Let men grumble, officers intrigue and correspondents scribble, Otter had no intention of replicating Ridgeway on the veldt. Drill had direct application to the nineteenth century battlefield, or at least it did until the Boers (who had not read the drill book) appeared on the scene. Most armies had yet to learn that war required intelligent self-expression while parades demanded implicit obedience.[18]

The obvious alternative to drill is marksmanship. Twenty Morris tubes, .22 calibre inserts for the service rifle, and 40 000 rounds had been shipped in the stores. With two ranges in the bows and 20 tubes, it would take 50 turns to put the battalion through once. An individual soldier could not have spent more than a few hours on the range from when the weather moderated on 6 November until the ranges were dismantled three weeks later. One veteran later wrote that only a few rounds per man were fired.[19]

On 12 November there was a break in shipboard routine. The Cape Verde Islands, which lie in the Atlantic a few hundred miles off Senegal and Mauritania, were sighted. The soldiers wanted a change and perhaps the opportunity to stretch their legs, see the sights, and enjoy a few hours away from the ship but it was not to be. The islands rose over the horizon, grew larger and more distinct, and then sank into the wake as the *Sardinian* throbbed through phosphorescent tropical seas.

As the ship made her way south and east, the sun climbed and the days changed from cold, to delightful, to downright hot. In an ill-advised attempt to harden the men, Otter ordered the battalion to parade barefoot, trouser legs rolled above the knee, shirts unbuttoned to expose the neck and chest to the sun, sleeves rolled above the elbow, and caps folded to deny shade to the face. The result was inevitable, not only from the intense sun, but also from the many steam pipes and overheated decks. Sun-burned, swollen, and peeling faces, chests, limbs, and even feet required medical attention. Mercifully, the order was soon cancelled.

Besides the drill and training there were preparations for the campaign to come. The loading had been done hastily, and many important articles were missing or buried under piles of baggage that would not be needed until arrival. Most of the difficulties were soon overcome, but Otter and Todd could not straighten out one particular "snafu." The stores were short 260 khaki tunics.

On the fourth day past the Cape Verde Islands the *Sardinian* met the *Rangatira* bound for Southampton from South Africa and all the more welcome for it. A ship's boat soon pulled towards her with two large bags of Canada bound mail. Few could have expected the news the boat bore. The Boers had won a series of victories and had seized the initiative. The battalion must surely see action.

There was renewed purpose to the preparations. Swords and bayonets were sharpened and resharpened, khaki covers for the water bottles were stitched by the nurses, and drill and rifle practice continued. Concoctions of tea were brewed to dye helmets and other articles various hues of drabness. Captain Bell had drilled his machine-gun section into form and occasionally the chatter of a Maxim would interrupt the throb of the ship as a stream of bullets crashed into a barrel bobbing in the wake of the *Sardinian*.

On the 27th the miniature range was dismantled, and preparations were begun for disembarking. The waters had become a little rougher and the top-heavy ship rolled villainously until on 29 November the bold top of Table Mountain loomed far through the morning mist.

Chapter

4 Mobilizing the Second Contingent

THE *SARDINIAN* had hardly left Canadian waters before the government offered a second contingent on 2 November 1899. Given Laurier's reluctance and the opposition to the war held by members of his Cabinet, the offer likely was a calculated response to the mood in English Canada.[1]

The British War Office believed that the planned army corps would be able to defeat the Boer republics and preferred to wait until the results of Buller's operations in Natal were known. Canada was politely thanked for the offer and told there was no requirement for more troops but should the situation change, the War Office "will have no hesitation in availing themselves of it. "Six weeks later, on 16 December, chastened by the series of disastrous defeats that came to be known as "Black Week" the British accepted the Canadian offer, adding "it is indispensable that men should be trained and good shots and should bring own horses." The call for trained men caused some difficulty until it was decided this could include men who could ride and shoot, rather than drill.[2]

The GOC prepared to mobilize a mounted rifle regiment, a company of scouts, and a brigade division of artillery with a total strength of approximately 1230 all ranks, 1124 horses, and 18 guns. The second contingent would be built around a permanent force cadre supplemented by militiamen who had completed at least one annual camp. The GOC had planned to recruit the three mounted rifle squadrons from the eastern militia cavalry. Except perhaps for the scouts, whose composition and recruiting area had not yet been set, this excluded the territories where men lived by the skills that were proving so valuable on the veldt. As the NWMP was organized on military lines and, despite its emphasis on policing duties, drilled as mounted infantry, Hutton later agreed that the NWMP would provide the regimental second-in-command, quartermaster, and the officers and noncommissioned cadre for a western mounted rifle squadron. The governor general, based on his experience in the North West Rebellion, felt that a greater proportion of the mounted rifles should be recruited in the west. Here he was at odds with Hutton, who leaned towards the militia establishment, and the government who knew where the Liberals lived. Minto's arguments must have carried some weight. In its final form the contingent included two battalions of Canadian Mounted Rifles, one drawn from the militia (1 CMR) and the other (2 CMR) based on the NWMP. The tactical limitations of a two-squadron battalion were of little concern to the government, which had finessed itself out of another controversy.[3]

The most urgent requirement was mounted troops who could hold their own with the Boers. The War Office, prompted by Minto, suggested that a reduction in the number of guns and a corresponding increase in the number of mounted men would be useful. As mobilization was well under way, the Canadian government was not prepared to back down. Minto had another card to play. He wrote Lord Roberts, an artilleryman himself, that "the artillery & other [mounted] troops cannot possibly represent a high standard of efficiency."[4]

The first contingent had been organized as a battalion of a permanent force regiment for a number of reasons. The practice was followed in the second contingent. C, D, and E Batteries were new units of the regular Royal Canadian Field Artillery, perpetuating A and B Batteries of the permanent force. In the case of the mounted rifles, the two battalions were seen as extensions of the permanent force Royal Canadian Dragoons and the North West Mounted Police, respectively.[5]

The permanent force had provided a cadre of officers and men for the first contingent. The second contingent drew even more heavily on the permanent corps and the NWMP. In the first battalion 8 of 19 officers, including the commanding officer, second in command, both squadron commanders, and the adjutant, came from the permanent cavalry. The NWMP provided 13 officers for the second battalion, including all the key appointments. In the brigade division, 9 of 20 officers were regulars, including the commanding officer and two of the three majors.[6]

Lieutenant Colonel François Lessard, who was serving with Sir John French's cavalry, was appointed commanding officer of 1 CMR. A product of the Quebec Garrison Artillery, he was commissioned in the permanent cavalry in 1884, served with his regiment in the North West Rebellion and had been appointed to command the Royal Canadian Dragoons on 1 July, 1899.

The commander of the second battalion, Commissioner Lawrence Herchmer, was by far the oldest of the three commanders, having been commissioned an ensign in the 46th Foot in 1858 at the age of 18. He had commanded the NWMP since 1886, not without controversy because of his abrasive personality and Conservative connections.

The third commanding officer was Lieutenant Colonel Charles Drury of the artillery, a permanent force officer since 1877 and North West Rebellion veteran. He was known as "the father of modern artillery in Canada" as a result of his innovations in training and tactics.[7]

The two battalion seconds in command (there was no such appointment in the artillery) were Major Thomas Evans of B Squadron, Royal Canadian Dragoons and Superintendent Sam Steele of the NWMP. Both had served in the North West Rebellion. More recently Evans had commanded the Yukon Field Force, while Steele had led the NWMP in the Klondike at the height of the gold rush. Command of the seven squadrons and batteries went almost exclusively to the permanent force and the mounted police, the exception being Major W.G. Hurdman of Ottawa's 2nd Field Battery. The squadron and battery seconds in command included one permanent and one militia cavalryman, two mounted police officers, and two regular and one militia artillerymen.[8]

Subalterns came from the units selected to provide drafts for the batteries and squadrons. Political influence surely played a part, at least in one instance. Major Harold Borden of the King's Canadian Hussars, the only son of the minister of militia and defence, left his medical studies to lead 4th Troop, B Squadron as a lieutenant. Before we criticize political influence in the selection process, though, we should note that it differed little from the practice of British officers joining expeditions by exploiting influence or pedigree. These Canadians were, after all, networking in pursuit of a chance to be shot at—not for the postmaster's job in Pump Handle, Ontario. In all, the officers appear to have been better qualified than those of the first contingent. However, it has been suggested that most of the mounted police officers in C and D Squadrons were "too old for the ranks which they held."[9]

The plan was for the permanent force to provide a troop or gun section to each squadron or battery in 1 CMR and the Brigade Division, while the militia manned the other troops and sections. However, the mounted police formed the nucleus in each troop of 2 CMR. The difference in approach was the result of the lack of any militia structure in the territories and the organization of the NWMP in a form that transferred easily into squadrons and troops. The mounted police formed a much larger proportion of the strength of 2 CMR than the permanent force did in either 1 CMR or the artillery.[10]

It was decided, perhaps because of the inclusion of mounted police in the contingent, to pay all ranks at mounted police rates of pay, which were higher than permanent force pay rates. As was the case with the first contingent, the Canadian government undertook to make up the difference between Imperial and Canadian pay rates. A private in the second contingent was paid seventy-five cents a day as opposed to fifty cents a day for his counterpart in The RCR, with corresponding disparities for the higher ranks. For the first contingent, from Otter to the privates in the ranks, the injustice inherent in different pay rates for men risking their lives for their country was more than a minor irritant. Otter appealed to Ottawa but was politely but firmly told that the matter was settled. He raised the subject again on his return to Canada but was told that he and his men had signed a contract and that they should be grateful that the government was giving them anything extra at all.[11]

Recruiting was soon under way: for A Squadron in Toronto, St Catharines, Peterborough, Ottawa, London, Kingston, and Montreal; for B Squadron in Winnipeg, Portage La Prairie, Brandon, and Virden, Manitoba and Yorkton in the Territories; Montreal, Quebec City, and Cookshire, Quebec; Sussex and Saint John, New Brunswick, and Canning, Nova Scotia. The 2nd Battalion was recruited at mounted police posts across the territories, but completed organization at the NWMP Depot in Regina where the men were allotted to troops and squadrons. C Battery was enrolled in Kingston, Gananoque, Hamilton, St Catharines, Toronto, and Winnipeg; D Battery in Guelph, Ottawa, London, and Port Hope; and E Battery in Quebec City, Montreal, and Granby, Quebec; Woodstock and Newcastle, New Brunswick; and Sydney, Nova Scotia. While E Battery included two sections from Quebec, both French Canadian gunner officers served in C Battery.[12]

The British had refused a number of offers of non-white troops, primarily from India, although many served as non-combatants. It is unlikely this was known in Canada, as in response to a query from Herchmer whether "intelligent half-breeds" could be enrolled, he was advised in the affirmative. At least two Métis, Jefferson Davis and Peter Villebrun, served in the 2nd Battalion.[13]

The CMR squadrons, lettered A through D were each six officers, 154 men, and 161 horses strong. A squadron, commanded by a major with a captain second in command, was made up of four, titled "first" through "fourth," troops, each commanded by a lieutenant. A troop was about 40 strong, including its share of the batmen, cooks, farriers (soldiers trained to assist a veterinarian), shoeing-smiths (soldiers trained to prepare and fit horse shoes), saddlers, and wagonmen. As mounted rifles, troops were trained to fight dismounted with one man in four acting as a horse holder. This, of course, reduced the rifle strength correspondingly. The men were armed with Lee Enfield rifles and bayonets and Colt revolvers. Colonel Lessard, based on his experience with French's cavalry, saw little use for revolvers and would leave them in stores, while the NWMP-based 2nd Battalion found pistols very useful, especially for searching buildings and in other close quarters. There was one important distinction in Canadian mounted rifles tactics. Unlike the British, who had adopted a double rank system, both the cavalry and the NWMP had retained the single rank system as "good enough for [J.E.B.] Stuart and [Phil] Sheridan," two famous cavalry leaders of the United States Civil War. Like the first contingent, each battalion included a machine gun section of two horse-drawn Maxims. These proved to be too cumbersome in the field and were replaced in due course by air-cooled Colts.[14]

Like the squadrons, the batteries, lettered C, D, and E, were commanded by a major aided by a captain second in command. A field battery of five officers, 145 men, and 137 horses, had three sections (right, centre, and left) each of two 12-pounder breech loading guns. Sections, commanded by a lieutenant, were trained to operate independently. A field battery (or section) could not defend itself against attack from close quarters as most of the men were "armed" with swords or bayonets, not rifles or carbines. Officers and drivers carried revolvers, and each gun carried two carbines strapped to the trail. As a result, a proportion of the available infantry or mounted rifles were detailed as escort to the guns. A shortcoming in the brigade division's organization was the absence of an ammunition column to resupply the guns, especially as the civilian drivers of the supply wagons were understandably reluctant to risk their lives.[15]

Besides the CMR and the artillery, the second contingent included four officers for instructional purposes, Lieutenant Colonel W.D. Gordon, a permanent infantry officer, Major J.L. Boulanger, the commander of the 1st Field Battery from Quebec, Major J.L. Biggar of the 15th Argyll Light Infantry from Belleville and Lieutenant J.E. Burch of St Catharines's 2nd Dragoons; a reinforcement officer for The RCR; an additional medical officer and four nurses; three chaplains; a post office detachment seconded to the militia department; Mister T.F. Best of the YMCA; and Dr G.S. Ryerson of the Red Cross Society. Twenty-three artificers, men possessing civilian trades in demand in South Africa, were also recruited to serve with the Imperial Forces.[16]

It would not have been Canada unless petty squabbling by meddlesome politicians intruded into the process. Borden and Hutton had set up a board headed by Colonel Gerald Kitson, the commandant of RMC, to purchase horses for the contingent on the Canadian market. In January Colonel Kitson was in southern Ontario purchasing horses when local Liberals complained to Borden that Kitson was buying Conservative horses. Hutton quickly travelled to Toronto to support his man where he encountered Robert Beith, a prominent horse dealer and Liberal MP, who had been sent by the minister to examine the horses without reference to the GOC. In the furor that followed Borden supported Beith instead of Hutton. The latter, enraged by this assault on his integrity, immediately returned to Ottawa and extracted an apology from Borden. The controversy raged again a few days later when the minister decided to review details of the purchases himself. For the record, little was found worthy of complaint in either the condition of the horses or the prices paid. This was only one of a series of unfortunate instances, and Hutton was soon recalled by the British, a euphemism for being fired by the Canadian government. Replaced by a more amenable officer, Hutton went to South Africa where he commanded the mounted infantry brigade that included the two CMR battalions.[17]

By late January the first of the contingent were ready to sail. Once again the logistics and engineering staffs had worked minor miracles. On 20 January 1900 D and E Batteries, with a party from 2 CMR and 14 attached officers, nurses and men, embarked on the Allen Line transport SS *Laurentian* at Halifax. The farewell was emotional and enthusiastic. The troops marched through the streets ringing with cheers. There were, of course, the inevitable speeches resounding with Imperial rhetoric and patriotism, bands playing lustily, and crowds enthusiastically singing the national anthem and other patriotic airs despite the wet, miserable weather. At last the gangways were hauled in, and the *Laurentian* cast off and moved out into Halifax harbour, where she anchored.[18]

The captain had wisely delayed sailing, as a storm was raging, and he was not satisfied that the equipment and stores, including 110 live sheep, were properly secured. The next day, as the city slept through a quiet Sunday morning the *Laurentian* steamed down the harbour past the grey forts and turned southeast into the open seas. The Canadians soon received a practical demonstration of the reason why their transport had been nicknamed the "Rolling Polly" when she was under prior ownership as the *Polynesian*. The grey, rolling seas broke over her and, because her scuppers soon plugged with debris, cold salt water accumulated on the stable deck. Most of the landlubbers huddled in misery were just too seasick to care.[19]

Major Hurdman, the senior officer on board, had appointed Lieutenant "Gat" Howard ship's quartermaster for the voyage. It was an inspired choice. Howard, an ex-United States army officer who had gained fame as "Gatling Gun" Howard during the North West Rebellion, was one of those invaluable individuals who combine common sense with charisma and enthusiasm. Not only did he take charge of the care and feeding of the horses, he was able to suggest little measures that made life more comfortable for the men. Gat was genuinely likeable and gregarious and hosted nightly talk fests and singsongs in his tiny cabin, where lies were swapped and friendships cemented.

From the very first, an active training program including a daily hour of gun drill for each gun detachment was instituted. The first days revealed four men with venereal disease, one case of appendicitis, and two stowaways. One of the latter, who claimed to have been discharged as supernumerary to the CMR, was enlisted in E Battery, while the second who was under age was "attached" to the battery.[20]

The weather soon cleared, and the passage would have been quite pleasant if it were not for the resurgence of the sickness that had killed 40 of E Battery's horses in Canada. During the voyage a further 26 horses died. The obvious course of action would be to drop the dead horses overboard. This had occurred to the army, too. To ensure that the books were in balance, and perhaps to discourage an illicit trade in horses, although the difficulties of selling horses on the high seas seemed to have escaped the bureaucrats, a board of officers had first to recommend that each dead horse be struck off the strength of its battery, and the senior officer on board had to authorize the write-off before the dead animal could be dropped over the side to the waiting sharks. Except for a short stop at the Cape Verde Islands, the *Laurentian* rolled her way across and down the Atlantic until on 17 February she arrived at Cape Town at virtually the same time as four other transports, two from Australia, one from England, and another from India.

On the same day that the gunners embarked in Halifax, 2 CMR paraded on snowy Parliament Hill. The March edition of *Canadian Magazine* effused:

Of the 325 officers and men under Colonel Herchmer 130 were policemen or ex-policemen. The rest were ranchers from the Territories. The whole body was drawn up in a hollow square in front of the broad flight of steps leading up to the main building on Parliament Hill. . . The Governor-General inspected the three lines of men, and Her Excellency presented three silk guidons for them, saying "I know I am giving these guidons into very safe keeping."

Despite their strained relationship, Hutton and the minister were both in Halifax seeing the first ship off rather than reviewing 2nd Battalion on the hill. The presence on the podium of Irish-Catholic and vehemently anti-British Richard Scott, who had argued in Cabinet against participation in the war, attests more to the demands of Cabinet solidarity than to his enthusiasm for the ceremony.[21]

Within a week 2 CMR embarked on the SS *Pomeranian*. Rather than repeat details of another voyage—heavy weather, sea-sickness, dying horses, training and sports—we will leap ahead to Cape Town, where the regiment arrived on Majuba Day in time to share in the thrill of the news of Cronje's surrender and the achievement of The RCR. The regiment, less a party that would travel with 1 CMR, had been fortunate in that only nine horses had died during the voyage. One other had died on the *Laurentian* and a further three would die on the *Milwaukee*.[22]

A general of a later war took considerable pride in boasting that his operations unfolded exactly as planned, when surely there is more to applaud in confounding the enemy by adjusting to changing circumstances. The Department of Militia and Defence soon had an opportunity to demonstrate its flexibility. SS *Montezuma*, the ship chartered for 1 CMR and C Battery, as well as small groups from 2 CMR and D and E Batteries, suddenly became unsuitable because of an outbreak of typhoid among her crew. While A Squadron and C Battery remained in Toronto and Kingston respectively to train, B Squadron, with troops in Manitoba, Quebec, and Nova Scotia, concentrated in Halifax and began to train as a squadron under the close supervision of the press. The next ship available, the SS *Milwaukee*, was still at sea and did not depart from Halifax until 21 February. The voyage was plagued by heavy losses among the horses; 13 from the artillery, 40 from 1 CMR, and 3 from 2 CMR, 56 in all. By the time she arrived at Cape Town on 22 March, Bloemfontein had fallen and it seemed that the war was nearly over. To make matters worse, the harbour was crowded with eight other transports already waiting to dock. It was a dejected lot of Canadians that finally disembarked on the 26th.[23]

Along with the formal offer of a second contingent, there had been a number of offers of volunteers. The Province of British Columbia had, for example, offered to raise a force of 100 mounted rifles. Although the offer had been accepted by the British government, which undertook to "defray the expense of any further contingent if enough to ship," volunteers were not forthcoming in sufficient numbers to complete the unit. This is probably due more to the recruiting of a glamourous regiment of volunteers than of concerns about the propriety of a province raising military forces, the exclusive purview of the federal government.[24]

On 31 December 1899 the Canadian high commissioner, Donald Smith, the Right Honorable Baron Strathcona and Mount Royal of Lochnell Castle of the United Kingdom, after discussions with the colonial secretary, informed Prime Minister Laurier by telegram that he proposed to raise and equip, at his own expense, a regiment of mounted scouts for service in the British army. On 10 January 1900 Lord Strathcona submitted his proposal to the War Office, which accepted it two days later.[25]

Officially Strathcona's Horse was a British, not a Canadian, regiment. On that basis it should not be included in any discussion of the second contingent. The distinction was of little account to the Canadian public, Canadian politicians, and the men who served in its ranks. While the British army compiled Strathcona's Horse casualties separately from those of the Canadian contingents, their decorations were gazetted as awards to Canadians. Like another unit of ambiguous status, the Canadian Scouts, the Strathconas were Canadian in practice, if not in theory.[26]

After the telegram of 31 December, Laurier had agreed to the use of Department of Militia and Defence resources to aid in raising, training and outfitting the regiment. The regiment was to be as well equipped as any that fought in South Africa. Khaki uniforms, including wide-brimmed stetsons; Lee Enfield rifles and Colt revolvers, three Maxims and a pom-pom; equipment including mounted police stock saddles and lariats; tents, blankets, pots and pans, wagons and harness; and, of course, the horses—all paid for by Lord Strathcona. By the time all the bills were settled he would spend \$550,083.02, a princely sum at the time.[27]

One of Lord Strathcona's conditions was that "the matter was to be entirely non-political, the only qualification being the thorough fitness of the officers and men for the service required." Lord Strathcona appears to have been powerful enough to prevent blatant political interference and nepotism. He was shrewd enough to set an example by avoiding the temptation to meddle himself. He had reserved the right to approve the nomination of the officers, subject to approval by the War Office. While Lord Strathcona may have preferred to have his old friend Sam Hughes command the regiment, he graciously supported the nomination of Sam Steele as commanding officer. When offered a captaincy in the regiment, Hughes imperiously refused any appointment short of regimental command.[28]

At the time Steele was second-in-command of 2 CMR and preparing to embark in Halifax. Hastily turning over his duties he quickly headed west to Ottawa where he confirmed a number of details including a regimental establishment of a headquarters of 53 and three squadrons each of 162, organized on the same basis as the CMR. One of his more pleasant tasks was to suggest a name for the new regiment which the high commissioner graciously accepted. The name, Strathcona's Horse, appealed to frontiersman and snob alike, and was a better choice than the original title, Strathcona's Rangers. Steele wasted no time in Ottawa and was soon off to the west to raise the regiment.[29]

The three squadrons of the regiment were recruited in the west, one in Manitoba and Saskatchewan, another in Alberta, and the third in British Columbia. As the unit would be part of the British army, nominations for commissions would require War Office approval. To no one's surprise, most of the officers came from the west, and a large number had served in the NWMP. Other nominees had seen service in the British army or the Canadian militia and one was a regular officer from the Royal Canadian Artillery.[30]

Strathcona demonstrated the acumen that had made him both a noble and extremely wealthy by neatly sidestepping the furor that erupted over the purchase of horses for the second contingent. Dr Duncan McEachran, the dean of the Faculty of Comparative Medicine and Veterinary Science at McGill University, was given the task of selecting and purchasing horses for the Strathconas. His task was complicated by the two perennial Canadian bugbears, climate and distance. It was the depth of winter, and the professor resided in Montreal. While there were many eastern horse dealers no doubt eager to supply good quality animals, the westerners would be mounted on cow-horses: tough, hardy animals trained in range work and life on the dry prairie.

By 10 March McEachran was able to report to Lord Strathcona that he had purchased 536 horses:

> "Ninety-five percent of them are thoroughly broken to cowboy work . . . horses which know nothing of stables or grooms, accustomed to be ridden half a day or more, and at night simply stripped of saddle and turned loose to find their food."[31]

By 1 March the regiment was settled in the Exhibition Grounds in Ottawa. On 8 March the regiment paraded on Parliament Hill in snow that reached above the horse's knees to receive its guidons, embroidered by the ladies of the civil service. On the 12th the regiment was off to Halifax, with stops in Montreal and Moncton for public ceremonies and presentation of flags.[32]

Lord Strathcona was as unstinting in paying for the transport to Halifax as he had been in everything else. His regiment rolled into the station in beautifully appointed pullmans and first class coaches. The farewell included addresses by the lieutenant governor and Dr Borden, who noted that "no doubt that the Strathconas would uphold the honour of the British flag and the reputation of the Canadian soldiers." On St Patrick's Day the regiment, 28 officers, 512 men, and 599 horses, with a party of three officers and 100 men to reinforce The RCR, sailed on board SS *Monterey*.

Like the rail cars, the *Monterey* was well-appointed, but the luxurious quarters had little effect on the ravages of seasickness. Men who faced blizzards and prairie fires without fear were soon retching and yearning for their beloved homes on the range. The Atlantic, however, proved even harder on the horses than the men. Accustomed to the cold, dry air of the prairies, the cow-horses developed respiratory problems and began to die. So many, 173 in all, died that the ship picked up its own entourage of sharks waiting for their next meal. A trooper remarked as he helped dump his horse over the side, "I guess we'll be Strathcona's Foot by the time we get to South Africa." The *Monterey* steamed into Table Bay and anchored on 10 April 1900. It was a severe blow to have lost so many horses, especially as a further 44 horses were found to be suffering from glanders and had to be destroyed.[33]

The first contingent had excluded the territories. Table 4.1, which is adapted from data collated by the Department of Militia and Defence in 1902, shows that the west was not denied the opportunity to serve: it includes the permanent force and NWMP, but not the officers, in the provincial and territorial figures. The reinforcement drafts for The RCR and the Strathconas are included in the above totals. The figures in the percentage columns are the percentage provided to the contingents and the percentage of population of the national total. British Columbia, for example, provided 233 men or 8.0 percent of the total from a population of 178 657, or 3.3 percent of the national population of 5 371 375 as tabulated in the 1901 census. The distribution provides a compromise between the power of the militia establishment and the availability of suitable manpower in the west.[34]

Table 4.1 - Sources for Canadian Contingents

Province/ Territories	1st Contingent	2nd Contingent	Strathcona's Horse	Total	Percent of Contingents	Percent of Population
British Columbia	61	0	172	233	8.0	3.3
Territories	0	345	324	669	23.1	3.9
Manitoba	61	89	46	196	6.8	4.8
Ontario	414	506	7	927	32.0	40.6
Quebec	263	149	7	419	14.5	30.7
Maritimes	311	135	6	452	15.6	16.7
Total	**1110**	**1224**	**562**	**2896**		

There was another body of men that has been included, somewhat deceptively, in the numbers of Canadians raised for South Africa—the 3rd Battalion, The Royal Canadian Regiment. The Imperial battalion in garrison in Halifax was the First Battalion, the Prince of Wales's Leinster Regiment (Royal Canadians). Originally raised in Canada in 1858 as the 100th Royal Canadian Regiment of Foot, this Irish regiment perpetuated the 100th Foot of the War of 1812. From time to time the Canadian government had expressed interest in repatriating the regiment, but the proposals proved fruitless. During early 1900 the matter had once again been the subject of correspondence with the Imperial government. While these discussions were futile, the Canadian government raised the subject of replacing the battalion in Halifax. On 2 March 1900 Prime Minister Laurier announced that the Imperial government had agreed to Canada's offer.

Implementation of the proposal required the same ingenious interpretation of laws and customs we have seen in the raising of the first and second contingents. The strength of the permanent force was fixed by statute. It was impossible to maintain necessary services across the country and garrison Halifax within the fixed ceiling. At the same time the government was reluctant to amend the legislation to allow a temporary measure. The battalion was constituted as a provisional battalion recruited from men already serving. A potential recruit was to belong to a corps in the active militia and be carried on the strength of that corps, have completed at least one year's annual training, and re-enlist in the active militia for a period of three years. Ex-militiamen wishing to enlist must first re-enlist in the active militia. The government rationalized that since these men were militiamen who agreed to serve in a provisional battalion for one year out of their three-year term, they were not members of the permanent force. As the prospect of active service that had attracted men to the contingents was absent, vlunteers were rather slow in coming forward, but eventually the battalion was raised, and the Irish sailed for South Africa.[35]

Except for a draft of reinforcements for the Strathconas and some individuals who made their way to the war as private citizens the Canadians who would see the first stage of the war through were all in South Africa. Despite political divisions and petty wrangling, The RCR, the gunners, and the three mounted regiments, as well as Canadians to fill a share of the supporting roles, had arrived more or less intact.

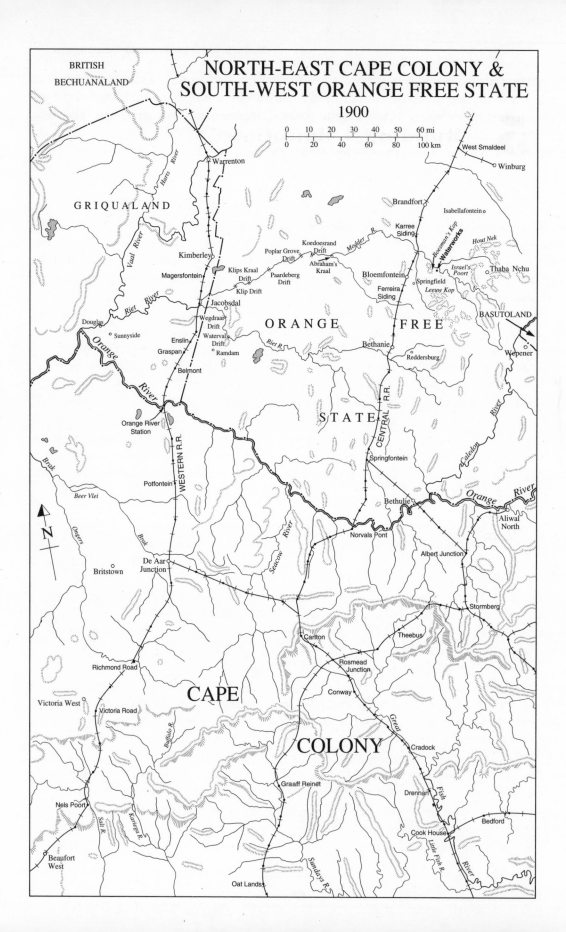

NORTH-EAST CAPE COLONY &
SOUTH-WEST ORANGE FREE STATE
1900

BRITISH
BECHUANALAND

0	10	20	30	40	50	60 mi
0	20	40	60	80		100 km

West Smaldeel

Winburg

Warrenton

GRIQUALAND

Brandfort

Isabellafontein

Karree
Siding

Boxman's Kop
Waterworks

Hout Nek

Kimberley

Koedoesrand
Drift

Molder R.

Poplar Grove
Drift

Abraham's
Kraal

Israel's
Poort

Thaba Nchu

Klips Kraal
Drift

Magersfontein

Paardeberg
Drift

Bloemfontein

Springfield

Leeuw Kop

Klip Drift

Riet River

Jacobsdal

Ferreira
Siding

BASUTOLAND

Wegdraai
Drift

ORANGE   FREE

Douglas

Sunnyside

Waterval
Drift

Enslin

Ramdam

Riet R.

Bethanie

Wepener

Graspan

Reddersburg

Belmont

Orange

River

STATE

CENTRAL R.R.

Caledon

River

Orange River
Station

WESTERN R.R.

Springfontein

Brak

Beer Vlei

Potfontein

Bethulie

Orange   River

Aliwal
North

N

Onsers

Brak

Norvals Pont

Albert Junction

De Aar
Junction

Britstown

Seacow

River

Stormberg

Richmond Road

Carlton

Theebus

Rosmead
Junction

Victoria West

Victoria Road

Conway

CAPE

Buffalo R.

Nels Poort

Sali R.

Kariega R.

COLONY

Great

Cradock

Fish

Graaff Reinet

Drennan

Bedford

Cook House

Little Fish   River

Beaufort
West

Oat Lands

Sundays R.

Chapter

5 Building A Battalion

setting

AS THE *SARDINIAN* steamed towards the harbour at Cape Town, the last few hours seemed to pass slowly, in part because the clear air made the shore seem much nearer than it was. The tiled roofs of Cape Town seemed to stretch away to the edge of the mountains guarding the harbour. At noon the anchor chain rattled into the depths of Table Bay. The bay was crowded with shipping: chartered transports, military troop-ships and warships.[1]

Soon a heavy, squat paddle-wheeler thrashed out from shore like a giant water bug towards the *Sardinian*. It was the official boat with Lieutenant Governor Sir Alfred Milner's aide-de-camp and a civic deputation on board. Also on board was Lieutenant Frank Duffus, a Nova Scotian serving in the Army Service Corps, who was responsible for organizing the move of the battalion forward.[2]

Both the visitors and access to newspapers brought confirmation of what many had suspected after the encounter with the *Rangitara*. The war, after a poor start, had not improved. After seven weeks of bloody encounters and pyrrhic victories, not a single shot had been fired on the territory of the Boer republics. At 6:00 p.m. 29 November the ship moved to the dock, accompanied by whistles from other ships and cheers from their passengers. Quite caught up in the spirit of the occasion, the Canadians replied with choruses of "The Maple Leaf for Ever" and "Canada for Ever." The lines were thrown ashore, the gangplank fell, and the Canadians felt themselves a part of the African continent.[3]

While formal disembarkation would wait for the morning, troops were allowed ashore to stretch their legs within the confines of the dock. There was little sleep that night because of the bustle and noise as the stores and horses were unloaded. At 8:30 the battalion formed up on the dock for the march to Green Point Common. As a result of the shortage of khaki tunics, and much to their disgust, F, G, and H Companies were dressed in the rifle green uniforms issued in Canada and escorted the baggage through back streets to avoid offending the eyes of the welcoming crowds.[4]

The main body, weighed down with nearly 100 pounds of kit per man, marched through the crowded streets to Green Point. Green Point was a cool, shaded camp providing a pleasant vista of sea and mountains. The battalion fell to work pitching tents, organizing the camp, and drawing khaki tunics for F, G, and H Companies. Civilians, including a number of expatriate Canadians, strolled about gazing curiously at the soldiers. There was time for sightseeing and recreation in Cape Town, and the men made the most of it. The battalion would move forward the next day, and officers and men could bring only their overcoats, a shirt and pair of socks, toiletries and a few personal articles, as well as one blanket per man packed in bales. All the rest, purchased so hurriedly in October, would be left behind in stores.[5]

The contingent included a number of individuals who were not members of the battalion. While the YMCA representative, the chaplains, the historical recorder and the press would accompany the battalion, the officers attached for instructional purposes, the extra doctor, the nurses, and Sam Hughes all went their separate ways. The four officers attached for instructional purposes were Lieutenant Colonel François Lessard and Captain William Forester of the Royal Canadian Dragoons, Lieutenant Colonel Charles Drury of the Royal Canadian Artillery, and Major Robert Cartwright of The Royal Canadian Regiment. The first three would play key roles in the second contingent, while Major Cartwright was posted first to a staff position at Orange River Station, and then to the staff of the 1st Mounted Infantry Brigade. The doctor and the nurses were hurried off to a British military hospital where they were told they could care for colonial, but not British, patients. The restriction was soon forgotten as the wounded and sick began to flow down the railways from the front. The only unemployed Canadian was Sam Hughes. The assessments forwarded by Hutton and others had done their job. Sam, however, had not come to South Africa to sit by while lesser men found fame and glory. His status as an MP gained him access to the corridors of power, where he began to lobby for an appointment.

Early on the first day of December 1899 preparations began for the move to De Aar station, several hundred miles up the line. Otter selected Lieutenant S.P. Layborn to command the rear party organized to secure the surplus baggage in Cape Town. He would be replaced by a series of officers recuperating from wounds or disease. The medical officers had identified a number of men who were not physically fit for active service, and these were among those detailed for the rear party. The colour sergeants made the most of the opportunity to get rid of the misfits that surface in any military organization. The rear party included one officer and 32 men and (temporarily) 33 others who were either drunk or absent without leave after the night on the town.[6]

The battalion, 40 officers and 933 men strong, marched to the station in two parties separated by the machine-gun section. The Maxim was mounted on a light carriage designed to be drawn by a horse. To the delight of the crowd the Canadian Maxims were pulled by two brawny machine-gunners. The population turned out en masse to see the battalion off, which inspired the *Cape Argus and Times* to gush:

> Surely never before did such a gigantic throng of people gather in the streets. . .
> Packed in rows on footpath and roadway they greeted the men off to the front with
> volley after volley of cheers. . . each vied with the other in giving voice to the
> admiration and half-sorrowful regret they felt for the gallant sons of the "Lady of the
> Snows" going light-heartedly to grapple with those who would dare assail the Old
> Lion.[7]

The battalion moved off on two trains two hours apart. Accommodation was in English-pattern third-class carriages with compartments six feet long by six feet wide and fitted with a small folding table. Troops were cooped up eight to a compartment in conditions that must have made the *Sardinian* seem spacious. Fortunately the solid, smooth roadbed, free from the ravages of frost, provided a superior ride to North American ones. At first the train passed through a "beautiful succession of farms, gardens, orchards and forest." By evening the train threaded its way in through the mountains of a low range. As it climbed from the coastal plain onto the veldt, the right of way was all grades and curves, so at one minute the train could be rushing along at 60 miles per hour, and at the next be slowed to almost a walking pace.

Morning brought the wide, arid veldt with strange colours and stunted bushes and shrubs, while barren mountains shimmered in the distance away to the east.[8]

There were stops along the route where one could stretch and get a quick snack. Crowds gathered at a number of the stops to cheer the troops, to which they naturally replied. This outburst of enthusiasm horrified Otter, who decreed that there was to be no more cheering, that the troops were to try to remember that they were soldiers now and not to act like a lot of "damned fools." Otter was always conscious that his volunteers were under the critical eye of the British army, and as a result he was very critical of his battalion.[9]

The first train rolled into De Aar station at three in the morning on 3 December, followed by the second train 90 minutes later. De Aar, a vital junction and supply depot where a spur line connected the western railway from Cape Town to Rhodesia with the central line from Port Elizabeth to Pretoria, was garrisoned by some Royal Engineers and the 2nd Battalion, Duke of Cornwall's Light Infantry. When it was light enough to see, tents were off-loaded and, while the cooks prepared coffee and biscuits for breakfast, the men pitched their tents in ordered rows, by company, exactly as sanctified in Otter's little red book.

After breakfast the men settled in to enjoy a pleasant Sunday morning, the heat made bearable by a light breeze that began to play among their tents. As the sun climbed in the clear, summer sky the wind increased and eddies of sand grew into "dust devils." Soon the air was a mass of driving sand; De Aar was in the path of a full-blown sand storm. Buildings a half mile away could not be seen and at times it was impossible to distinguish objects 50 yards distant. Neither work nor worship was possible from early morning until dusk. After the event comments were offered that a Manitoba blizzard was preferable to a South African sandstorm any day of the week.[10]

The next morning a cool breeze greeted the men as they rose for a six o'clock parade. Training began at once in accordance with the drill book, modified by belatedly learned lessons of war on the veldt. The burning sand, the glare of the scorching, blistering sun, and the never-ending thirst could be borne patiently if for no other reason than the prospect of action was near. For three days the battalion sweltered and trained at De Aar, while rumours of heavy fighting raced through the ranks. Here, as well, the battalion was issued with transport mules and wagons and water carts, with their native drivers.[11]

On the third day word came that the battalion was to move to Orange River, the next major station north on the western railway, at once. That night the trains were loaded and by 6:30 a.m. the battalion was climbing northward in two trains across the brown expanse of "sand, wilderness, rockstrewn hill, dried river bed. . . [where] flocks of sheep nibbled the dry grass that grew between the stretches of sand; flocks of goats cropped the brown plains or browsed among the rocks of the unpicturesque kopjes . . . Farm houses—so they were called—were dotted on this everlasting wilderness at intervals of about six miles."[12]

It was not until noon, after a tedious trip under a blazing sun in open cars, that the first train arrived at the cluster of houses and white British army tents at Orange River station. The battalion took over a recently vacated space next to the Second Battalion the King's Shropshire Light Infantry, in a camp made up of Cape Artillery, First Battalion the Gordon Highlanders, Royal Horse Artillery, and the Shropshires. Many hoped the halt would be temporary, but the authorities ordered the Gordons, who had arrived at Cape Town hours before the Canadians, forward instead. When the Scots lost heavily at Magersfontein on the 11th, the disappointment was not as keenly felt.

The tents did not reach the camp until 6:00 p.m. and the work of pitching them began with vigour. Only a few tents had been pitched when black clouds began to roll ominously up over the surrounding kopjes. Soon the wind swirled, the tents flapped like sails catching the wind, and the heavens opened. Drenched soldiers huddled miserably in dripping uniforms and soaked boots until the storm moved on across the veldt, and then set to pitching tents again.

The first night at Orange River offered little chance to dry clothes and equipment. Boer Commandant Prinsloo had cut the line at Enslin north of Belmont. All ranks slept fully clothed, ready to respond to a call to arms. The temperature dropped sharply after nightfall, and teeth chattered as the men huddled in clammy clothes beneath sodden blankets.[13]

The next day was busy, if frustrating. From some of the outposts, the distant hills around the forward outpost at Belmont could be seen. Two hundred men under Captain R.K. Barker, the Officer Commanding (OC) C Company, were detailed to build a railway siding and platform near the station. Despite the heat, the Canadians fell to work with a vengeance. By the end of the day they had constructed three-quarters of a mile of roadway with ties, laid a quarter mile of rails, and built a platform 150 feet long. By any standard it was a good day's work. The accomplishment was made all the sweeter when a train drew into the station and Lieutenant Colonel G.P.E. Girouard alighted. Girouard, a French Canadian in the British army, had built the railway that supported Kitchener's victory in the Sudan. To no one's surprise he was chosen to maintain the South African rail routes from the ports to the front. The cutting of the line between Orange River and Belmont provided an unscheduled opportunity for a brief meeting with his countrymen. He inspected their work and proclaimed that regulars could not have done better, and none but Canadians could have done it in so short a time. This may have been chauvinism fueled by rubbing shoulders with his countrymen (and being able to chat in his mother tongue), but it does not diminish the achievement.[14]

That night saw the regiment take its share of outpost duty, with six officers and 200 men posted on various kopjes. The realization that Boers were in the vicinity kept them awake and alert. Lieutenant Armstrong and his men from E Company on Mount Cheviot kopje could see the signal light busily telegraphing messages from Kimberley, 77 miles away. It would be two months before French's cavalry would finally relieve the beleagured town that seemed so near in the clear night air.

In the cemetery behind the military hospital at Orange River the battalion discovered a Canadian resting on the barren Karroo far from his native Nova Scotia. Lieutenant Charles Wood had died of wounds on 10 November 1899. The great grandson of United States President Zachary Taylor, he had graduated from RMC in 1896, and probably was the first Canadian to die in South Africa during the war.[15]

Spirits were raised when it was learned that the rail line forward to Lord Methuen's army had been repaired, and the battalion was to move forward without delay. Surely action must now soon follow. The four companies of the right half battalion entrained in the early morning of 9 December, glad to be rid of Orange River Station. After 20 miles of brown treeless veldt the train shuddered to a weary halt at the little hamlet of Belmont which the British had captured after a sharp fight on 23 November.[16]

The combination of ridges and railway at Belmont had to be denied to the Boers if the army was to be fed and supplied. It was a rather unimpressive place, consisting of about six single-storey houses, closed-up stores, and station buildings, all of which bore the scars of battle. A few Australian gum trees gave a little relief to the everlasting brown of the grassless landscape. The only animals that seemed able to survive were a few stunted goats and sheep and some ragged ostriches. To the west sprawled the Karroo, covered with low sage scrub stretching to a ridge of kopjes five miles away. To the north and south along the railway line the ground was slightly more undulating, while three successive kopjes to the east culminated in Scots Ridge, named for the successful assault on it by the Scots Guards during the Battle of Belmont. About the camp were the white bell-tents of a sizable garrison made up of Highlanders, Munster Fusiliers, Australians, and Royal Horse Artillery.

Water in the camp was in short supply, so the Canadians were marched to a nearby farm to bivouac for the night. After a week on the veldt the men were heartily sick of the constant dust. The farm was a godsend. In the brown barrens it was a place of soft green grass and ample sweet, cool water. The men drank their fill and then scooped small holes in the sand. Tarpaulins from the transport wagons provided liners for impromptu baths, rinsing grime and grit from the men's bodies and depression from their souls. After the respite, reality returned. The men were ordered to sleep in their uniforms to be ready to stand to at a moment's notice, the norm for months to come. Through the night watchful pickets guarded the surrounding countryside.

In the morning the men learned that this oasis had been a temporary resting place. In typical army fashion, they had to return to the camp at once. Tents were struck after breakfast, and the men marched back to the station to find the Highlanders and Australians gone. The Munsters were awaiting the arrival of the left half battalion before they, in turn, departed for Honeynest Kloof about 19 miles up the line. The right half battalion piled arms on the battlefield and patiently waited for the train. De Aar had welcomed the Canadians with a sandstorm and Orange River with a thunderstorm. Now Belmont was to spring its own surprise. Half an hour before the train was to arrive, rain fell in torrents and thoroughly soaked the men. At noon, while the rain was still pelting down, the remaining companies arrived looking like 400 drowned rats. The Munsters immediately struck camp and hurried off on the same train, as the Canadians occupied the newly vacated ground in front of the station. The Royal Canadians were now responsible for the defence of this dreary backwater on the lines of communication.

The station was flanked by ridges and kopjes within rifle range to the east. Boers on the ridge would make life very uncomfortable for the defenders of Belmont station. The railway could also be cut in a number of likely places, so the surrounding country had to be patrolled to deny the Boers an unopposed approach. And the undulating ground in both directions along the line itself provided a covered approach for any enemy who evaded the patrols, so Otter had to guard against this possibility.

Otter posted a company on Scots Ridge and small parties 800 yards north and south of the station along the railway track. Mounted infantry patrolled from Wittiputs to Graspan. Every afternoon outposts were sited to cover approaches to the station, especially on the various hills of the Belmont battlefield. In the settlement itself trenches were dug in the baked, rocky earth on the north side of the station.[17]

The obvious question is why Otter only placed trenches to the north when the enemy could appear from any direction? The answer, somewhat oversimplified, is that the ridge, not the station, was the key to the defence of Belmont. The company on Scots Ridge sat on the enemy's approach from the east and southeast and secured the station from attack from the northeast to the southwest. The trenches north of the station blocked the remaining approaches. In addition, the British were facing the Boers on the Modder River a few miles to the north. While Prinsloo had cut the line just days before, the arrival of British reinforcements—Gordons, Australians, Canadians—allowed Lord Methuen to build up his forces and secure his lines of communication. As long as there was a large British force on the Modder, the Boers would be reluctant to detach a force large enough to successfully assault Belmont. However, any slackening of the defences would almost certainly result in an unwelcome visit. As long as the ridge remained in friendly hands a battalion with a company of mounted infantry and a section of field guns could deny the station to the Boers.

After "Black Week" (10-15 December 1899) Belmont would not be quite so secure. British reverses, as well as proximity to the Boer republics, had resulted in rebellion in the western and northern Cape Colony. Douglas, a long day's ride to the west was a particular hotbed and threatened the flank and rear of any advance over the Modder River, while Boers roamed at will from safe havens in the Orange Free State.

In the meantime companies prepared defences on the various kopjes and then practised occupying these positions in response to alerts. There was little free time, as two companies continuously manned the defences while the other companies provided outposts and patrols each night. Each morning well before first light all ranks stood to, fully dressed and armed against a surprise assault from lurking Boers who may have evaded the outposts. The battalion continued to drill and train and perform the necessary housekeeping required to maintain a unit in the field.

Otter took his responsibilities as station commander and the officer charged with the defence of Belmont seriously and delegated command of the battalion to Major Buchan. Every day companies under Buchan's direction marched out on the veldt and exercised in the new tactics dictated by the unhappy experiences of the early battles. Buchan, unlike Otter, was a gregarious individual who, despite putting the troops through difficult and strenuous training, seems to have been liked by the men. Training took cognizance of the bitter lessons already learned by the British army in encounters like the one where Lieutenant Wood had lost his life, properly and elegantly dressed. Officers and NCOs took their place in the ranks, dressed in issue uniforms without visible rank badges. The battalion drew 32 Lee Metfords from the British for the officers. The tried and true practice of firing volleys shoulder to shoulder from steady ranks was abandoned for the new heresy of skirmishing forward in long lines with several paces between the men. Prone men practiced firing and then moving, either by short rushes from cover to cover or by crawling like cursing khaki lizards. The hot, dry days built a battalion that would come to be considered the equal of any in the British army.[18]

Definite opinions had been formed about their clothing and equipment. The useless little glass water bottles were replaced by the British pattern. The Oliver web equipment, canvas uniforms, and Mills pattern bandolier proved to be uncomfortable, impractical, or both. Working on the grass is always greener principle, the British felt the bandolier was superior to the cartridge pouch and later adopted it.

Water originally was brought from a nearby farm by ox cart. The inadequate supply was made available on a first come, first served basis. Later the situation improved, when under the direction of a British officer, water was brought from Orange River by rail, and eventually a well was sunk and a canvas bath filled with water. Lice appeared at Belmont and became constant, unwelcome companions for the duration of the campaign.

The British treasury has always been particularly prone to economize on the supply of food for its army on campaign. Bread took the form of hard, solid loaves transported to Belmont in railway cars open to the elements. On arrival the loaves, burnt on the bottom and hard on the inside, were kicked or tossed from the cars to roll across the ground like aristocrats' heads fresh from the guillotine. By the time the bugle sounded "Come to the Cook-House Door, Boys, Come to the Cook-House Door" the bread had a patina of South African grit and grime, not all of which could be removed. On occasion hard tack, thick army biscuits, would be substituted for bread. Meat was canned bully beef or stringy local livestock. Perpetually famished young men soon dubbed Belmont "Hungryfontein." An unnecessary irritation was the lack of a dry canteen. Dry canteens sell extras such as soap, tobacco, candy, jam, and writing paper for the men. Otter, feeling that his men were adequately rationed, would not allow the battalion to operate one and even objected to the efforts of the YMCA to provide an area where men could write letters and relax. He was dead wrong on this, and most other questions requiring a basic understanding of human nature.[19]

In any military organization, as in any other community, there is a continual drain from illness, death, and accident. The Canadians were no different, individuals being lost to various causes, including one soldier who was observed to have been "acting oddly," and was evacuated to England as insane. Private M.C. Chappell of G Company died of tonsillitis on 13 December, the first of many to perish of disease. Unfortunately the effect of several weeks of inadequate diet, poor sanitation and general dehabilitating conditions intensified what the army insensitively calls "wastage." By 22 January 1900 37 Canadians had been hospitalized. The battalion was probably fortunate that there were not more than three fatalities during the stay at Belmont.[20]

To the military mind reporting sick provides an opportunity for the faint-hearted to shirk duties. If going on sick parade is made as difficult as possible, then only the truly sick will parade. Men reporting sick were marched to the battalion medical section with full packs, helmets, weapons, and equipment. Examination by a medical officer would surely have revealed malingerers and hypochondriacs more accurately than an ordeal akin to a medieval test for witchcraft. Once in action, stretcher-bearers and medical officers alike would display incredible gallantry caring for wounded under fire. In Belmont, before battle, the situation was different.[21]

Difficulties were exacerbated by the intense heat of summer 4000 feet above sea level on the veldt, which produced "unbearable sweltering days . . . The sentry found it impossible to sit upon the heated rocks and stood leaning on his rifle and gazing in a sort of stupor into the shimmering haze of the distance. The flaps of the tent had been rolled as much as possible to admit of a breeze . . . So hot was the iron of the tent-pole that to touch it meant a blister, and that in the shade." Conditions on outposts were, if anything, worse. There was little shelter from the direct sun. The stench of dead horses choked the nostrils and turned the stomachs. Hastily buried bodies of Boer dead were everywhere on the old Belmont battlefield.[22]

Traditionally the army has made extraordinary efforts to come up with a special meal on Christmas Day, especially on active service. The Canadians, like every other unit in South Africa, were determined to set a special table for the feast. A party was despatched to purchase fowl, fresh fruit, and all the trimmings in Cape Town for the men's dinner. The officers took up a collection for their own meal and pressed the purchasing party into service to shop for them at the same time. Whether from incompetence or just plain bad luck, the supplies did not arrive until Christmas morning. The fowl were alive and had to be hastily killed and cleaned, while much of the fruit had spoiled after several days in the heat. Despite the handicaps, both the officers and men were able to enjoy the fellowship of a traditional, if spartan, Christmas dinner. The men made the best of the opportunity and seemed to have enjoyed their dinner and went so far as to stage an impromptu serenade of the officers' mess as well as some other horseplay fueled by high, not liquid, spirits. Otter decided his duties as station commander took priority over greeting his troops, but Buchan emerged to wish the men a Merry Christmas and to enjoin them, as they were issued a bottle of warm beer each, to not get too drunk. The men loved it and cheered Larry Buchan to the skies.[23]

After Christmas command of Belmont passed to Lieutenant Colonel Pilcher of the Bedfordshire Regiment and Otter was able to devote himself to the battalion. The station had been reinforced with two companies and a machine-gun of the Cornwalls on Boxing Day and then with two companies of Queensland Mounted Infantry on 29 December until the garrison numbered nearly 1700. Pilcher was offensive minded and began to exercise columns in forced marches followed by mock attacks and a fighting withdrawal through a firm base back to Belmont. He also increased local security and restricted the movement of civilians, white and black.

By year's end it was time to deal with Boers terrorizing Douglas, a short distance to the west. In the early afternoon of the last day of 1899 Pilcher led a force made up of the Irish and Australian mounted infantry, a section of Royal Horse Artillery, the Cornwalls, and C Company and the machine-gun section of the Canadians against them. Normally the appearance of a column riding into the hills and ridges towards Douglas would have put every Boer for miles around on the alert, but the various exercises had created a false sense of security. Indeed, on the 30th a column had struck deeper to the west than usual, but returned to camp, like all the excursions that preceded it. The infantry were carried in springless open wagons, which, while uncomfortable, were not appreciably slower than mounted infantry. Besides, riding beats walking. Night marches were the exception because of the presence of patches of ironstone which made compasses unreliable and the lack of trustworthy guides and maps.[24]

After five hours of hot, thirsty work the column halted at Thornhill, about 20 miles from Belmont. Pilcher had taken every precaution to prevent word of their approach reaching the Boers. Guards had been dropped off at the little farms and native kraals to prevent any communication with the enemy. The next morning, the first of 1900, the little force, less the Cornwalls who manned a firm base, moved off at 6:00 in the morning. Now luck intervened on their side: a wind rose and created dust devils and clouds that obscured the cloud of dust raised as the column crossed sandy patches. By 9:00 scouts had located the enemy and shortly before 11:00 tents could be seen on the north end of Sunnyside kopje. Action was now a virtual certainty.

The veldt to the right was clear and the two 12-pounders trotted forward to come into action on a convenient knoll a mile from the camp. Shortly after 11:00 the first round screeched downrange to burst over the laager. Within five minutes shrapnel spraying the camp had sent the Boers scurrying to the top of the kopje where they opened rapid but ineffective Mauser fire on the guns. With the Boers' attention concentrated to their front, the Queenslanders worked forward on the left while the Munsters swept wide on the north to cut off the line of retreat.

The panting, sweating figure of the Associated Press correspondent, whose journalistic ethics did not preclude him from doing his bit, relayed orders to Captain Barker. Leaving one section to guard the guns, C Company was to advance to a kopje about 1200 yards from the enemy position. To reach the ridge the men had to cross a stretch of open ground, usually a prescription for disaster. The lessons had been learned, and the boys from southern Ontario doubled across the veldt with eight paces between men. The Boers opened heavy fire but it takes more than marksmanship to hit a running man at a mile.

When the Canadians reached the ridge, the men crawled and wiggled into fire positions and opened rapid fire on the hill. The hail from three score Lee Enfields soon had its effect as the returning fire lessened noticeably. The heat and sun now were more of a threat than the enemy, and the men were relieved when the command was received to move forward to another kopje well within effective Mauser range.

Sections advanced by rushes from cover to cover, crawling when they must, doubling across open spaces, dodging behind rocks and into hollows, while rifle bullets sang around their ears. When the kopje was gained, Barker found again that not a man had been hit. C Company, roasting under the hot sun and cursing the touch of hot rocks, cautiously crawled into fire positions, while they waited for the order to assault the hilltop.

Concentrated fire on the enemy position began to have the desired effect. Boers began to slink away, especially when bursts of fire to the west signalled the approach of the Australians. Barker ordered "fix bayonets," and C Company dashed forward under fire to join in the assault. Incredibly their luck held. Helmets and tunics were nicked, but not a man was hit. Up and over the kopje swept panting, cursing soldiers from opposite ends of the Empire. Bearded men in dusty civilian clothing threw down their weapons and raised their arms in surrender, barely a moment too soon for excited soldiers with their blood up.

The tally was very much in Pilcher's favour. His column suffered two killed and three wounded, none of them Canadian, while they counted 6 dead, 12 wounded and 35 prisoners scattered about Sunnyside. Surprise and audacity had paid off. There was a bit of luck involved too, but luck in battle depends more on preparation than chance. Surprise, effective covering fire, and the skilful use of ground enabled the men to approach unscathed, while the Munsters sweeping around the right encouraged a number of the enemy to opt for discretion over valour. In this case success must be measured in the number of enemy taken out of the war. If Pilcher had acted differently, his force could have occupied an abandoned camp.[25]

The rest of the day was spent destroying captured supplies and equipment that could not be carried away with the column. That night, after a meal courtesy of the enemy's commissariat, the soldiers rested on the battlefield expecting to return to Belmont in the morning.

The task was not yet done. The party on Sunnyside was only a small part of the enemy in the area. Pilcher could have justified ending the excursion as it was known that the Boers held Douglas in strength. He probably counted on surprise and the fog of war to work in his favour. Instead, the column pushed on to Douglas near the junction of the Modder and Vaal rivers, held by 300 Boers, mostly Cape Colony rebels. Word of the affair at Sunnyside probably had demoralized them, and survivors had no doubt exaggerated the size of the British force. The Boers chose not to contest Douglas and the Union Jack flapped, temporarily, over the little town. Douglas had been used as an enemy supply depot, and the troops set to destroying large stocks of ammunition and other supplies they were unable to carry away.

The enemy would react in strength to the presence of this little force, and no time was wasted in completing the task and heading east towards the sanctuary of Belmont. A large number of civilians, mostly of British extraction, accompanied the column in wagons and carts. It fell to the Canadians to provide a close escort and security for them, and to guard against any attempts at sabotage or signal by fifth columnists in their ranks. The column rolled back through the Cornwalls' firm base, collecting the guards at the farms and kraals until finally on 4 January 1900, C Company with 80 civilians passed through the pickets and halted in the dust of Belmont. Incredibly, this well-managed little foray was the first real success for British arms in weeks. Part of the impact of this success appeared, at least in Otter's mind, to have been due to a compliant correspondent and Pilcher's flair for self-promotion. The expedition may have been overpromoted in the press but it still was a success and showed that Boers could also be caught napping.[26]

Regrettably it also demonstrated that foot-borne infantry were of limited utility in a mobile war. The lesson had not been lost on the British. Every infantry battalion in South Africa, including the Canadians, was ordered to detach a company for service as mounted infantry. Otter cleverly deflected the bullet by insisting that the Canadians must retain their national identity, preferably by fighting as a company in one of the Canadian Mounted Rifles battalions being raised for service in South Africa. That, he reported to Ottawa, was the last he heard of it.[27]

January 1900 brought no real change in the routine at Belmont. The build-up of forces continued as the Canadians languished in a searing, dusty wasteland. There were some distractions, including a sports day where the Australians dominated the field. The soldiers also took up a pastime that nearly a century later conjures up wild images. Flocks of ostriches wandered about the area and sometimes strayed through the camp and its various outposts. Otter described them as being as tame as dogs and a nuisance, continually poking their heads into tents and appropriating whatever struck their fancy. In a burst of perverse inspiration, someone decided that he would like an ostrich plume to send home as a souvenir. It soon became "in" to sneak up on an unsuspecting bird, wrestle it to the ground and pull feathers from wildly thrashing wings or tail. Frantic birds yelped and dashed for safety pursued by laughing, shouting soldiers. After a few men were laid low by kicks from muscular legs the sport lost some of its popularity, but it seems never to have died out completely. In more than one instance, hungry young men decided that they might as well carry the process through to the logical end, and cooked and ate the unlucky bird.

In January the battalion lost two more members from its ranks under happier circumstances. Major Septimus Denison, a regular infantry officer and a member of the first

RMC class, was selected to serve on the staff of the commander-in-chief, while Lance Corporal C.R. Molyneux from Montreal was commissioned in the 2nd South African Horse, a locally raised mounted regiment. He was the first of many from the Canadian contingents who would become officers in the British and colonial forces during the war.[28]

On 9 January the Belmont garrison mounted a raid which included the Maxim section and A, B, and part of H Companies under the command of Major Pelletier, on Commandant Lubbe's farm near Jacobsdal in the OFS. Intelligence must have been very good, because it was only by a fluke that the commandant and a party of his cronies were not captured as they sat down for dinner. The farm was pillaged, anything portable carried away with the rest destroyed, and the raiders returned to camp the next morning. The Canadians missed much of the excitement as it was their turn to secure the firm base. The results of this raid, coming so soon after the Douglas operation, resulted in Pilcher being ordered forward to command a mounted infantry corps. This did not sit well with Otter, who believed Pilcher had used Otter's plans for his own advancement. He must have been even more disgruntled when an *engineer* officer replaced Pilcher at Belmont.[29]

Another less successful raid was mounted on the 21st towards Thornhill. There were several contacts with enemy outposts and a patrol of the Victorian Mounted Rifles, who had replaced the Queenslanders, was fortunate to escape from an ambush with only one wounded. The presence of enemy in force resulted in G, soon reinforced by A Company, occupying Richmond farm, where both remained for three weeks.[30]

On 8 February "Bobs," Field Marshall Lord Roberts, VC, the commander-in-chief, and his chief of staff, Major General Lord Horatio Kitchener of Khartoum spent a few minutes in a quick inspection of Belmont and a short meeting with Otter. The next day it became apparent that they must have approved of the Royal Canadians. The battalion, which had attacked every kopje for ten miles around Belmont, was to join the newly created 19th Brigade along with the Cornwalls, Shropshires, and Gordons, with whom they had shared the dust, heat, and boredom of lines-of-communications duty. On the 10th the brigade commander, Brevet Colonel Horace Smith-Dorrien, arrived for a quick visit.

At 4:00 p.m. on 12 February the battalion bid farewell to dusty, desolate Belmont. The Royal Canadians were off to war.[31]

Chapter

6 Paardeberg

BY EARLY FEBRUARY 1900 Roberts was ready to take the offensive. The most obvious course was an advance along the central line, the very option that had formed the basis of pre-war planning. Roberts, however, decided to base his advance on the western railway. The commander-in-chief with 37 000 men and 36 000 horse, mules, and oxen would strike 80 miles across country to the central railway below Bloemfontein, with a detour to relieve Kimberley. Roberts' striking force was made up of a cavalry division, 6th and 7th Divisions from the United Kingdom, and the newly organized 9th Division, which was made up of the Highland Brigade and 19th Brigade, formed from battalions, including 2 RCR, on the lines of communications. As can be seen from Table 6.1 the division was deficient in supporting troops, a situation that would persist until after Paardeberg.[1]

Table 6.1 Ninth Division Lieutenant General Sir H.E. Colvile

3rd (Highland) Brigade	19th Brigade
Major General H. Macdonald	Major General H.L. Smith-Dorrien
2nd Black Watch	2nd Duke of Cornwall's L.I.
1st Highland L.I.*	2nd Shropshire L.I.
2nd Seaforth Highlanders	1st Gordon Highlanders
1st A. and S. Highlanders	2nd Royal Canadian Regiment
Cape Vol. Bearer Coy	7th Divn. F.H. Bearer Coy
3rd Co. Field Hospital	No. 1 Section Cape F.H.

Divisional Troops
82 Fd Bty**   65 How Bty 2 RN 4.7in.   2 12-prs 7 Coy, RE
                          2 RN 4.7 in. 2 12-prs

Notes: * Remained at Magersfontein.
    * *Replaced in March by 83, 84, and 85 Field Btys

To cut the army away from the railway required special arrangements for the supply of the army. A large supply park of ox-drawn wagons resupplied from depots established along the railway would trail the army. To mobilize this large transport network required pooling unit transport and the collection of nearly 2000 supply wagons and 20 000 draught animals. Units were restricted to ammunition mules, a water cart, an ambulance or two, and a few baggage wagons to carry no more than the barest of shelter and two days food and forage. While this reorganization has been criticized, reliance on unit transport would have resulted in chaos in South Africa.[2]

There is a certain irreducible minimum that must stay with the soldier: boots, clothing, webbing, and helmet; a field dressing; a weapon and as much ammunition as possible; and some food and water. (In 9th Division only The RCR retained their greatcoats, which were carried rolled and slung across the body.) Everything else can be dispensed with, at least for short periods. Unit transport was available to carry a blanket per man and a rubber groundsheet for every two. Spare uniforms, tents, and such frills would come along later, if at all. Like the men, the animals had to be fed by forage carried with the army.

On the afternoon of 12 February the Canadians steamed up the track to Graspan, the next station up the line, to join the rest of the brigade. Graspan was the jumping-off point for the British offensive and the cavalry division, and two infantry divisions were already marching into the Orange Free State. Nineteenth Brigade would trail the army on the morrow. The brigade bivouacked under the stars and before dawn began to march east towards Waterval Drift on the river Riet, which flows northwest to join the Modder near Modder River Station. The first day's objective was the hamlet of Ram Dam. The 13th was a desperately hot, dry day and progress was slow. Upwards of 50 men dropped out. Though most straggled in later on their own, 14 Canadians were unable to continue the march. Ram Dam, a desolate farm squatting at the foot of a ridge, was reached in the early afternoon. Columns of dead-tired troops in salt-caked khaki and burning boots wheeled into position and halted. Where was the water? All that was available was a slimy pool, alive with unnameable wriggling things and churned into mud soup by hundreds of animals jostling for space with men filling their canteens. Thirsty soldiers after a hot march are not discriminating and these gulped down canteen after canteen of the foul stuff.[3]

The Ninth Division was to cross Waterval Drift, swing north and capture Jacobsdal. After a march of 12 miles as hot and trying as the day before, the Canadians reached the drift in the early afternoon of Valentine's Day 1900. If the troops were ready for a rest, they were in for a rude shock. Two naval guns were stranded at the drift. The combination of a mud-bottomed river, a few tons of heavy gun, and soft, sandy banks were too much for the 32 oxen hitched to each gun. The Canadians were detailed to assist in the passage of the guns over the drift. Teams of 200 soldiers grasped long ropes hitched to the gun wheels and hauled the obstinate dead-weights through the drift and up the banks to the flat open veldt on the far bank. It was nearly 6:00 before the guns were across. After a welcome meal the men, less sentries and mess orderlies, were soon rolled up in their greatcoats, fast asleep. Reveille came at 3:00 a.m., and the column was on the march again at 5:00.[4]

This time it was the Canadians' turn to lead 19th Brigade, detailed to protect the rear of the army. Leaving a further seven men unable to proceed, the battalion moved off at first light. The sky was hazy and a pleasant breeze was blowing, which made the march seem more of a stroll than a forced march. Before 9:00 a.m. the battalion had covered nine miles to the day's objective at Wedgraal Drift and thrown out a screen to cover the arrival of the brigade.

The same day General French relieved Kimberley in a wild charge that swept through the Boer defences. Meanwhile, back at Waterval Drift, the ox-drawn supply train was waiting to cross the Riet, guarded by a small force of mounted infantry. Christiaan De Wet with 1000 riders swept up the Cape side of the Riet, brushed aside the escort, and fell upon the wagons loaded with several days' supplies. Roberts, after some vacillation, decided that he must abandon the convoy. As he was not yet aware that Cronje would offer himself up for destruction, Roberts had to balance the possibility of jeopardizing his grand design against the shortage of supplies. Roberts persevered with his plan, the convoy was lost, and the army went on short rations. Fortunately, the seven Canadians were unharmed as De Wet disappeared to reappear at Paardeberg.[5]

Meanwhile, 7th Division had already captured Jacobsdal five miles from Wedgraal after a sharp skirmish with its Boer defenders. Cronje finally appreciated, after Kimberley was relieved and his flank was turned, that a noose was being tightened about Magersfontein. That night he abandoned his strong position on the north bank of the Modder and started along the Bloemfontein road to the east. Meanwhile French, out of contact with the main army, was pursuing Kimberley's besiegers to the north. On the morning of 16 February Kelly-Kenny's 6th Division on the Modder spotted the dust from Cronje's convoy and began to race him for the series of drifts over the Modder. Boers hindered with wagons and families could still easily outstrip marching British infantry. The British had to stay close enough to catch Cronje before he could cross his entire party over a drift and escape behind a mounted rearguard. A hastily mustered force was able to prevent a crossing at Klip Drift. The next crossing place was near the little hill called Paardeberg.

Contact was regained with French just after dark and that night he dashed, if that is the correct term for weary men on exhausted horses, for the Kimberley-Bloemfontein Drift. The situation was very much in doubt.

Nineteenth Brigade marched through Jacobsdal. While the town had been captured on the previous day, and the brigade advanced guard had swept through the town, the Canadians were canny enough to search for lurking enemy, and food. At this time, which was no later than mid-morning, Roberts, who had established his headquarters at Jacobsdal, still had not realized that the Magersfontein position had been completely abandoned. He first directed 9th Division to guard against an enemy advance from the south, but later ordered Colvile to start towards Kimberley that evening. Shortly after 6:00 p.m. the orders were changed again, this time to march to Klip Drift.[6]

On a grueling night march that did not end until Klip Drift was reached before dawn, 19th Brigade left Jacobsdal. The brigade rested until late afternoon and, after a hasty meal, set out on another overnight march. The men trudged all through the night on the heels of the Highland Brigade. Marching by night was more comfortable, as the temperature cooled to the merely warm. Against this there was the poor footing and the danger of injury as men cursed and stumbled over the plain.[7]

Cronje had reached Vendutie Drift, just upstream from Paardeberg, and halted for rest and a meal in the late morning of 17 February. Oxen were outspanned, horses unsaddled, and a number of burghers lay down for a quick nap. Suddenly there was a boom, a swish and the explosion of a British shell. Smoke drifted lazily over a hill a mile and a half to the north. General French, with 1200 cavalry and two horse artillery batteries, had arrived in the nick of time. The sensible thing to do would have been to salvage as much of the army as possible. Cronje refused to abandon the families and supplies and resolved to make a fight of it from a hasty laager on the north bank of the Modder midway between Koodesberg and Paardeberg drifts. Once his wagon and animals pulled into the laager, the Boers began to extend outposts upstream and downstream along both banks of the Modder. This not only prevented any approach by the British, but kept open an avenue of escape, at least for riders, and, if they could extend far enough west, for the wagons at Paardeberg Drift.

Cronje had no great opinion of British fighting abilities and expected to be relieved before the British could pound him into submission.

The old fox had been run to ground, but the trap was still not closed. The road to the south lay open. Soon a cloud of dust approaching along the Modder from the west heralded the approach of mounted infantry. For the time being Cronje would be in a trap of his own making as the British built up a cordon around him, but the issue was still in doubt as commandos under De Wet and Ferreira had been summoned. It would depend on who got there "firstest, with the mostest."

Cronje's laager lay on the north bank between two drifts across the Modder, which snakes in a deep, wide gorge across the veldt. The usually shallow Modder was in flood, with the current running at nine miles per hour. A series of kopjes ringed the veldt, close to the river in the west at Paardeberg, swinging out a few miles in the north, approaching the river again at Koodesberg, and running rather closer along the south bank. The dominant feature was a high peak, soon to be dubbed Kitchener's Kopje, near the southwest extremity. The position resembled a shallow oval platter, with a gouge down the long axis.

The laager formed a large semicircle on the north bank with Boers entrenched on both sides of the river. Cronje's men began to extend their positions downstream to within a mile or two of Paardeberg Drift. The Boers dug narrow, deep slit trenches, scattering the soil so that they were invisible from ground level. By the end of the battle many trenches would include a dugout in the walls to provide protection from the searching lead balls of British shrapnel.

Before dawn 19th Brigade began to arrive south and west of Paardeberg Drift. All around were the signs of battle to come. The Highland Brigade had deployed to the east of the drift and would later attack northwards at about the same time as The RCR forded the Modder. The attack would prove futile, although a number of Scots were able to cross the river between Paardeberg Drift and the Boer outposts at the bend. Beyond them were the men of 6th Division and some mounted infantry holding the ground they had taken up to block Cronje's escape. During the day, in response to Kitchener's orders, they would mount unsuccessful frontal assaults north and south of the river. Batteries were steadily pumping shells into the wagon laager, just visible in the distance. Away to the east French's men were blocking Koodesberg Drift and warily probing the Boer trenches. In the early morning light of 18 February Smith-Dorrien halted his three battalions, with the fourth, the Duke of Cornwall's Light Infantry (DCLI), still on the road escorting the division's transport, and awaited orders. Lieutenant General Colvile, the division commander, was with Lord Kitchener, who had assumed command because of the sudden illness of Roberts. The first order was to take up a position near some field guns south of the river. There was no time for breakfast; instead a cup of coffee, a biscuit, and a hurried rum ration was gulped down by tired men on empty stomachs.

Soon a staff officer galloped up to Smith-Dorrien with orders to cross the river and secure a feature, Gun Hill, three or four miles across the veldt to the northeast to prevent any escape in that direction. When Smith-Dorrien asked where his brigade was to cross, the staff officer replied, "The river is in flood, and as far as I have heard, Paardeberg Drift, the only one available, is unfordable; but Lord Kitchener, knowing your resourcefulness, feels sure you will get across somehow." With these helpful words, he turned and galloped off, leaving Smith-Dorrien to his own devices. The brigade commander, who, as a 20-year-old lieutenant had survived Islandawna by a combination of guts and good luck, was not one to waste time. Ordering his brigade to follow, he galloped to the river. He must have still been fuming, for he unhesitatingly plunged his horse into the rushing stream upstream of the drift. After regaining the bank with some difficulty and somewhat chastised by his brush with death, he moved to the drift. Here he found that his horse could just get across without swimming, but the current was very strong and the river at least 50 yards wide. It was too dangerous for tired infantry encumbered with weapons and packs to cross unassisted. The engineers got a rope across which they securely anchored on both banks. Some men crossed by the rope, while others linked arms for support. The brigade, as well as its supporting battery, struggled across through rushing mud-brown water that reached up to the men's armpits and completely submerged the field guns. Besides the guns and limbers, the only other vehicle able to cross was one of the Canadian machine-guns, the other being temporarily out of action with a damaged wheel. By 10:15 a.m. the crossing was complete except for the DCLI guarding the transport and two companies of KSLI. As the brigade crossed the first battalions swung to the west to avoid Boer fire. The Shropshires secured Gun Hill by 11:00 a.m., after which the Gordons were ordered to extend the line to the northeast. As The RCR crossed they were directed to work up the bank and prolong the line from the Shropshires to the river. The guns and the Canadian Maxim came into action at Gun Hill and began to engage the Boers in the donga and along the river bank.

Gun Hill, and the troops extended either side of it, threatened the Boers and made their withdrawal east along the river back to the laager inevitable. This makes what happened later during the day all the more tragic.[8]

Smith-Dorrien seemed to have been seized with an uncharacteristic bout of inertia and allowed the Canadians to proceed in accordance with his ambiguous orders despite his perspective from Gun Hill. It may be that he intended for Otter to piquet the crest and extend northwards in front of the Paardeberg feature. Smith-Dorrien felt his task was to prevent any escape to the northeast, while Otter believed that 9th Division had been ordered to attack with 19th Brigade left (north of the Modder) and the Highland Brigade right on the south bank. Otter was not one to question orders, and the Canadians, lulled by Sunnyside, had yet to experience how handily an unseen enemy could shoot down exposed soldiers. Nineteenth Brigade was newly formed and had not trained together. It was up to Smith-Dorrien to make his intentions perfectly clear to Otter, which he did not.[9]

As companies emerged from the drift they swung right behind a hill and ridge extending from the bank where a track ran from the drift towards Gun Hill. The plan and formation was simple: A Company would lead, followed by C close behind, with D and E as their support. The remaining companies would remain in reserve. Major Buchan would advance with the firing line, with Otter and Major Pelletier doing the same with the support companies. The spacing between men increased to five paces as the companies moved steadily forward, crested the knoll, and headed down the long, open forward slope. Private James Halkett Findlay, a 27-year-old from central Ontario, was struck by a bullet in the heart, the first member of the battalion to die in battle. The open ranks of hunched men in wet, leaden khaki advanced steadily in long, thin lines until they were within about 300 yards of the Highlanders and within accurate rifle range of the greenery lining the banks. The order to lie down was given, and the men dropped into the cover afforded by the little folds and rock-hard anthills that dotted the veldt. On order sections rose and doubled forward 30 paces or so, to drop and crawl into concealed fire positions again. Concealed sections should cover moving ones by fire; the presence of friendly troops to the front effectively prevented this. The advance progressed slowly down the hot, barren slope as bullets snarled and screamed. Here and there, dark stains on still khaki forms dotted the field as Boer fire began to take its toll. Sergeant William Scott, the "celebrated oarsman," died leading his A Company section in one of the short rushes. Finally, the line reached a point from 500 to 800 yards from the enemy trenches; an A Company NCO estimated this had required no more than three or four rushes per section. Here the advance halted and opened fire, in a position Smith-Dorrien felt was "rather closer . . . than necessary" and well within effective range of the Boers. The firing line was reinforced first with C Company, then with D and E and part of B. The rest of B as well as F and G were a few hundred yards to the rear in support with H in reserve, but still under fire. As the firing line was built up, fresh troops were superimposed on men already in place so that officers found themselves commanding troops from a number of companies. While the advance by a series of short rushes, the reinforcement of the firing line and the retention of supports and reserve behind the firing line were all in accordance with British doctrine, not all the problems of adapting tactical drills to South African conditions had been solved.[10]

The troops huddled in the available cover and scanned the banks for a glimpse of the enemy. The day was very hot, the men had not eaten since the previous afternoon, and the sun burned down unmercifully. Those who had been prudent enough to save a biscuit or two in their pockets found that the river water had reduced hard tack to pulp. To shift in an attempt to find cover was to invite Boer bullets. In the early afternoon a violent thunderstorm soaked the men without relieving their thirst or improving their position. Among the men with rifles, who at least had the satisfaction of being able to shoot back, moved other brave men, medical orderlies, ammunition carriers, and chaplains, who courageously exposed themselves as they moved from rear to front and made the return trip. Casualties steadily mounted. Captain Arnold, the A Company Commander, was shot through the head as he raised himself to scan the banks through his binoculars. Two stretcher-bearers ran to Arnold and were shot down. Two more followed, and one fell. Finally Surgeon-Captain Eugene Fiset was able to reach Arnold and, after bandaging his wounds, bear him from the field with the aid of the remaining stretcher-bearer. It would have been impossible for the Boers to identify the red cross armband worn by medical personnel. Several, including Father O'Leary and Privates Curphy and Page, had narrow escapes as they selflessly laboured in aid of their fellow man. Smith-Dorrien ordered the KSLI forward to relieve pressure on the Canadians and moved his supporting field battery to a position where it was able to fire directly down the length of the donga and along the river bank. These moves had some effect, but fire from the donga persisted. The Boers in the donga had not been located by some of the Canadians and their fire was taken for overs from Gun Hill. This resulted for calls to hold fire, which in turn resulted in an increase in the fire from the donga. The Canadian advance on the right, that is on the river side, may have actually outflanked the nemy. Unfortunately, the well-intentioned enfilading of the river from Gun Hill prevented troops from moving along it to turn the Boer line.

Otter felt that while he was faced by 1200 Boers, the situation was not difficult. (His assessment probably includes those extending along the Modder holding the Highland Brigade and 6th Division at bay.) He was pleased by his men's steadiness and fire discipline in their first action. The Boer fire was termed "slow" as the enemy husbanded their ammunition until a Canadian exposed himself. Unfortunately fate, or British generalship, intervened in the person of Horatio Herbert Kitchener.

Cronje could not escape without outside assistance. If the cordon could be maintained, it could only result in his capitulation and victory without heavy casualties. Kitchener would have nothing to do with a waiting game. All day he ordered attack after attack on the Boers. Finally, Kitchener turned to 9th Division's baggage guard. Without reference to Smith-Dorrien, Colvile was directed to order Lieutenant Colonel Aldworth of the Cornwalls to cross the river and carry the Boer position. Taking three and a half companies Aldworth forded the river and moved forward into the Canadian lines. Some writers have claimed Aldworth was overwrought or even deranged and hastily launched an unauthorized attack on his own. Otter's report tells a different story. At about 4:00 p.m. Aldworth arrived and imperiously told Otter that he had been sent to resolve the situation at the point of the bayonet. One of his companies moved into the firing line almost immediately, followed in about 30 minutes by the others. In the meantime Aldworth and Otter were discussing the enemy situation and the form of attack from a point just behind the firing line. Lieutenant James Cooper Mason of B Company overheard part of the rather heated discussion and organized covering fire for the Cornwalls as they moved into position.

Finally at 5:00 Aldworth decreed that a general advance would take place. At 5:15 bugles sounded the charge. Canadians, frustrated by a long, hot day under fire, leaped to their feet and joined in as the Cornwalls passed through their lines. A number of officers shouted for the Canadians to join the charge. Douglas Williams, C Company's bugler, stood to attention on an anthill and sounded the charge. Bugler A.J. Cawdron of D Company, the ex-bugle major of Ottawa's Governor General's Foot Guards, found his bugle cords tangled with his rifle and to his chagrin was forced to adopt a more unconventional position. There were cries on all sides to fix bayonets and join in. The attack was a frenzy of cheering men running towards "the hateful line of foliage which had been spitting out death and destruction at us all day." At least 1000 men must have joined in the charge: 600-700 Canadians, 100-200 Highlanders and MI, and 300-400 Cornwalls. Some troops had fallen asleep from strain and fatigue and literally slept through the charge. As well, Otter had arranged to keep elements of G and H Companies back as a reserve. The number that did not charge could not have effected the outcome. The defenders' position was too strong for a rush to succeed. In one officer's opinion, "It was a hopeless undertaking to cover 600 yards of open ground where the enemy had the exact range. When we started to move the bullets fell like a perfect hailstorm and the men fell by dozens all around me." The main body of the charge faltered to a halt 300 yards from the Boers, although some managed to get much closer, and two Canadian bodies were found in the Boer trenches. Lieutenant Mason and Privates "Boss" Baugh and Richard Thompson all later wrote that they were within 100 yards of the Boer trenches. Aldworth, his adjutant and bugler and many of his men died. Others lay groaning in agony. Dead was Private John Todd of A Company, a Spanish-American war veteran whose last words were, "Come on, boys; this beats Manila hollow." Dead too were White of B Company and Lester of E Company, the tallest man in the battalion. With them fell Manion of C and Lewis, seconded from the NWMP, of D, and several others. Mason, who had charged with Aldworth, was shot diagonally from left to right through the chest; he would receive the Distinguished Service Order and eventually rejoin the battalion. Private James Bradshaw would have bled to death had not Richard Thompson laid across him and staunched his wound for seven hours. Poor Bradshaw lay close enough to the Boer lines for Thompson to make out the features of the bearded Boer who shot his helmet off as he crouched over his wounded comrade. Others lay groaning and writhing until their comrades were able to creep out and retrieve them after nightfall.[11]

Smith-Dorrien was horrified. His first impression was that the Canadians had mounted an unsupported assault. Only later did he find that the charge had been ordered by Kitchener. Diplomatically he noted, "It was quite irregular that my troops have been ordered to execute such an important movement, except through me, as any possibility of my supporting the charge with the rest of the Brigade was effectually prevented, for by the time I realised what was happening, the attack was over, since it only occupied a minute or two." Always the loyal subordinate, Smith-Dorrien told Otter no more than that he had not ordered the charge, leaving Otter in the dark as to the origin of the order. The first impulse is to blame Aldworth. But Aldworth was not the only one whose actions do not stand close scrutiny; he was only the one unable to defend himself after the event. Could the attack have succeeded? Possibly, if orders had been passed through Smith-Dorrien and a coordinated operation mounted. There are claims that an attempt to contact Smith-Dorrien by heliograph failed because the weather was too cloudy! Otter had estimated the Boer strength at 1200. While this may have been high, the enemy had already halted an attack by the Highland Brigade and were able to shoot down nearly 100 in a few minutes. One of the battalion wrote, "Of that ill fated charge of the Canadians, Cornwalls and A&S Highlanders the less said about it the better. It was a charge that never should have been made." That is a poor epitaph for brave men.

To make a dark day darker, Boer fortunes took a turn for the better. De Wet with over 300 men appeared from the south and seized Kitchener's Kopje, unaccountably guarded by only a small party. If De Wet could repel British attempts to oust him, not only might Cronje extricate himself, but Roberts' army, already in a precarious supply situation, would be threatened.

Dead and wounded lay all across the field, and the Boers continued to fire at any movement. After nightfall the Canadians collected their dead and wounded and withdrew to the area of the drift. There could be no accurate assessment of the losses until daylight. The first count was not encouraging. Fully half the battalion was absent. The crowded field hospital about a mile behind the lines was already busy with wounded from the long day on the slope. Through the night dead and wounded were brought in by search parties while other men straggled back to a rationless, barren bivouac. When all were accounted for several hours later, the picture was not nearly as dreadful as first thought. This, however, is small consolation.

It had been a bad day, 18 February: 19th Brigade had 228 casualties, the Cornwalls suffered 79 and The RCR lost 18 killed plus three, including Captain Arnold, mortally wounded, and 60 wounded, or nearly 10 percent of its strength. Total British casualties were

don't discuss Boer deaths

some 1300. Five battalions lost more heavily than the Cornwalls and the Canadians on the first day of Paardeberg. Clearly this could not continue.

Through the next morning, 19 February, the battalion was occupied with the depressing task of searching for wounded and clearing the battlefield. The Canadians buried their dead, including 17 in a long common grave near the banks of the Modder.[12]

In the late afternoon the Canadians were ordered to occupy an outpost line some three miles away. By 6:00 p.m. the move was complete. It was not until two and a half hours later that the men had their first real meal in 36 hours, and the last meal had mostly been rum and coffee. The next day 19th Brigade occupied a line within 1000 yards of the Boer trenches. The RCR, flanked by the KSLI and the Gordons, spent a day under heavy Boer fire, including the nerve-shattering experience of being on the receiving end of fire from a pom-pom. The firing line was protected by a ridge line, but some rounds cleared the ridge and dropped on the reserves. Only four Canadians, all in reserve, were wounded despite a day under fire. The day was very hot and once again the men suffered from hunger, with only a single biscuit each, and thirst, as the Boer fire drove the water cart from the front lines whenever attempts were made to refill empty water bottles. It was after 6:00 p.m. when the bone-weary soldiers fell in and marched back to the barren plain by the Modder for another night.

That day Smith-Dorrien advised Roberts, Colvile, and Kitchener that a frontal assault was out of the question. Instead, he proposed a gradual tightening of the noose, night by night, culminating in an attack when the time was right. Roberts bought the plan, but Kitchener urged Smith-Dorrien to attack immediately, suggesting he would be a "made man" if he succeeded. Smith-Dorrien declined the opportunity.[13]

Despite the natural strength of the position it had not been a good day for Cronje's beleagured force. The laager was shelled heavily, a pattern that persisted through the rest of the siege, and wagon after wagon caught fire and burned into a heap of twisted iron and ashes. The Boers could do little more than crouch in their trenches and wait until darkness provided a respite from the ordeal. The slaughter of animals, a legitimate military target, was incredible. If, as estimated at the time, three-quarters of the horses, and perhaps the same proportion of other animals died, then at least 3000 animals perished in the laager. The Boers attacked the problem with characteristic directness. The dead animals were dumped into the river to be carried downstream towards Paardeberg Drift. The destruction also effectively eliminated the possibility of escape from the laager.

The 21st was a day of relative rest and quiet for the Canadians. There was a break in the rations when a little fresh meat appeared, if not on the (non-existent) tables, in the pot. During the night the battalion took its turn on outpost. Thursday morning (22 February) the men were fresher than they had been since leaving Graspan hardly a week earlier. Nineteenth Brigade marched handily out of the camp to line a ridge line against the threat of a large body of Boers marching to Cronje's relief. The enemy failed to materialize. What did appear was a furious rainstorm that lashed the countryside and soaked the men. The rain fell the rest of the day and night. Friday threatened rain during the day but then it rained all night again. Conditions were miserable. The regimental transport was on the other side of the river, and the men were without their greatcoats and still on short rations, thanks to De Wet. Blankets had been pooled to provide some extra comfort for the wounded, so many of the troops did without.

In the meantime De Wet had been resisting all attempts to dislodge him from Kitchener's Kopje. Finally on the 23rd, after five days and nights, De Wet reluctantly left Cronje to his fate. The British cordon was not airtight. Brave men crept in and out of the laager with messages, the last actually leaving in the early hours of the 27th. While there still was a possibility of outside assistance, Cronje had discouraged any large-scale attempts to break out. By the time he accepted that relief was impossible, it was too late for more than a handful to get away. It was the Canadians' turn for a spell in a sorely needed rest position near the river on the 24th. Eight hundred and ninety-six Canadians left Belmont on the 12th; this morning the battalion mustered 708 officers and men fit for duty. The combination of battle casualties, exhaustion, injury, and disease had depleted the ranks by 20 per cent in less than two weeks. Heavy rain flooded the bivouac, and the troops spent another miserable night. At sunrise the battalion rescued their kit from the mud and water and carried it to higher ground. The day was passed drying kit and enduring the horrible, sickly sweet stench from the carcasses in the only source of water. Otter noted a new carcass appeared every two minutes or so. The troops noted there was a distinctive taste to the tea!

The next day, 26 February, normal rotation saw the Canadians replace the Cornwalls in the forward trenches facing the west end of the laager. A Company crossed the Modder by a pontoon bridge near a Royal Engineers observation balloon and occupied a trench on the south side. C, D, and E Companies moved into a long trench that was anchored on the river and extended a quarter mile inland. The remaining four companies were in reserve a few hundred yards to the rear.

Twenty-seven February was the anniversary of the Boer triumph at Majuba in 1881, a debacle that had rankled the British ever since. A veteran of Majuba, Major General Hector Macdonald, wounded leading the Highland Brigade on the 18th, wrote Roberts from his hospital bed, pleading that Majuba be avenged and the army's honour restored by forcing Cronje to surrender on the 27th. "Fighting Mac" was a national hero and his plea must have carried particular weight with Roberts. Majuba would be exorcised.

Attempts by the Boers to relieve Cronje had failed, and the slaughter of the horses effectively prevented any break-out in strength. Conditions were terrible; the din of the shelling; the shortage of rations; and, especially, the stench of carcasses that had not been dumped into the river. Shelters had been dug into the river banks, and the wounded and non-combatants were leading a safe but uncomfortable existence. Cronje accepted that he must capitulate. The question was when. Every day he resisted was a day that delayed the British march. The symbolism of Majuba Day was not lost on the Boers, and Cronje decided that he would surrender, but not on the 27th.

Roberts' decision was more than a reaction to a plea by a wounded hero. Smith-Dorrien's preparations for an assault were complete. Nineteenth Brigade had been reinforced by the Argyll and Sutherland Highlanders and two companies of the Black Watch as well as 7th Company, Royal Engineers. The forward Canadian companies were in trenches anchored on the river 500 yards from the Boer lines; to their left rear the Gordons, Shropshires, and Black Watch lay on a north south line threatening the laager from the west. Behind them, facing outwards, the Argylls and the Cornwalls protected the rear of the brigade and the artillery on Gun Hill.

Smith-Dorrien appreciated the key to the laager was the Boer position facing him. If he could capture or dominate these trenches, his troops would be able to fire directly into the laager and the dugouts on both sides of the river bank. His plan was to advance and seize the trenches by stealth. If surprise was lost before the trenches were assaulted, the troops would dig in where the advance was halted. The main attack along the bank would be mounted by the Canadians and the engineers. The Gordons were to be prepared to follow up the attacks. The Shropshires and Black Watch would support the attack with rifle fire from the flank when the attackers were engaged. Darkness precluded any artillery support for the attack.[14]

The RCR would advance with six companies, C through H, in line in two ranks. The front rank would have bayonets fixed and rifles ready, prepared to cover the rear rank and the engineers who had the vital task of digging in if the advance was halted before the trenches were reached. The men in the rear ranks were to advance with rifles slung, carrying shovels. When surprise was lost they would drop flat and, covered by the front rank, dig in where they lay. To keep direction the ranks would advance shoulder to shoulder, with left arms grasping the rifle of the next man. Buchan would command the left flank and Pelletier the right. Otter would move just in the rear of the left.

At last light the depth RCR companies, less B in brigade reserve, moved up to the forward trench. Smith-Dorrien accompanied by his brigade major and aide-de-camp joined The RCR in their trenches about 10:30 p.m. That night there was a "very heavy dew, wetting everything, but mercifully no fog, from which we had suffered on two nights lately." He would advance with his brigade and the sappers, on the right near the river. Finally, the supporting Gordons moved forward to occupy the Canadian trenches. All were awake and at their places by 1:45 in the morning of Majuba Day. At 2:15, with a slight scuffing sound and the creak of equipment, 240 Canadians climbed from the trenches, paused slightly to set alignment, and moved off into the dark. The rear rank, the engineers, and the brigade commander and his staff followed.

It was only about 500 yards to the Boer trenches. At 20 yards a minute the advance would reach its objective in 25 minutes, but Smith-Dorrien found that "although I did not realise it at the moment, we were going slower than that even, and thinking it over afterwards I was not surprised, for it was a stealthy step-by-step advance in perfect silence, except for the occasional breaking of a twig or kicking of a stone—a movement most creditable to the troops." By 2:45 a.m. Smith-Dorrien was very anxious, anticipating perhaps that direction had been lost and the advance was veering across the front. Suddenly there was a rattle of rocks in cans hung on wire, followed almost immediately by a shot, a cry of pain and desperation, and then the flash and crash of a volley of rifle fire from the Boer lines. With the first shot the men dropped flat, avoiding most of the fire, and the front rank began to return fire, while the rear rank literally dug for their lives. On the left the night winked with flashes as the Shropshires and Highlanders volleyed into the laager.

Incredibly, casualties in the first engagement were light, except in F and G Companies who lay closest to the trenches. Night firing is a tricky business, and the tendency is to fire high. Steadily, minute by minute and stroke by stroke, the trench deepened. Progress was quickest on the right, where the ground provided complete protection for the engineers and H Company, who would escape without casualties that night.

A group of Canadian officers. This picture was taken a few months before the outbreak of war. Most of these officers would serve in South Africa.
Courtesy of National Archives c 12278

Major General E.T.H. Hutton. Hutton's fights with Canadian politicians have overshadowed both his place as an outspoken proponent of Mounted Infantry and his achievements as an able and successful commander of mounted troops.
Courtesy of National Archives c 6359

Farewell to the Manitoba Transvaal Contingent. The large crowd provides a demonstration of the enthusiasm generated by the war across English Canada.
Courtesy of National Archives c 12272

D Company of the First Contingent. This company was recruited in military districts 3 and 4 in Eastern Ontario. The picture was probably taken in Quebec prior to sailing as the men are dressed in rifle green serge uniforms.
Courtesy of National Archives c 7981

On the *Sardinian* - A group of Canadian officers. Officers exchanged their swords and tailored uniforms for rifles and issue uniforms before the battalion saw action.
Originally published in Canada's Sons on Kopje and Veldt by T.G. Marquis, 1900.

The First Contingent preparing to board the *Sardinian* at Quebec. The "SARDINE" was probably the least suitable troopship used by the Canadians during the war.
Courtesy of National Archives c 12276

A group of Boers. Note the modern rifles and full bandoliers. The clips of ammunition evident in some of the rifles enabled the Mauser to achieve a higher rate of fire than the British rifles.
Courtesy of National Archives c 128778

In camp before battle. Compare the drab khaki drill with the green serge in the picture of D Company taken in Quebec.
Courtesy of National Archives c 7994

Three Canadian Rough Riders. A camp scene of the Second Contingent. Note the western saddles on the horses picketed in the right of the photo.
Courtesy of Canadian War Museum 75-840

Left Section, D Battery Royal Canadian Artillery. This section and the Royal Canadian Dragoons would fight off a series of determined Boer mounted charges at Leliefontein.
Originally published in With the Guns in South Africa by E.W.B. Morrison, 1901.

Private Harry Dougall Black. A studio photograph of a member of the first contingent.
Courtesy of Canadian War Museum 71-4375

The Battle of Pretoria. This photo shows how open terrain and excellent visibility have affected operations.
Originally published in Blue Shirt and Khaki by J.F.J. Archibald, 1901.

Canadian Non-Commissioned Officers en route to South Africa. These men can be identified as members of Strathcona's Horse by the high brown boots. Other Canadian contingents wore low ankle boots and long cloth puttees.
Courtesy of National Archives c 16599

Canadian transport at a difficult drift. Note that two teams are being used to haul the wagon up the slope.
Originally published in Blue Shirt and Khaki by J.F.J. Archibald, 1901.

The Officers of B Squadron, Royal Canadian Dragoons. Left to Right: Rear row Lieutenant F.V. Young (wounded), Lieutenant H.L. Borden (killed), Lieutenant C.T. Van Straubenzie, Lieutenant R.E.W. Turner (wounded); Front row Major V.A.S Williams, Capt. H.S. Greenwood (transferred to Imperial Military Railway). Turner was the only officer of this group present at Leliefontein where he was wounded and won the Victoria Cross.
Courtesy of National Archives c 115280

Canadian Mounted Rifles in camp. The beards and worn uniforms are indicative of conditions on campaign. Note the Colt revolvers thrust into the belts.
Courtesy of Canadian War Museum 82-7264

After the battle. A vivid illustration of the poor quality of medical care available, in this case, at Paardeberg. The troops include men from both brigades of 9 Division.
Courtesy of National Archives c 26179

Major Arthur L. Howard, Commanding the Canadian Scouts. Gat Howard is wearing the ribbon of the Distinguished Service Order he won while commanding the machine gun section of the Royal Canadian Dragoons. The strain of active service is beginning to show on the 54-year-old Howard.
Courtesy of National Archives c 26179

A trooper takes a break. While this photo is of a British soldier, the equipment carried on his horse was more or less standard throughout the army.
Courtesy of Canadian War Museum 71-66

Lieutenant Colonel L.W. Herchmer, Commanding Officer, 2nd Battalion, Canadian Mounted Rifles. Herchmer, who also was the Commissioner of the North West Mounted Police, was surely the unluckiest senior Canadian officer of the war.
Courtesy of National Archives c 12277

The battalion was in good hand and reacting properly to orders. The brigade commander noted that the Canadians were firing volleys as the digging went on. Private Tweddell and his section mates in E Company were taken aback to hear a voice call from the right, "Retire." At first the men thought the order was to fire, but a lieutenant leaped to his feet, repeated the order, and bolted to the rear. Men began to drop back in response to the order, and the example set by the officer. The Boers poured fire into the confusion and men fell. Panic, or at least the sense of self-preservation, spread down the line. Not all the soldiers heard the order or retired immediately. Private Richard Thompson found himself alone while reloading his magazine during a pause in the firing and retired until he found the firing line a short distance to the rear. A private in C Company wrote that, once they came under fire, "we dropped flat, and gradually worked our way back to cover." This implies that some troops, perhaps most, retired under control. G and H Companies under Lieutenant Macdonnell and Captain Stairs ignored or did not receive the word and stood their ground and fought as their comrades fell back. The latter is the more likely, for the heaviest casualties, 12 and 15 respectively, were suffered by F and G Companies, and a gap in the line, except for dead and wounded, likely ended any spread of panic from left to right. In the Canadian trenches the Gordons stood by, peering into the dark, wondering what was happening a quarter mile to their front. Suddenly, along with the crack of bullets passing overhead, came the thump of boots and dark shadows leaping into the trenches.

Otter returned disgustedly and set about reorganizing the battalion for the morning. He knew that two companies and the engineers were still in position, and all was not lost. It was small consolation for an officer who, for the second time in his career, had had his men break and run about him. Otter and Forbes MacBean, commanding the Gordons, knew that Smith-Dorrien was still forward, though they could not know whether he was dead or alive. By the time a coherent picture began to emerge it was within short hours of dawn. There was nothing to do but wait it out.[15]

When the forward trench was completed the Maritimers had gratefully dropped into it and continued the fight. Finally the sky lightened to the northeast over the laager and objects became clearer. The trench anchored on the river bank dominated the Boer trenches and, as expected, allowed fire from covered positions into the laager and the dugouts in the river bank. A building across the river provided cover for riflemen to shoot the length of the Canadian trench. Smith-Dorrien hastily sent orders back, and A Company captured it without incident. Checkmate!

The grey light of dawn revealed huddled forms lying on the open, coverless field. From the main trench men could make out a body near the Boer lines that seemed to move as if writhing in pain. Was he alive or not? A corporal in the Cape Bearer Company asked for a volunteer to attempt to find out. Private Richard Thompson, who had saved Bradshaw's life on the 18th, lay his rifle down, lit his pipe, nodded to his comrades and drew himself out of the trench. There was silence in the trenches as Thompson coolly covered the long quarter mile to the body, and the waiting Mausers. The Boers rarely respected the red cross, not as much from brutality as from ignorance of the conventions of war, and usually would shoot anyone who approached their lines, except perhaps under a flag of truce. Inexplicably the proverbial luck was with the Irish-born Thompson. He reached the body and knelt beside it. A quick examination by the ex-medical student showed his ordeal had been unnecessary, the man was dead.

Pausing only to retrieve some personal effects, he returned to the Canadian line and jumped into the protection of the trench. A short time later, Thompson left the trench once again to go to the aid of another man who appeared to be in need of assistance. Thompson's bravery, on the 18th and this occasion, was rewarded with the award of one of the four scarves crocheted by Queen Victoria for award to the "four most distinguished private soldiers in the Colonial Forces of Canada, Australia, New Zealand and South Africa." In an era that made a fetish of personal courage, Thompson stands with the very bravest in an army of brave men. His award was recognition of an unselfish act that conquered fear in the harsh light of dawn, not in the heat of battle.[16]

There had been attempts by some of the enemy to give up, but the troops had heard too many stories of feigned surrenders to take them seriously. Smith-Dorrien called to the enemy to surrender. The trenches sprouted a sea of white, and bitter bearded men began to emerge and throw their rifles to the ground. So many popped out of holes in the ground that Smith-Dorrien was prompted to remark that it was just like the resurrection. Soon a large white flag was raised over the laager itself. Paardeberg was won.

Otter had spent an unhappy few hours following the retreat just when it seemed that success was near. Not only had his troops broken, but he and his second in command had been unable to stem the tide. To make things worse his other major, Oscar Pelletier, had returned to the Canadian lines with what Otter considered a minor wound, leaving his two forward company commanders directly under the control of the brigade commander. The blossoming of the white flags surely restored his spirit; in the flush of victory the retreat would soon be forgotten. With long lines of Boers trudging into the British lines and the personal congratulations of the commander-in-chief fresh in his ears, he discreetly let the matter drop. He would have been even more inclined to accept the inevitable that afternoon when he received a personal note and two bottles of champagne from Fighting Mac. It is doubtful that knowledge of the withdrawal was widespread. Smith-Dorrien glossed over it in his memoirs, the Gordons's historian barely mentioned it, and Sir Arthur Conan Doyle called it a planned manoeuvre in his history of the war. Occurrences of this type are more common than armies care to admit. The Highland Brigade had broken and run twice at Magersfontein, so fingers were unlikely to be pointed.[17]

The unanswered question is who or what caused the sudden retreat? Recent historians have speculated the order to retire came from Boer lips, or even from a renegade Canadian. However, at the time few suggested the withdrawal was the result of a Boer ruse. Marquis wrote, in an attempt to put the matter to rest, that the culprit died that night. The command, "Retire and bring in your wounded" is quoted in Otter's formal report submitted after the battalion returned to Canada. It is not clear that Otter heard the order himself. Otter's first report to Ottawa and the staff diary only mention the word "retire," once with reference to a call to bring back the wounded, and the other without mention of any such call. Tweddell, who heard the call, recorded it as "Retire," although there may have been other, later calls to bring back the wounded. The intent of the order is ambiguous. The intention may have been for the front rank to fall back and occupy a trench, which was not yet complete.

Perhaps a company officer or a section commander decided to regroup his men in an attempt to outflank the enemy trenches and or to move to a less-exposed position. The rear rank, lying prone and hacking at the hard ground with shovels, could not have known the order was not for them and dropped back. If the front rank could not find an obvious place to stop, the tendency would be to retire until told to halt. Withdrawals under fire are notoriously difficult, most so at night. It is not clear how many men actually heard the order and how many merely passed it on, perhaps changing an attempt to regroup into a call to return to the trenches. Circumstantial evidence suggests the order came from the lips of someone in E or F Company. Whatever did happen, within hours it mattered not. The Boers surrendered, Roberts lavished praise on the Canadians, and the matter was discreetly dropped.[18]

Was the attack necessary? Both sides attached an enormous amount of importance to Majuba Day itself. Emotion and symbolism played a part but were contributing, not overriding factors. Smith-Dorrien had reported to Roberts that his preparations were complete on the 26th. It has been suggested that the attack was unnecessary as Cronje was going to surrender anyway. It was obvious Cronje must eventually surrender, but not when. Roberts, therefore, would be inclined to attack when preparations were complete, but not a moment earlier. From his perspective, to attack at this time was the proper military decision.

Smith-Dorrien had reported the early surrenders opposite 19th Brigade to Colvile and Roberts, followed by the welcome report of a general capitulation. In return the Field Marshall ordered 19th Brigade to occupy the Boer laager. By 9:30 a.m. khaki-clad infantry advanced past the Boer trenches and forward to the devastated laager. The infantrymen who advanced warily with bayonets fixed and rifles at the ready found a little corner of hell on the veldt. For the first time soldiers had a chance to examine the effect of over 100 guns and howitzers accurately directed at flimsy wagons and carts. Virtually all the Boer wagons and carts were shattered, burned-out hulks. Clustered where they fell were the loathsome, reeking carcasses of dead animals that had not been tipped into the Modder. The laager had a perimeter of two miles or so in an arc anchored on the river bank. Given the number of defenders who emerged unscathed from the deep, narrow trenches it would have been a very tough nut to crack. Altogether over 4000 Boers surrendered along with 1000 horses, 5000 rifles and five guns. The more perceptive noted that despite the shelling there had been fewer than 300 Boer casualties. The Boers had suffered a lot of discomfort, but little lasting harm. Dispersion and digging saved lives.[19]

The laager was an unpleasant place, but the troops waited there until Lord Roberts finally appeared to thank them at 4:00 in the afternoon. The commander-in-chief was a busy man. Since shortly after dawn, Roberts had met Cronje and accepted his surrender, issued orders for the handling of the prisoners, addressed himself to the resumption of the advance, and sent off his despatches. The first despatch, which set London agog, merely said:

PAARDEBERG, Feb. 27, 7:45 A.M. - General Cronje and all his force capitulated unconditionally at daylight and is now a prisoner in my camp. . . I hope that Her Majesty's Government will consider this event satisfactory, occurring, as it does, on the anniversary of Majuba.

Reports from correspondents arrived during the day and fueled endless speculation. Paardeberg was the first real victory of the war, and it only waited for the official despatch to allow a more accurate tally. Finally the following was received from the front:

From information furnished daily to me by the intelligence department it became apparent that General Cronje's force was becoming more depressed, and that the discontent of the troops and the discord among the leaders were rapidly increasing . . . Each night the trenches were pushed forward towards the enemy's laager so as to gradually contract his position, and at the same time I bombarded it heavily with artillery . . . At 3 A.M. today a most dashing advance was made by the Canadian regiment and some engineers, supported by the First Gordon Highlanders and Second Shropshires, resulting in our gaining a point some six hundred yards nearer to the enemy and within about eighty yards of his trenches, where our men entrenched themselves and maintained their positions until morning, a gallant deed worthy of our Colonial comrades, and which, I am glad to say, was attended by comparatively slight loss . . . [20]

Chapter

7 Bloemfontein

AFTER SPENDING 28 February 1900 collecting the spoils of war, the Royal Canadians rested for five days on the south side of the river at Osfontein. Food was scarce, heavy rains flooded the camp and there were so many rotting animal carcasses lying about that the bivouac was christened "Deadfontein." In their sodden lines the troops joked of staging regattas and greeted each other with manic quacks. On 6 March the Canadians gladly bid farewell to Paardeberg.

The Boers held a line of kopjes that extended for several miles from north of the river, south through Table Mountain to the Seven Kopjes feature five miles from Osfontein. At the first sign of a British advance the burghers fled, except for a few stalwarts under De Wet who fought a masterful rearguard action. The infantry occupied positions vacated by the Boers, while the cavalry slowly advanced with frequent halts to rest their horses. The RCR marched about the battlefield but did not fire a shot. The British had won the field, but not the battle.[1]

The army rested for a day before resuming the advance. On 9 March the Canadians crossed the Modder at Poplar Grove Drift and bivouacked. Shortly after 5:00 a.m. in the grey chill of dawn the Canadians led 19th Brigade towards the anticipated battle at Abraham's Kraal 18 miles ahead. As the sun tracked across the sky, and the heat layered on, the brigade trudged dreary mile after dreary mile, but it did not take part in the battle. Although the British lost 300 men, they counted 210 enemy dead and captured four guns and a number of prisoners. On the negative side 1500 Boers held off 10 000 British soldiers for a day.

It had been nearly a month since the march had started, a month without changing clothes or cutting hair. Uniforms were dirty, worn, and caked with sweat. Boots, ravaged by rock and wet, were falling to pieces. Some men were actually barefooted, others wound their puttees or pieces of raw sheepskin around their feet. The marches were hard and many men dropped out, to stagger into camp behind their comrades. On one dreadful day, on a ten-mile march from Driefontein to Aasvogel, 100 fell out. The climate, poor diet, and physical strain were having an effect on the the army, both men and animals. In four days the army lost 796 mules and 3500 oxen, plus an undetermined number of horses.[2]

On the morning of 13 March Roberts accepted the formal surrender of Bloemfontein. As its name suggests (*Bloem* = flower, *Fontein* = spring or fountain) the capital was a pretty little place of neat red bungalows, mature trees, colourful flower gardens, and tasteful government buildings with a population, including natives, of 4000. The Canadians, still on the road, finally staggered into Ferreira Spruit Siding. That evening, as heavy rain fell, ears turned towards a sound they had not heard for a month, the whistle of a train. Contact with the railway was absolutely necessary, not only to feed and clothe the army, but also to stockpile supplies for the march on the Transvaal and to replace the thousands of animals that had died in the past month.

There had been an incident on the march that could have had tragic results. Two British officers had seen Private A.W. Belyea of D Company grab a stray chicken that crossed his path. Looting was anathema to the army, and Belyea was court-martialled. To set an example for the troops the brigade was formed up in a hollow square to hear the verdict. For poor Belyea the ordeal was terrifying as he stood alone, head bowed, awaiting the decision of the court. The verdict was hardly in doubt, and the offence could draw the death penalty. The officers who made up the court realized the maximum punishment did not fit the crime. Belyea was confined to barracks for 56 days, a meaningless punishment on the veldt.[3]

Roberts believed the Boers must soon surrender and was prepared to wait for nature to take its course. However, the burghers vowed to fight on and even managed to regain the initiative about Bloemfontein. Even if the Boers had entered into negotiations, the army, suffering from poor rations and water and the exertions of the past month, would still have needed food, fodder, clean water, and remounts.

All of this was beyond the immediate interest of the Canadians who squatted on the muddy field like tramps. An epidemic of enteric (typhoid) fever swept through the army and threatened to undo the victories of the past weeks. Tragically, there was a proven immunization available, but it caused a severe reaction and was not in general use. The army had arrived at Bloemfontein with no more than 200 patients in its hospitals. Within ten days the figure was 1000. The situation was made worse by an archaic medical organization. A civilian practitioner remarked after touring a military hospital that he thought he was visiting a museum. A Canadian officer, a medical doctor in civilian life, wrote that he was ashamed of the professional standards in a military hospital he had visited. Even with proper medical care, enteric fever was often fatal, but with the medical staff overwhelmed and the hospitals inadequate a bad situation was made worse.

Over 100 Canadians were soon hospitalized with more reporting sick daily. Disease was no respecter of rank, striking officers, NCOs, and men indiscriminately, and recovery was slow. The more serious cases were shipped to the United Kingdom and then to Canada, where they were invalided out of the army. Even the less seriously ill could be lost to the unit for a matter of months. Far too many others were laid to rest on the veldt.[4]

A number of officers had been lost to the battalion over the past few months: Denison to Roberts' staff; McLean to the Royal Field Artillery; MacDougall, Stuart, Temple, and Wilkie sick; Panet to the Second Contingent; Arnold dead; and Major Pelletier and Lieutenants Mason and Armstrong wounded. Others would be lost in the next few weeks: Bell with fever; Peltier with sunstroke; and Lieutenant Pelletier to the British army. Four of the eight companies had new commanders: Blanchard in A; Burstall in B; Macdonnell in G where he had replaced Weeks, appointed quartermaster behind Denison; and Leduc in F. Meanwhile, Ottawa was raising a reinforcement draft of three officers and 100 men and a fourth officer had sailed with the second contingent.[5]

The generally accepted view in the army was that the war would soon be over. The British had declared a general amnesty for all, except the Boer senior leadership, who would surrender their arms and equipment and pledge to not take up arms again. The Boers did not consider a pledge coerced at gunpoint valid, while the British failed to grasp the implications of Boers turning in rusted relics instead of Mausers. It did not take much encouragement for a burgher to retrieve his Mauser from its hiding place, saddle his pony, and take to the field again.

Boer columns had easily parried clumsy British thrusts to Karee Siding 20 miles north of the capital and into the hills east of Sannah's Post. The British column led by Colonel Broadwood that had struck to the east had met little resistance and finally halted at Thabanchu. The column could only return by one route, crossing the Modder at the site of the water supply for Bloemfontein. On the night of 30 March 1900 De Wet went with 2000 men to capture the waterworks, and to ambush the returning column. Shortly after dawn on 31 March Broadwood, pressed by Boers approaching from the east, rode into De Wet's trap. The burghers captured his supply train and one of his Horse Artillery batteries, while the other battery wheeled into action a scant 300 yards from the Boers. Unable to silence the fire from the spruit, the gunners were shot down as they served their guns in the open. Their action, however, had bought time for Broadwood and an opportunity to avoid a complete catastrophe.

Roberts had issued orders to Colvile the day before to cover Broadwood's withdrawal. At 5:30 a.m. 9th Division marched from Bloemfontein. The British outnumbered the Boers and could have driven De Wet away from the waterworks, but Colvile misread the situation completely. Ignoring an urgent appeal from Broadwood, he directed his division to Waterval Drift several miles to the north. The RCR saw little of the battle, having been left to secure Boesman's Kop and the wagons, while the remainder of the division advanced. Ninth Division achieved so little that its presence escaped the attention of both De Wet and many historians. Sannah's Post cost Broadwood 600 men, 80 of his 90 wagons, and 7 of his 12 guns. Moreover the British also lost the waterworks and, with the arrival of Boer reinforcements, were unwilling to attempt its recapture.[6]

The British had been administering the pledge and collecting weapons in the southern OFS until the Sannah's Post debacle prompted their recall. De Wet surrounded a retreating force at Reddersburg and captured over 400 British on 4 April. After this success De Wet could threaten the lines of communications or attack the post at Wepener. The situation was worse than embarrassing for Roberts. His army controlled no more than their bivouacs and garrisons. To advance into enemy country from an insecure base would be taking too serious a risk.

On the same day as the disaster at Reddersburg, Roberts learned of a conference of Boer leaders on the Leeuwkop, about 20 miles south-east of Bloemfontein. Ninth Division and the remnants of a cavalry brigade (130 men and four guns) were ordered to crash the party. Warned in late morning the force set out shortly after 2:00 p.m. on a march of six hours. The march resumed before first light, although 19th Brigade, bringing up the rear did not immediately move off. The advanced guard met light resistance some four miles ahead and the division prepared to attack the conference site. However, either the intelligence was faulty, or the birds had flown. The column retraced its steps to Rietfontein to wait for further orders. In late afternoon just as dinner was ready a torrential downpour began, and the men "were drowned out and wet through by night but managed to build a shelter of our blankets."[7]

The force returned to Bloemfontein on 6 April, after a fruitless 40–mile march feeling pretty well done in. For The RCR there was a pleasant surprise. For two months the men had lived in the open, each sheltered from the elements by a single blanket, ground sheet and greatcoat. The tents left in Belmont in February had arrived and had been pitched by the men left behind in the bivouac. The supply situation steadily improved over the next two weeks.

Train loads of clothing and equipment came up the line, and "comforts" began to arrive from Canada.[8]

Even De Wet was not immune to lapses. Rather than strike into the Cape or the southern OFS behind Roberts and delay his advance indefinitely, he chose to attack 2000 despised South African volunteers at Wepener on the border with Basutoland. Suddenly the British were provided with an opportunity to cut De Wet's retreat and clear the way for the march on the Transvaal to begin. General French was ordered to march to the relief of the Wepener with his cavalry division and 11th Division. Third Division, which was already in action against the enemy forces about Wepener, was also put at French's disposal.[9]

Eighteenth Brigade was covering the Boers at the waterworks from a position at Springfield. Smith-Dorrien was ordered late on 20 April to move at dawn to relieve 18th Brigade. As this march was believed to be a three-day foray, the Canadians left four officers and 169 soldiers in camp to continue their recuperation. Only 27 officers and 584 men headed north from Bloemfontein. Companies that had proudly paraded 125 strong in Quebec now were fortunate to muster 70 rifles. The march was uneventful, and 19th Brigade settled in around Springfield as 18th Brigade marched away to the east on the morning of 22 April. Soon the sound of heavy firing was heard from the direction of Leeuwkop, the location of the so-called conference in early April. Fighting continued all day as the Boers attempted to prevent 18th Brigade from blocking an escape route.[10]

That evening the brigade commander received welcome news. The brigade would join General Ian Hamilton's mounted infantry division, which had been ordered to recapture the waterworks and strike towards Thabanchu. From now on 19th Brigade would have little contact with 9th Division and General Colvile. The change pleased Smith-Dorrien, who wrote, "From now on I enjoyed every minute of the campaign. He [Hamilton] was a delightful leader to follow, always definite and clear in his instructions, always ready to listen and willing to adopt suggestions, and, what is more important, always ready to go for the enemy and extremely quick at seizing a tactical advantage, and, with it all, always in a good temper."[11]

The British attempted to envelop De Wet with forces advancing east from the railway and north from the OFS towards the Basutoland border. The Boers were able to block the progress of these columns long enough to allow De Wet to disengage his forces besieging Wepener and to ride for safety north of Thabanchu. The arrival of Hamilton's division as well as actions by other troops had finally pushed the enemy out of the waterworks on 23 April and back towards Thabanchu. On the 24th Smith-Dorrien's brigade crossed the drift and occupied the Sannah's Post battlefield of dark memory. Ian Hamilton proposed to Roberts that he should advance to Thabanchu to block the Boers' retreat northwards. On the 25th Hamilton's column marched east away from the waterworks.

East of Bloemfontein and the Modder the ground turns rocky and undulates away to Basutoland in a succession of ridges. The town of Thabanchu lies at the foot of the feature from which it takes its name. Initially the route from Bloemfontein follows the bottom of a long, wide valley. As one approaches the town the walls close in and rise higher and higher. At the east end of the valley, only six miles from Thabanchu, the road is commanded by a line of kopjes at Israel's Poort. The enemy held it in strength, lining both the left (northerly) wall of the valley and the kopjes plugging the bottleneck at valley's end.[12]

Hamilton's division advanced with Brevet Colonel C.P. Ridley's Mounted Infantry Brigade well in advance. Shortly before noon the first sounds of what would be an all-day battle were heard by the main body, and Smith-Dorrien was ordered to advance as quickly as possible to confront the Boers holding the bottleneck. He would hold the enemy with his forward battalion, which would advance to within 600 to 800 yards of the enemy and then halt and engage the enemy with small arms fire. With the enemy occupied by the threat from the front Hamilton intended to launch two left hooks. In the first, and shallower one, Smith-Dorrien would use his remaining forces to clear the enemy lining the valley wall. Meanwhile, Ridley's brigade would cut in behind the Boers to threaten their retreat. Hamilton appreciated that the twin threats would lever the enemy out of the plug, and that the troops threatening from the front need not brave the Boers' deadly rifle fire at close range.[13]

The RCR was the lead battalion of 19th Brigade. The battalion arrived opposite the strong position in the early afternoon of the 25th and prepared to advance straight up the valley with a mounted infantry unit, Marshall's Horse, on their right. There would be no headlong charges that day. Otter deployed the battalion in four lines, each of two companies in single rank. The men were 12 to 15 paces apart, while the lines were separated by 150 yards. Major Pelletier, newly rejoined after having been wounded at Paardeberg, commanded the forward two lines, while Major Buchan led the supports. Otter accompanied Pelletier and the four forward companies.

The battalion advanced steadily on a front of some 2000 yards, while the 12-pounders of P Battery Royal Horse Artillery fired over their heads at the kopjes. Eventually a wire fence was reached just under half a mile from the kopjes. No sooner had the men halted than the enemy opened heavy fire on them. Otter decided to pull the battalion back a short distance to a donga. A withdrawal under fire is tricky. The situation became confused, and some of the men began to waver. However, the officer and NCOs were able to restore order and the movement was completed deliberately. Whatever the men might have thought of Otter in camp, they had no reason to question his courage. Both the colonel and his adjutant, Lieutenant J.H.C. Ogilvy, had stalked the line, steadying the men as they dropped back. Otter remained standing in the open while the rest of the battalion dropped into the donga. What followed was inevitable. Boers were always quick to fire on anyone obviously giving orders or otherwise drawing attention to himself. Just as Otter was about to jump into the donga he was struck by a bullet that grazed his right jaw and passed through his neck, narrowly missing the jugular vein. Another bullet clipped the badge of rank from his left shoulder-strap. The wound was bloody and painful, but Otter was able to stay on the field.

As the battalion lined the donga and raked the kopjes with rifle fire, the Cornwalls supported by the Shropshires and a half battalion of Gordons (the other half was the baggage guard) advanced along on their left. These movements, together with the threat from Ridley's men, appeared to unsettle the Boers. By 3:15 p.m. the Boers began to abandon the line of kopjes. The Canadians recognized that the enemy's fire was slackening and correctly deduced the reason. Captain Burstall, commanding B Company, had located a donga leading obliquely towards the kopje. He volunteered to lead his company up it and assault the hill from the open flank. Stealthily B Company, followed by D Company, advanced under cover unnoticed by the remaining Boers. The appearance of khaki uniforms behind their defences was the last straw for the Boers. "By 4:40," wrote the brigade commander, "we were penetrating the position everywhere; the Canadians were charging forward . . . I ordered up the guns . . . and signalled back for our baggage."[14]

The battalion spent the night on the line of kopjes. Casualties had been very light, considering how long the men had been under fire. Private J. Defoe of H Company was dead, and three men including Otter were wounded. Although he was officially classified as "slightly wounded," the colonel had had a close call and was evacuated to hospital. He would be absent for a month. In the meantime command passed to Major Buchan. The loss of Otter was greeted with mixed emotions in the ranks. For some "a great deal of regret was expressed on all sides over Colonel Otter's wound," while others reported that not a lot of sympathy was felt. One wrote sarcastically, "Didn't the men go into mourning when a bullet scraped his jaw? Certainly. But what for?"[15]

Before first light on 26 April the army was on the move again. Ridley's men led the way again to seize a gap in the hills where the road from Dewestsdorp, 25 miles to the south, passed through the hills. Once this pass was secure, mounted infantry reconnoitered another poort seven miles to the east where the road passed in front of the steep slope of Eden Hill. The infantry followed at dawn, leaving a company of Gordons and some mounted infantry to hold Israel's Poort. It was the Canadians' turn to play the passive role—the battalion with a section of guns and a company of mounted infantry was detailed to hold a poort on the Dewetsdorp Road—while the other battalions of 19th Brigade occupied a line of low kopjes west of Thabanchu village facing entrenched Boers across the valley. Some 3000 Boers and 200 wagons had slipped through the gap en route to Ladybrand in the morning. By the time the mounted infantry had arrived, the enemy were too far away to follow, especially with Boers entrenched on the flank. Once again the enemy had escaped by skilful delaying tactics and a lack of drive on the part of the British.

It is possible that, if Ridley's brigade had pushed on to Thabanchu, he might have put a plug in the escape route. While the Boers were being pursued by a strong force from the south, it is unlikely that the burghers could have been surrounded and forced to surrender without a river to trap them against. It is possible, however, that a major battle might have resulted. All of this seems to have been unknown to the Canadians, who spent the rest of the day preparing defences in light of the expected arrival of the Boers. One rarely erred by preparing for the worst in South Africa.[16]

In the morning French's cavalry column passed through the RCR position at the poort and then swung east around Thabanchu. French was soon followed by Rundle's 8th Division. On his arrival French assumed command from Hamilton. Now that the army had linked up, the need to secure the pass was gone. The Canadians gladly marched back to camp, in the process passing two pretty young girls playing tennis, evidently oblivious to the war around them.[17]

The Boers were not ready to abandon the Thabanchu–Eden Hill position without a fight. On the same day (27 April) there were a series of contacts between the enemy and mounted infantry patrols north and northeast of the village in the area of the most westerly of a series of kopjes running down from Eden Hill. Ordered to support the mounted infantry, Smith-Dorrien sent the KSLI and two guns forward in the early afternoon with instructions to return to camp once the kopje was captured. At dusk Lieutenant Colonel Spens, CO of the KSLI, received a report that the kopje had been captured by Kitchener's Horse, an irregular mounted unit. After a frustrating afternoon under Boer shell fire, Spens wasted little time in returning to the 19th Brigade camp.

Within a short time of their return a messenger arrived with news that Kitchener's Horse was in difficulty, and 19th Brigade was to send a battalion to their aid. All this was the result of a blunder—the enemy had detected Kitchener's Horse in the act of abandoning the hill. As usual the Boers were very quick off the mark. Kitchener's Horse was soon closely engaged and cut off. French's orders sent six companies of the Gordons reinforced by B and D Companies of The RCR marching north to the assistance of the mounted infantry. The night was dark, and the guide lost his way. The battalion spent a frustrating night wandering on the veldt, and dawn found it five miles south of the camp. There was nothing to do but to march back to camp, tired, footsore, and frustrated. The battalion did not rejoin the brigade until it was too late to take part in the forthcoming operations. Despite later accusations, the guide, Major Cookson of Kitchener's Horse, was guilty of dreadful navigation, not treachery. In the meantime, Kitchener's Horse had extricated itself with ten casualties.[18]

Thabanchu was a roughly semicircular feature with its steepest side facing the British. On the east it provided a shallow bowl sheltering a large number of Boers. With Rundle's division as a firm base in the area of the town, French planned to use Hamilton's column and his own cavalry division to lever the Boers out of their position and, if possible, to cut off and surround some of the defenders. As a first step 19th Brigade would secure the ridge running to the west from the end of the mountain. Ridley's mounted infantry brigade and a cavalry brigade would swing around the north end of the mountain, while another cavalry brigade would force its way through a pass in the south. Leaving a company of Cornwalls on Thabanchu Hill and still without the Gordons, the brigade supported by a field battery and a young war correspondent, Winston Churchill, marched before dawn.

By 7:30 the Shropshires had occupied the first kopje. Smith-Dorrien and his staff rode around the base of the hill and, leaving their horses, went forward on foot to take a look at the country ahead. The enemy were closer than he had expected, and his party beat an undignified retreat with bullets whizzing about their ears. Soon the forward positions of the Shropshires came under heavy fire from some kopjes half a mile to the north, and Boers were observed moving towards another kopje near the foot of Eden Hill. The Cornwalls moved, supported by The RCR, to a position from which they were able to drive off the Boers and then occupy the kopje. Before the day was very old, 19th Brigade was on its objective, facing the enemy to the north and on the slopes of Eden Hill. Meanwhle Ridley's mounted infantry had seized another kopje two miles to the left of 19th Brigade and then pushed farther north. Soon in contact, Ridley signalled for assistance to Smith-Dorrien, who prepared to march with two battalions and four guns, leaving one battalion lining the ridge. The manoeuvre was stillborn. French ordered 19th Brigade to stay in place as a cavalry brigade was to pass through their position and swing around Eden Hill.

The RCR had spent the day on the right flank of the brigade under sporadic fire from the crest of Eden Hill. From their position they were able to watch the cavalry ride off to the northeast under shell fire. Following a report that several thousand Boers had trekked away to the east, the troops were ordered to return to camp. It was late afternoon and the cavalry retraced their path towards the village of Thabanchu, closely pursued by the enemy.

Smith-Dorrien had left one battalion on the ridge and started back to camp. The march was hardly under way when his orders were changed again. At about 4:00 p.m. he ordered The RCR to seize Eden Hill to secure the cavalry's line of retreat. By 5:40 the six Canadian companies had scrambled up the steep, rocky slope and occupied a position just below the crest. It was shortly before dark, and the battalion prepared for a long night. It was obvious that if the Boers turned their attention to the Canadians, things would go from bad to worse.

Smith-Dorrien had appreciated the gravity of the situation by late afternoon and made his case to Hamilton who directed that all positions must be held until last light. After dark Smith-Dorrien was to abandon the position and return to camp. It was a cardinal rule that forces in contact were to withdraw only under cover of darkness. At 7:00 p.m. The RCR began to creep down the steep slope, which in places could better be described as a cliff. It was a difficult task to collect the men and to descend the slope without injury and without alerting the enemy. A retreat down the mountain under fire would have been disastrous. It took 90 minutes to clamber down and another two and a half hours to return to camp.[19]

The Boers had handled the British once again. The double envelopment around both ends of the mountain was beyond the capacity of the British forces. Three mounted brigades riding around the northern end (or at least two mounted brigades and an infantry brigade) might have levered the Boers out; two were just not enough. An infantry division sat in camp all day. While this division was tired after its march north, at least one of its brigades could have been used. It seems the British had seriously underestimated the enemy's strength, as Churchill noted that a helpful censor had changed "more than 2,000 Boers" to "small parties" in a story he had written two days before the battle.[20]

There was little action for 19th Brigade on the next day, although at least one round of Boer artillery fired over Eden Ridge landed within 200 yards of the bivouac area. Of more importance, Hamilton had received orders from Roberts to march on Winburg, via Jacobsrust, as the right column of the general advance on Pretoria. At Jacobsrust he would be reinforced by Bruce Hamilton's 21st Brigade, Broadwood's cavalry brigade, two field and one horse artillery battery and two 5-inch guns.[21]

Hamilton's immediate task was to clear the enemy from the Hout Nek position ten miles from Thabanchu. The road from Thabanchu to Jacobsrust ran across the open veldt with enemy-controlled ridges on the right flank. As the troops marched away from Thabanchu they could distinguish the ragged line of the Hout Nek and Thoba Mountain rising above the veldt to their front. Hout Nek crossed a ridge that ran out from the escarpment and lay across the road. On the extreme left, flat-topped Thoba Mountain rose some 600 or 700 feet above the veldt with a near-vertical face on its western extremity. The enemy paralleled the advance on the ridges, carefully watched by a mounted infantry flank guard. At 7:30 a.m. on 29 April the right flank guard became engaged while the advanced guard approached Hout Nek.

Both the shape of the ground and the presence of the enemy in strength precluded any other option than to seize the mountain to turn the position. The mounted infantry moved onto some low kopjes on the right to block Boer movements from that direction. On the left Kitchener's Horse were directed to seize Thoba Mountain, which appeared to be lightly held. The actions of 19th Brigade bear a certain resemblance to those taken at Israel's Poort. The leading battalion, the Shropshires, deployed to the front and, with some field guns and three Maxims, engaged the enemy at long range. The Cornwalls, baggage guard for the day, ringed the column's transport, which was watered and outspanned in an open area at long artillery range from the enemy. The other two battalions halted and waited for orders. Soon Kitchener's Horse were seen working their way up the southern edge of the mountain, and two companies of Shropshires and the Gordons were sent to reinforce the position. By 1:00 p.m. these troops had reached the plateau, despite being shelled by two guns firing from a flank as they advanced. It soon became evident the enemy were reinforcing the north end of the mountain. Buchan was ordered to send first two companies, then a half battalion, and finally the whole unit to join the troops on the plateau.

The movement took place in broad daylight, diagonally across the enemy's front at long rifle range but well within effective artillery range of the enemy. One soldier credited the wide dispersion between the troops and the speed of the advance for lack of casualties. Another credited Divine Providence as shells had struck all about the men as they advanced. Incredibly there was only one casualty-Private Harry Cotton of Ottawa was killed.

The enemy held two rocky knolls a short distance apart on the southwestern edge of the plateau, as well as the northern end of the plateau. The Gordons with the Shropshires companies were clinging to a precarious position along the south edge of the plateau while The RCR were on a spur part way up the slope and overlooked by the more southerly of the two knolls. Smith-Dorrien visited his battalions clinging to the plateau and ordered them to remain in place during the night. In the morning the two knolls and the saddle between them would be taken as a first step in capturing Thoba Mountain. The troops spent a cold night without food or water, lying with magazines charged and bayonets fixed seeking cover from the cold wind and sporadic rifle fire. One Canadian noted that the only hope was to complete the capture of the hill and drive the enemy out as "we are fairly surrounded."

As dawn approached and men could see to shoot, firing broke out all along the line. Smith-Dorrien arrived to take charge of the operations to clear the plateau. The more northerly knoll was secured by the Gordons before 8:00 a.m. on 30 April while a half-company of Shropshires led by the Colour Sergeant worked into the saddle between the two features and split the Boer position. In the south The RCR advanced towards the other knoll as soon as it was light enough to see. Progress was slow as the men crawled and dodged from cover to cover. Just below the crest the advance was stalled by heavy fire. Captain Burstall led a section from B Company towards some rising ground that commanded a full view of the enemy position. Private C.K. Rorison, the first man on the rise, was wounded as he turned to wave his comrades forward. He was soon followed by the rest of his section who swept the knoll with a hail of .303 bullets. By 9:00 a.m. the knoll was secure and the southern end of the hill was firmly in British hands. Besides Rorison, Lieutenant Ross and four other men had been wounded. In the meantime, the enemy had reinforced the far end of the mountain and the battle was far from over.

Hamilton had wired for reinforcements the day before and their timely arrival turned the tide. Ridley's mounted infantry and the cavalry rode in a turning movement around the western edge of Thoba Mountain to take the enemy in the rear. The immediate result was an increase in the shelling of the troops on Thoba, but within an hour guns were seen moving off, soon followed by some wagons that had been laagered behind kopjes facing the Shropshires on the plain. Smith-Dorrien pressed his troops forward along the plateau. The RCR were pinched out of the action, while the brigade commander led the Gordons and the Shropshires across the plateau under heavy fire. At the far end cheering troops charged with fixed bayonets, and "the enemy were flying down the north side of the mountain, while we were merely out of breath." Hamilton's column was in camp a few miles north of the pass before nightfall. That evening the battalion had its first meal since 4:00 p.m. on the preceding day. At least one soldier felt "Hout Nek was the hardest fight we took part in, always excepting Paardeberg."[22]

Chapter

8   Chasing Shadows in the Dust

IN THE EARLY MORNING light of 17 February 1900 the quarantine officer's launch cast off from shore and puffed importantly to a waiting steamer with the distinctive white-on-red funnel of the Allen Line. The second contingent had arrived. As the clear light of a southern summer bathed Table Bay the SS *Laurentian* drew up to dock in the busy harbour of Cape Town. Soon lines were heaved and waiting stevedores secured hawsers around bollards on the dock. The *Laurentian* took up the slack and slowly winched herself snug to the foot of the dark continent.

As the men stepped ashore they were greeted by their popular CO, Lieutenant Colonel Charles Drury, and Captain Henri Panet, detached from F Company in the first contingent. While the stores were being off-loaded on the 18th, a party had been preparing the camp-site at Green Point Common. The camp had seemed a pleasant green oasis to the first contingent during the southern spring. Now Green Point, scorched by the hot, summer sun, was swept by blowing sand "necessitating the wearing of goggles which were hot and uncomfortable . . . the cure being as bad as the disease."[1]

Drury had spent the previous months along the western railway, and his only communication with Ottawa had been by sporadic cablegrams. He was taken aback at what he found, especially the absence of an ammunition column from his brigade's organization. To make things worse, the arrival of his third battery was delayed because of the outbreak of disease on board the SS *Montezuma*. Drury resolved to improvise an ammunition column out of his own resources. As for the delayed C Battery, he could only hope that it would arrive before too much time had passed. In the meantime the first step would be to replace the missing horses. On 20 February demands were submitted to the remount authorities for 17 riding and 49 draught horses. To no one's surprise, slightly less than half of the horses could be provided by the remount department.[2]

That same day the unit took part in a ceremonial parade for the general officer commanding, Lines of Communications. The troops, Canadians, Australians, Imperial Militia and the City Imperial Volunteers finished the parade with a march into the town along streets thronged with large, enthusiastic crowds. Following the parade there was a Naval and Military Tournament, where a team from D Battery pulled its way into the finals of the tug of war before succumbing to a team from HMS *Doris*, while Gunner Williams won the half-mile race.[3]

Shortly after their arrival in Green Point the Canadians had noticed a nondescript man in civilian clothes strolling through their lines and taking in the sights. To their chagrin after he had left the camp the Canadians found that he was none other than Rudyard Kipling. Kipling may be in some disfavour today but he was extremely popular then, especially with soldiers. Chaplain Cox and Lieutenants McCrae and Morrison made a point of visiting his hotel in the hope of a glimpse of the voice of the Empire. To their delight Kipling took time from his busy schedule to chat with them. He proved to be an approachable and pleasant gentleman in the best meaning of the word. When the Canadians told him that they were sorry to have missed him the day before, Kipling replied, "That's all right—I heard you cursing considerable—could tell that you were up to your eyes in work." He advised them to boil their water and, shaking their hands, bid them good luck and adieu. Kipling was a "superstar" in an age when the printed word was the major means of communication. A chat with Kipling was as exciting as an audience with the Queen.[4]

Slowly progress was made. On 21 February the Canadians drew 29 horses. For the meantime that would be all. Until more animals arrived the batteries were not fully mobile. The troops paraded in marching order, the guns were cleaned and their sights tested and gun drill was practised under the eagle eyes of the battery sergeants major (BSMs). Meanwhile drivers fussed over their horses under the watchful eye of Veterinary-Major Massie. On 23 February Drury was elated to receive orders to move by train to Kimberley in two days' time. All ranks set to with a vengeance, buoyed by the prospect of seeing action before the (imagined) imminent end of the war. It was not to be. The order was cancelled the next day. The 25th was occupied by church parades and passes into Cape Town instead of a trip to the front. One suspects that not a few Canadians were unrepentantly hung over the next morning.[5]

On 26 February the SS *Pomeranian* arrived from Canada carrying 2 CMR, less a troop travelling with the 1st Battalion. Even for the population of Cape Town, who had witnessed many an unusual sight since the start of the war, the CMR was something completely different. The local population gawked unashamedly at the westerners with their cowboy hats, Colt revolvers, and strange saddles. The British (and the Boers) seemed to have been conditioned by lurid stories of the Wild West to believe that Canadians routinely killed and scalped their enemies.

The battalion had been together since early January—an advantage compared with many of the hastily raised South African units. A third of the men were members of the NWMP while others had had recent service in the force, the Canadian militia, or the British army. There had, however, been little time for training in Canada, and a long sea voyage provided few opportunities for anything but lectures and some small arms training. While not well drilled as mounted infantry or overly addicted to the finer points of military discipline, the Canadians could ride and care for their horses and had some aptitude in scouting and patrolling.[6]

The battalion faced one potentially disastrous problem—their Lee Enfield rifles did not shoot straight. In Cape Town a quick trip to the range showed that the rifles fired well to the right and a British armourer advised Herchmer that the wrong sights had been fitted to the rifles. The problem, the result of a design error and faulty testing, was not unique to 2 CMR, although the battalion seems to have been the only Canadian unit affected. In Canada the NWMP carried Winchester Model 1876 rifles. The Lee Enfields had been issued from militia stocks. Therefore, the NWMP officers and men would not be familiar with the Lee Enfields. While the British had adopted the Lee Enfields as standard, the regular army was still using Lee Metfords as an economy measure. The problem had recently been discovered when Lee Enfields had been issued to the Imperial Yeomanry. The Canadian permanent force had been equipped with Lee Enfields long enough to have identified and corrected the problem, and to have considered it water under the bridge. It seems that with the pressure of the mobilization no one had remembered to warn the NWMP.[7]

On 27 February came word of Cronje's surrender. Gunner Walter Bapty, with a keen eye on priorities, noted in his diary it was pay day, ending his entry with a curt "Cronje surrendered." Captain Henri Panet, snatched from F Company on 12 February and sent back to Cape Town to join (delayed) C Battery, wrote in a letter home that he felt a bit down on his luck and that the authorities "could have let me know that "C" Battery was not coming till March. It is too bad. I do my best not to think of it, but I tell you I feel pretty sore . . . We are afraid this may end the fighting."[8]

Throughout the war the loyalty of much of Cape Colony was tenuous. The first action for 2 RCR had been at Sunnyside in the Far North Cape against rebellious colonists, not Boers from one of the republics. This had the desired effect on the actions, if not the loyalty, of the settlers around Douglas. While Cronje was being invested at Paardeberg, rebellion erupted again over a large area west of the western railway from Douglas to Carnarvon and Kenhardt. It was serious enough that Roberts sent his chief of staff, Lord Kitchener, to put down the uprising. As part of Kitchener's punitive expedition, Brigadier General Sir Herbert Settle was ordered to put down the uprising in the Karroo west of the railway. While Settle prepared to lead a column from Orange River Station through Prieska, Upington, and Kenhardt, he ordered Colonel Sir Charles Parsons to lead another force to Carnarvon and Van Wyks Vlei before linking up with his column at Kenhardt. The CMR and the artillery were ordered to join Colonel Parsons' column.

First to move was D Battery on Sunday, 4 March. Warned at 11:45 a.m. the battery, less the left section, marched out of Green Point Camp at 1:15 p.m. Before the battery left the station they were treated to the sight of the arrival of a load of prisoners taken at Paardeberg: "a dirty looking lot, smelt bad, all ages and all sizes, but mostly old men and young boys." Left disgustedly cooling their heels in Green Point Camp were Lieutenant Morrison and his 54 men who "all said the same thing in fifty-five different ways."[9]

A 36-hour train journey brought the battery to the whistle-stop of Victoria Roads where the column was concentrating. It was not a beauty spot, even compared with dry, dusty Green Point Common. D Battery camped on the veldt away from the pro-rebel settlement to wait for the arrival of the remainder of the Canadians. In camp the only diversion to relieve the monotony and heat was watching lizards and giant beetles scampering through the lines. Outside camp, the countryside was not secure. There had been the occasional incident of sniping at sentries, and the Canadians could see enemy signalling from the low hills a few miles away. Outposts were prepared, and guns and ammunition readied to repel any attack. Fortunately, the dangerous interlude would not last long. Back in Green Point the other Canadians were ordered to prepare to entrain. The CMR soon followed D Battery on the long climb up the escarpment and away from the fertile coast onto the dry veldt. On 9 March the remaining gunners drew some mules and wagons as well as a few horses to make up deficiencies in transport. Mules are not as glamourous as horses, but in many ways they were better suited for the task to come. At 9:00 the next morning orders came to entrain at 11:30. With their arrival at 5:00 a.m. on the 12th the Carnarvon Field Force was virtually complete.

The enemy in the western Cape Colony were believed to be some 2000 to 3000 strong with two guns. The British, actually mostly "colonials," were outnumbered but this was offset by the Canadians' 12 field guns and two machine-guns. The Carnarvon Field Force was made up of 2 CMR, a company each of Western Australian Mounted Infantry, Derbyshire Yeomanry, and New Zealand Mounted Infantry, D and E Batteries, and wagons with supplies for seven days.

That morning the troops left the security of the railway to move a few miles to Victoria West as the first stage of the push to Kenhardt. The field force moved in three groups a few hours apart. The first party, a CMR squadron and D Battery, commanded by Major Hurdman, was followed in the afternoon by the remainder of the CMR and other troops under Lieutenant Colonel Herchmer. The next day (13 March) Lieutenant Colonel Drury brought up the rear with the remaining troops and the supply train. Before the main body had reached Victoria West, the advanced guard had already left the settlement on its way to Carnarvon. On 14 March the main body left the dubious security of Victoria West for Carnarvon via rebel-controlled territory. The plan was to join Settle's column at Kernhardt where the combined forces would either defeat or disperse the enemy. As the crow flies distances did not seem to be that great. The Karroo, at best near-desert, stretched away in brown sheets shimmering in the heat and clouded by blowing dust and swarms of locusts. Herchmer described it as a "sandy waste without a blade of grass, relieved here and there with a few small bushes which the native animals consume. The country is entirely destitute of trees, except a few small willows &c., near the dams and wells."[10]

The Carnarvon Field Force was hardly the fast, hard-hitting instrument that usually exists only in the fertile imaginations of military theorists. The column stretched along several miles of road, from the wary scouts to the last riders of the rearguard eating the dust of the creaking, groaning supply wagons with their native drivers and herds of attendant animals. Heat radiated up from the baked, arid surface and limited the progress of the column to 17 miles one day, 20 the next, and then 16. While a better pace might have been possible for a short time, the limiting factor on the Karroo was always the condition of the animals. This was especially true for the CMR horses, which had not yet lost their thick winter coats.

Sir Charles Parsons seems to have adopted a somewhat unusual means of conveyance, no dashing steed for him. Sir Charles drove out from Victoria West to join the advance guard in a cape cart, easily overtaking Drury shepherding the main body through the dust and heat. One suspects the monotony of the march was relieved by comments from the cracked lips of saddle-sore cowpunchers and swagmen as the cart and its distinguished passenger jauntily rolled away across the Karroo.

Carnarvon was occupied on St Patrick's Day after an uneventful march of some 80 miles and without any contact with the enemy. The inhabitants had all heard of the recent British successes and were either outwardly loyal, except in prices charged for food, or sullenly neutral. The local women, rather reluctantly, had prepared a good spread for the hungry and thirsty little army. Rebels were fleeing before the column, and whole districts were opting for loyalty. One can only wonder how long the pro-British sentiment would endure once the troops moved on.[11]

The occupation of Carnarvon was only the first stage in the suppression of the rebellion. If the enemy would not stand and fight, then the column would go in search of the enemy. From Carnarvon the British would press on to Van Wyks Vlei and then to the small settlement of Kenhardt. In the meantime, it was time to attend to matters spiritual, rather than temporal. The next day, Sunday, the return of Carnarvon to the fold was celebrated with a church parade, in the heat of the day amid colossal grumbling by the men. As one Canadian dourly observed, there is nothing like the comfort of religion in troubled times, but "a little common sense is not a bad thing."[12]

Suddenly 2 CMR found itself seriously under strength in senior officers. In Canada, Sam Steele, the second in command, had been appointed to command Strathcona's Horse just days before sailing and had not been replaced. Major Gilbert Sanders, the officer commanding D Squadron, had been sick for much of the voyage and had been left behind seriously ill in Cape Town. Joseph Howe, the remaining major, had been incapacitated for three days by an eye ailment, but would recover in time to lead his squadron on the next phase. The situation was serious enough that Herchmer asked Sir Charles Parsons to request that a senior officer from 1 CMR be sent forward to join 2 CMR on its arrival. Now on 19 March, Herchmer wrote in the staff diary, "Must have suffered from the sun, as my head has not been right since, and the extra work occasioned by Major Sanders's illness and the temporary illness of Major Howe, rendered me for a few days unfit for duty." Major Howe subsequently reported to Ottawa, "20 Mar.—Assumed comd due to sickness of Herchmer by comd of Sir Charles Parsons. Herchmer granted 2 weeks sick leave. Lt. Col. Herchmer has since returned to Cape Town, where I have been informed he has received a staff appointment." It was a bad start and the battalion never completely recovered from it.[13]

By 21 March the main body was ready to resume the march north to Van Wyks Vlei, although small groups had already moved on. After an early reveille the force moved off at 5:30 a.m. Even with stops to water and rest animals, 20 miles were made that day, which may indicate that the rest had been of some benefit. On the downside horses still gave out and died in alarming numbers. Morrison painted a sad picture of the typical fate of an exhausted horse:

> It is pitiful to see the old troopers play out on the line of march. We, of the artillery, will be trudging on through the sand when we will come upon a horse of the advanced guard standing by the roadside, swaying groggily on its legs, its neck stretched out and its eyes glazing in death. When it hears the clank of the guns and the trampling of the horses in the column it will reel forward in a game effort to join the ranks, only to tumble in a heap. The battery passes on and a minute later the sharp crack of a pistol announces that some more horse flesh is fertilizing "the wild and waste Karroo."[14]

By necessity the column was to be self-contained, carrying its own food and forage and marching from well to water-hole to spring. One Canadian, perhaps with a dry tongue firmly in his cheek, wrote that "it will give you some idea of the way good water is valued in this country to explain that if a man is giving you a drink he hands over the bottle of whiskey and makes you say 'when' to the pouring of the water." To satisfy needs such as fires for cooking and warmth on the treeless Karroo the men adopted the local fuel, dried goat dung, which was cut like peat from the kraals where the animals sheltered at night.[15]

The first members of the column to reach Van Wyks Vlei were the New Zealanders and the right section of D Battery who had left Carnarvon on 19 March. The foray proved successful as three unwary rebels were captured. After a hot, dry march the little force was reunited in the settlement with the arrival of the main body on the morning of 23 March. That afternoon the skies opened to end a two-year drought. The downpour washed out the road through a number of dongas. As a result both men and animals were on half rations for ten days. After a long night one officer wrote, "It was a wet, dreary night, the camp being entirely inundated, and the horses half-leg deep in water and mud. The guard and picket had no place they could bed down and they spent a night of hardship . . . with the lines of bedraggled horses strung in dripping lines between the guns." Rain fell for four days, until finally on the 26th the weather began to clear. The weather may have been clear but the parched earth had turned to deep, sticky mud.[16]

A "flying" column including a CMR Squadron and Lieutenant McCrae's section had left Van Wyks Vlei on 22 March and slogged through the mud to Kenhardt. The rest of the advanced guard under Colonel Parsons soon followed along the muddy tracks and across flooded dongas. After the exertions of the march Kenhardt, occupied on the 31st, was a disappointment. It was a miserable little place with a population of 12 whites and 500 natives, although a number of the more loyal locals had previously fled to safer areas. Despite its size, the symbolism of the reimposition of British power was important. The Boers had sortied to the Kenhardt area and annexed it on the outbreak of hostilities. Now Sir Charles Parsons personally welcomed the inhabitants back into the bosom of the Empire. The population, with little choice, cheered as the Union Jack was run up the flag pole.

Dysentery and rheumatism plagued the column during its five-day stay, and the men were not impressed by the miserable little town in a sea of mud. Discipline broke down and on one occasion 19 members of the CMR found themselves in the local jail after a monumental spree. The incident prompted threats to order the Canadians out of the field. The squadron commander, Captain Archibald Macdonnell, managed to both placate the British ire and convince his men they were bound for the rear areas unless they shaped up.[17]

Back in Van Wyks Vlei the main body combated boredom, mud and disease. On 27 March there had been an attempt to follow the advance guard to Kenhardt, but the column was halted by the flooded Haartbeeste River. The next day the river, which had fallen during the night, was crossed with difficulty, and the main body followed the advance guard's trail towards De Naauwte Poorte. Word soon came from Parsons that the roads were impassable, and Drury opted to return to the semicomfort of the little hamlet.

Camp was set up outside the town where a dam provided an adequate water supply. Soon after the arrival, while watering the teams, Driver Robert Bradley of D Battery was thrown from his horse when it floundered in deep water. Bradley could not swim, and although Driver Hal Walters jumped in and began to assist him to shore, Bradley slipped from his grasp and sank. Other Canadians and some Western Australians jumped in and began to dive for him in the muddy water. Private Thomas Firn of the West Australians found him on the bottom in 15 feet of water and brought him to the surface. He was revived, but soon became delirious, and died a few hours later. Bradley and a New Zealander, Private T.H. Hempton, who died of enteric fever on 4 April, lie together at the foot of a kopje out on the Karroo, surely two of the loneliest war graves ever. A number of the troops had been struck down by illness (on 31 March there were 24 sick at Carnarvon and 50 at Van Wyks Vlei) and although most recovered and rejoined their units before the field force was withdrawn, some were left behind. One, Private J. Woolcombe of 2 CMR, died of pleurisy and dysentery on 23 April and was buried at Carnarvon.[18]

With the occupation of Kenhardt the rebellion was over, for the time being at least. General Settle ordered the column to return to De Aar by 14 April following the route

Carnarvon, Vosburg, and Britstown, which meant a difficult cross-country march to the railroad. A suggestion that instead the column move from Carnarvon to the railway at Victoria Roads was turned down, and preparations for the march were begun. Life was not all hard work, mud, and death—mail from Canada actually made its way from the railroad to the Carnarvon Field Force on 3 April. At 7:00 a.m. on the 4th the main body bid a heartfelt farewell to miserable little Van Wyks Vlei. Even with D Squadron, the Kiwis (New Zealanders), and McCrae's section detached, it still was a relatively large force of 611 troops and 118 native drivers, 10 guns, 57 supply wagons, 559 horses, 571 mules, 96 donkeys, and 32 oxen.[19]

On 10 April the first riders of the Carnarvon Field Force reached De Aar, a day ahead of the deadline. Three days later the Kenhardt column joined the main body. The Carnarvon Field Force was dissolved, and the two CMR squadrons soon rolled up the line towards Bloemfontein.

With the departure of 2 CMR, the Royal Canadian Field Artillery (RCFA), less C Battery, was left along the railroad from De Aar to Belmont. Soon the unit would be dispersed even more and in fact would not be re-united until the trip home had begun. The disposition of the unit on 10 May is typical of the time:

Headquarters Staff	De Aar
C Battery	Rhodesia
Left Section D Battery	De Aar
Centre Section D Battery	Orange River
Right Section D Battery	Victoria Roads
E Battery	Griqualand

The Griqualand foray was a continuation of operations that paralleled those of the Carnarvon Field Force. For this reason, and because there was another Canadian element to the story, we must retrace our path to Cape Town in the days prior to the arrival of the second contingent. As a member of parliament, Sam Hughes had been able to reach a variety of influential ears, including the high commissioner. Energetic and persistent, he finally obtained a staff appointment on the lines of communications. While he may not have volunteered the information, the improvement in his fortunes probably owed at least as much to an intervention by Lord Minto as to his own efforts. Soon he moved steadily up the ladder, as shown by these extracts from orders:

Line of Communications Order 30, 30 January 1900
Lieut.-Colonel Hughes, Canadian Rifles, has been appointed Railway Staff Officer, Naauwpoort, from 29th January 1900.
Line of Communications Order 54, 23 February 1900
1. Subject to approval by Secretary of State for War, Lieut.-Colonel S. Hughes, Royal Canadian Rifles, is appointed Special Services Officer from the 1st December 1899.
Line of Communications Order 105, 15 April 1900
4.b. Further to Lines of Communication Order No 54 (1) of 23rd February 1900, Lieut.-Colonel S. Hughes, Royal Canadian Rifles, is graded as an Assistant Adjutant General from 1st December 1899.

Sam, never one to miss the main chance, had somehow managed to convince the authorities to backdate his appointment, and his entitlement to pay, to 1 December, very nearly the day that he had first become available for service in South Africa. The pay was not as important as the symbolism. It was a poke in the eye with a sharp stick for Hutton and his despised permanent force toadies.[20]

The appointment of 23 February proved particularly significant for another reason. Brigadier General Herbert Settle, the commander of the Orange River Station sector of the Lines of Communications and one of the officers Sam had met at Cape Town, was hastily assembling a column similar to the Carnarvon Field Force. He was faced with a real dilemma; he must jury rig a force strong enough to pacify the Karroo, while not jeopardizing the efficient flow of supplies forward to Roberts' army. The newly arrived colonial officer was an obvious candidate for a job in the field. Colonials were felt to have innate abilities as scouts and skirmishers. Settle could not have known that Hughes was from Victoria County, Ontario, hardly the wild frontier, and Sam Hughes was not likely to correct his error. Sam was appointed to the dual role of column intelligence officer and chief of scouts.

The campaign was similar to that of the Carnarvon Field Force—long, dreary, and difficult. The column pushed along the Orange River through Preiska to Upington, re-establishing British authority over the turbulent settlements and threatening Kenhardt from the north. Hughes and his orderlies, Privates G. Phillips of Belleville and "Dick" Turpin of Cobourg, Ontario, were in the van of the advance, ranging far to the front and flanks of the column in search of rebels, weapons, ammunition, and forage for the column itself.

Hughes' command was not very large, probably no more than a couple of dozen men, but effective in the time and place. Sam found many kindred spirits among his men, while they in turn shared his contempt for the regular army's red tape and parade square mentality. During the sweep he and his men ranged far and wide across the Karroo often under terrible conditions: scouting Preiska, accompanying Settle to Kenhardt, and capturing Upington, the last centre before German South West Africa.

In this last operation he demonstrated an unexpected flair for the unconventional side of warfare. The same torrential rains that plagued the Carnarvon Field Force had bogged down Settle's column 40 miles west of Prieska. Sam was ordered to lead a scratch force of his scouts and some irregular cavalry to Upington, where some 300 rebels were believed to be located. Progress of even this small force was too slow for Sam. Leaving most of his men behind, he rode on ahead with six men. In two days the little party covered the 90 miles to Upington with only a few contacts with scattered rebels. Sam must have realized that rumour and uncertainty would have magnified his numbers in the enemies' minds. He decided on a colossal bluff. As soon as the town came into sight he ordered his little force to charge raising as much dust as possible to make the enemy believe that they were faced by a much larger force. As Hughes' "column" galloped into town the small enemy rearguard left just as quickly, only pausing to trade a few ill-aimed shots. The little force, aided by 20 natives (who would have been shot by the Boers if found with weapons) armed by Hughes to aid in the defence, spent an anxious night. There was no doubt that there were enemy in the area: eight were captured when they rode too close to the town in the early evening. The impact of the loss of both Upington and Kenhardt on the same day dealt a severe blow to the rebel cause. The arrival of Settle's force three days later completed the demoralization started by the bluff. Rebels began to come in and surrender their arms. It was the end of the rebellion south of the Orange River, at least for the time being. Sam Hughes' audacity had paid off handsomely, but there must have been some doubts about the wisdom of some of his actions. However, his stunt had worked, and that is all that matters in war.[21]

Without great loss of life on either side a relatively small force had pacified an area the size of Ontario. Of lesser import in the big picture, but a matter of real satisfaction, the gunners had earned the nickname "Rebel Chasers From America" from their RCFA shoulder flashes. Now by mid-April most of Settle's and Parsons' men had returned to the railway and moved up to the front. There was little for Sam to do other than chafe at the tedium of restoring civil authority.[22]

While the vast stretch south of the Orange River had been pacified, Boers were still active in Griqualand west of the railway. Lieutenant General Sir Charles Warren was ordered to clear the enemy as part of the general advance that was to end the war. If Warren could secure Douglas (the same town captured by Pilcher in early January), Campbell, Griquatown, and Kuruman, he would deny the enemy its source of supplies. He could then turn his attention to the main enemy, a Transvaal commando led by Piet de Villiers. With de Villiers dead or a prisoner the rebellion would quickly run out of steam.[23]

In early May Sir Charles began to muster his forces. Back at the Cape he had made the acquaintance of Hughes and must have been aware of Sam's exploits in Settle's command. Opting to reinforce success despite any lingering doubts about the events at Upington, he appointed Sam as his intelligence officer. Other Canadians would march with Warren. On 9 May Major J. Hunter Ogilvie's E Battery began to march north from De Aar to join Warren at Belmont, while Captain H.J. Mackie was selected to command the 17 men of the modestly dubbed "Warren's Scouts."

Warren's column seems to have followed the pattern used for Settle's and Parsons' commands—a mixture of colonial and yeomanry units—freeing British regulars to take on the main enemy forces. Besides the scouts and the Canadian battery, the column included the 8th Battalion Imperial Yeomanry and the Duke of Edinburgh's Own Volunteer Rifles (DEOVR), a South African colonial unit. Other troops temporarily taken from garrisons along the railway would see action in a strike on Douglas. Later another yeomanry battalion, the 19th (or Paget's Horse), would join the march north through Griqualand. Little time was wasted preparing for the offensive. E Battery had reached Belmont late on the afternoon of 13 May and, leaving the left section in garrison, accompanied the DEOVR to Rooi Pan two days later. Major Ogilvie noted, unlike the Royal Canadians a few months earlier, that the country was beautiful. While there is no accounting for taste, the major had just spent several weeks on the Karroo. On 20 May the build-up was completed and Sir Charles was ready to march. Douglas, once more a hornet's nest of rebels, was a day's ride away. Warren could not risk leaving Rooi Pan unguarded, so the centre section of E Battery, half of the 23rd Yeomanry Company, and a half company of the DEOVR were left to hold a firm base. At 10:00 p.m. Captain Mackie lead his scouts past alert sentries and west towards Douglas. The column included the right section of E Battery, Imperial Yeomanry, Cape Police, Munster Mounted Infantry, and the DEOVR less a half company. After a short march through the black African night the main body halted, while the scouts cleared the route through a pass.[24]

With the first glimmer of dawn on 21 May the column marched on Douglas. When the advance guard reached the hills overlooking the settlement they could see the enemy on a line of ridges across the river. After three months of waiting E Battery was ordered into action. The two guns, with limbers and wagons, galloped up the column and swung into action on the ridge. At 8:30 a.m. a 12-pounder field gun barked and a round whistled towards the distant ring of wagons. Once on the target rapid fire was opened. As yeomanry, scouts, and police skirmished forward, Boers began to inspan and withdraw. Others stayed to fight. The guns moved forward in late morning to enfilade a donga sheltering a party of enemy. The enemy may have been scattered, but they had not run away. It took darkness to finally put a stop to the action. Incredibly, there had been only one British casualty during several hours' fighting.[25]

When the column left Douglas on its march north it included the 8th and 19th Yeomanry, DEOVR, the scouts, and E Battery, less the Maritimers of its left section left to bolster the garrison. This would have been a fairly large force, were it not for the necessity to occupy the towns along the lines of communications. As in bungee jumping, forward momentum is absorbed by the stretched tail, and eventually the whole thing slows to a halt and recoils. While the column slowly probed forward the enemy fell back on Campbell, where they were reinforced by de Villiers. Warren finally opted to wait for supplies at Faber's Put. His choice was not a good one and may have been due to the presence of a comfortable farm house that he appropriated for his living quarters. The little farm was overlooked by ridges within close rifle shot. Sir Charles Warren had stuck his head in a noose and offered de Villiers a chance to be the hangman.

During the night of 29 May 600 Boers surrounded the camp just out of earshot of the outposts. De Villiers and a small party crept through the outpost line and into the camp. Here luck deserted the enemy. Dawn was still at least a half hour distant when a surprised sentry raised the alarm. The Boers poured heavy fire into the yeomanry lines, killing men and stampeding scores of horses. In the dark and confusion, startled soldiers rolled from their blankets and began to return the fire. The yeomanry and colonials were not soldiers of long standing and had not yet learned to wait for orders. In the Canadian lines, next to the yeomanry, gun detachments ran to their four guns, while drivers harnessed the teams and led them to cover. It was still too dark to distinguish the enemy and Ogilvie ordered his men to lie down by the guns.

The scouts and the DEOVR, who had bivouacked near the farmhouse, had escaped the close range fire. As the sky lightened Hughes, Mackie, and Lieutenant Colonel Spence of the DEOVR hastily organized a counterattack, while the yeomanry engaged the enemy at close range. Ogilvie was ordered to move two guns to a small hill to his right front. Finding the fire too heavy to bring the horses forward, the gunners manhandled their guns across the fire-swept field and came into action. Bombardier William Latimer of Granby, Quebec was killed and seven others wounded from the two nine-man gun detachments in the process. The other two guns engaged the enemy over a wide arc to their left. As the British counterattacked, the guns were masked and began to fire over the infantry's heads, bursting shrapnel behind the crests in an attempt to stampede the Boer horses. Ogilvie reported that this seemed to work, as the enemy began to retire. No doubt the counterattack by a few hundred men also played no inconsiderable part in the withdrawal. After the initial shock, the enemy had been outfought at their own game.

However, casualties had been heavy, 27 (including Lieutenant Colonel Spence killed), and 41 wounded. The Canadian share of the butcher's bill was one killed and 11 wounded. The names of three wounded were listed in the battery diary, but not in the official return, which records Canadian casualties of one killed and eight wounded.[26]

Warren tried to paint the picture in the best possible light. Glossing over the casualties, the loss of a large number of horses, and any embarrassing questions about how the enemy was able to approach so close to his poorly sited camp he reported that a victory had been won. From Warren's perspective that was probably true, and the resistance had been a nasty shock to the Boers. However, his impetuous intelligence officer had already drawn some unfavourable conclusions about his commander. One could never accuse Sam Hughes of keeping his feelings to himself. He managed to get his views of the affair printed in South African papers, virtually at the same time Warren was praising Sam in his despatches. Besides Sam Hughes, 30 other officers and men were mentioned in the same despatch, including three other Canadians—Major Ogilvie, Captain Mackie and Surgeon-Major Worthington. Sam was later to claim that Warren had promised him the Victoria Cross twice, for his actions at Douglas and Faber's Put. At best this was selective interpretation of praise, and at worst wild fantasy. Whatever the true story, Hughes soon provided Warren with good reason to renege on any promises of decorations.[27]

Through June Warren followed up his advantage, pushing into Griqualand. Sam often rode with the scouts, taking advantage of any signs of weakness and harrying the enemy. Word was received that nearly 300 men led by de Villiers were holed up in Kuruman and wished to surrender. Sir Charles sent Sam to scout the town, with strict instructions to do no more than investigate, and under no circumstances to enter into negotiations. Sam, who clearly felt he knew better than Warren, rode into the town and demanded the surrender of de Villiers and his men. Bravado almost worked, and if it had not been for second thoughts on the part of de Villiers and 50 of the more stout-hearted, it would have been a major coup. Warren was enraged when he found that, despite the capture of 220 enemy with their weapons, the big fish had escaped and, contrary to orders, Sam had granted the rebels generous terms.

Like the precipitate action at Upington, Sam's foray to confront de Villiers was dramatic, but unnecessary. Now his lapse in judgement combined with official displeasure to an indiscretion on his part would lead to the end of his career on active service. He had written to cronies in Canada criticizing the British as military incompetents. To make political hay in an election year the letters were printed in a number of Canadian papers. Minto wired Roberts in mid-June, urging that Sam be muzzled before he inflicted any more damage on Imperial relations. Roberts' demand that "Hughes either give a satisfactory explanation or be deprived of his command and sent back to Canada by [the] first ship" coincided with the escape of de Villiers and an unwelcome call for an explanation from an outraged high commissioner. Warren had also learned of the criticism of his conduct at Faber's Put in the Cape Town papers at about the same time. If de Villiers had surrendered unconditionally, Warren might have gone to bat for Sam. Now, Sir Charles was presented with a convenient scapegoat. Hughes was ordered to Cape Town on 27 June and the commander-in-chief wasted no time in making good on his threat. On 18 July the Toronto *Globe* reported that Roberts had dispensed with Hughes' services.

Sam seems to have been convinced to the end of his days that he was the victim of conspiracy or obstructionism. Back in Canada he conveniently glossed over the reason for his return and embarked on a campaign of self-aggrandizement.[28]

During his long career as a militia officer, politician, and cabinet minister this three-month period was his only taste of action. Despite his claims, he was not a military genius. It is important to put his achievements, creditable in their own right, in perspective. He never commanded a body of troops even as large as a troop of mounted rifles and except for Faber's Put saw little hard fighting. The capture of Upington was brave and audacious, while his attempted bluff at Kuruman bears the hallmark of an egomaniac, or a man on the make. Hughes was brave, bold and decisive. These virtues, however, are liabilities in an officer without judgement and common sense.[29]

While E Battery had been campaigning in Griqualand, D Battery had been deployed in sections disgustedly guarding dreary stations along the railway south of the Orange River. Now, with the end of the rebellion D Battery would join 2 CMR east of Pretoria, while Drury's headquarters would join C Battery in the western Transvaal and northern Cape Colony. E Battery would be the only Canadian unit not to set foot in the Transvaal, but would continue to pursue rebels across the extremes of the Cape Colony and parts of the OFS. Ironically the battery had fought in what was, with the exception of Leliefontein, the most desperate situation faced by the Canadians in South Africa and received the least recognition. They surely deserved better.[30]

Chapter

9 The Relief of Mafeking

THE DELAY CAUSED by the change in troopships meant that C Battery had spent an unexpected six weeks in Tête-du-Pont Barracks (now Fort Frontenac) at Kingston. At last the battery and 1 CMR sailed on the *Milwaukee* on 21 February 1900. Once disembarkation was completed in Cape Town on 27 March the Canadians followed the route taken by their comrades to Green Point Camp. The first priority was the horses. Fourteen had died during the voyage, and others were in poor condition. With fresh air and plenty of water and space the animals rapidly recovered, the battery diarist writing that "our horses . . . in the short interval of rest have picked up wonderfully." The first Canadian mail arrived on the 29th and the battery recruited two more men, one a member of the *Milwaukee*'s crew and the other a Canadian who presented himself at the camp.

On 4 April the battery and 1 CMR left Green Point for Stellenbosch, to replace the horses lost at sea and to prepare for operations. Roberts was concentrating forces at Bloemfontein, and first B Squadron, and then the rest of 1 CMR, left on the long railway journey to the front. C Battery, however, remained behind, seemingly destined to spend the war far from the scene of action.[1]

Finally at noon on 13 April came orders, expected by Battery Commander Major Joseph Hudon, if not by the always-sceptical gunners, to move to Cape Town to embark for Beira. Striking camp that afternoon the battery marched through the night, arriving at the ship, the SS *Columbian*, at 8:30 a.m. Guns, wagons, horses, harness, and ammunition were all loaded by noon. Sergeant W. Kiely, from Winnipeg's 13th Field Battery, proudly wrote home that a staff officer appeared at 12:15. This worthy individual, seeing Canadians seemingly waiting for direction, ordered them to load the guns.

"All loaded, sir" was the reply.

"Go on loading horses, then."

Again, "All loaded, sir."

"Then go on with the ammunition." Once again the same,

"All loaded, sir."

Exclaiming "Impossible," the staff officer hurried away to wire Roberts. The reply, ordering the ship to sail, and complimenting the men, was not long in coming. By mid-afternoon the transport was at sea on her 1500-mile voyage through the Indian Ocean.

At Beira the battery would disembark and move overland to join the Rhodesian Field Force in an attempt to relieve Mafeking.[2]

Mafeking was a miserable little whistle-stop on the western railway. The Boers had laid siege to it on the outbreak of war. By any measure the town should have fallen months ago, but Mafeking, led by Major General Robert Baden-Powell, a mildly eccentric cavalry officer and later founder of the Boy Scouts, had held out for seven months and captured the public's imagination as a symbol of British pluck. Despite its negligible strategic value, the loss of Mafeking would be a catastrophe for the war effort and British prestige.

Why was it necessary to make such a long and difficult journey to relieve Mafeking? The most direct route was up the railway from Fourteen Springs, north of Kimberley. A column, largely irregular mounted units with an RHA battery, led by Brigadier General Bryan Mahon, was concentrating near Kimberley. However, there was little advantage in banking all on a single option, and Roberts had decided on a two-pronged advance. The other prong, the Rhodesian Field Force led by Colonel Herbert Plumer, had to be strengthened before it could move on Mafeking. The only guns with Plumer's small force were three small 7-pounder muzzle loaders and a lone 12-pounder. Lord Roberts selected C Battery to reinforce Plumer because it was colonial and available.[3]

The passage to Beira, some 1500 miles, was uneventful except for a near grounding when the *Columbian* lost her way on the approach to Beira. Little time was wasted unloading and the drivers and the horses left for Bamboo Creek, 60 miles inland, by a large train of 42 cars on the narrow gauge railway at 8:40 p.m. on the 23rd. The next day, 24 April, the remainder of the battery disembarked and immediately boarded another train with 100 Queenslanders as escort. Few could have been sorry to see the last of Beira with its well-earned reputation as a fever-ridden pest-hole. The novelty of the trip through low marshland and then banana and coconut plantations very likely did not last. The train was crowded—so crowded that some men were forced to sit on top of the cars, and others found seats on the guns and wagons and the bags containing the harness and tack. At Bamboo Creek the battery transferred to a wide-gauge line and moved off again on four separate trains. The funnels of the wood burning engines spewed out clouds of thick smoke and embers from the supply of dubious fuel. The men were kept on the alert, fighting fires that threatened the open cars loaded with guns, wagons, and ammunition. By the time the battery was complete in Marandellas, 351 miles from Beira, on the 27th the men had had very little sleep for four days. With a few exceptions the expectation of being in on the relief of Mafeking kept spirits high.

The horses had suffered from heat, shortage of water, and the swaying and jolting of the closed boxcars. It was the height of the dry season, and the country was tinted brown by dried vegetation. The horses could not make a 300 mile cross-country dash. Hudon and the chief staff officer of the Rhodesian Field Force, who had come to Marandellas to organize the battery's cross-Rhodesian trip, put their heads together. In fact, much of the planning had been done prior to the arrival of C Battery, as an unknown genius had anticipated that there would be difficulties.

Mail and passengers travelled to Bulawayo by stagecoach. Normal service was suspended, and the stagecoach line was requisitioned to move the battery, less two guns and the horses and drivers, forward. Hudon, Lieutenant Leslie, 23 men, two guns, and a wagon left on 30 April escorted by 17 members of the horseless Queensland Mounted Infantry. Much the same arrangements were made for the other two parties, two guns and an ammunition wagon under Lieutenant King and two ammunition wagons under Captain Panet, that left the next day about 12 hours apart. The gunners had a taste, unique for Canadians, of life on safari. Unlike the veldt farther south, the country was savannah with frequent trees and bushes. At night lions were heard, and during the day game could sometimes be seen. Conditions were terribly cramped in the stagecoaches, and some men rode on the guns. It must have been quite an ordeal, jolting along on unimproved roads and choking on thick Rhodesian dust.

The 300-mile trip was completed in about six days. The rate of 50 miles a day was achieved by changing teams at the relay stations every 10 miles or so, and this must have severely strained the resources of the stagecoach line. At some of the stations oxen replaced the mules and, surprisingly, had no trouble keeping up the pace.

After a short stop in Bulawayo the battery moved by rail to Ootsi, arriving on 11 May. Hurried preparations were made for action and the battery, 62 all ranks, accompanied by the dismounted Australians and some guides, marched again at 4:30 p.m. On 14 May there was an emotional rendezvous as the Canadians and Australians joined the ranks of the 800-strong Rhodesian Field Force at Sefeteli. It is indicative of the conditions that 300 members of the field force were on the sick list. The arrival of the reinforcements as well as recent contact with a patrol from Mahon's column made the end of their ordeal seem near. In an outpouring of emotion they stood and cheered as the reinforcements entered the camp.

By early afternoon the whole force—men of the British South Africa Company Police, the Rhodesia Regiment, the Southern Rhodesia Volunteers, and now a dismounted company of Queensland Mounted Infantry and the left and right sections of C Battery, Royal Canadian Field Artillery—were moving south. Plumer's force contacted Mahon and his men at Jan Massibi about 30 miles west of Mafeking on the Molopo River on the morning of 15 May. Mahon's column was made up of the Diamond Fields Horse, the Kimberley Light Horse, the Imperial Light Horse, some Cape Police, and an RHA battery. The combined force outgunned the Boers threatening Mafeking, and both sides knew it. Boers, however, were never pushovers, and victory was not a foregone conclusion.

With scouts well to the front and flanks the relief column pushed forward in two columns on 16 May. Soon word was received that the enemy were dug in across the route to Mafeking. They clearly intended to make a fight of it. Hudon moved the battery forward, the guns were unhooked from their teams of mules (the contribution of the native mule drivers has largely gone unrecognized) and manhandled forward under shell fire. A Canadian sergeant shouted "fire" and his number two tugged the lanyard clipped to the T shaped friction tube. With a sharp crack the first round fired in anger by Canadian gunners in the war whistled towards a target 5000 yards away.[4]

After a quarter hour in action the battery leapfrogged to a ridge about 1000 yards further east, still under fire. Hudon later wrote:

> We opened fire on a stone laager at 3700 yards against artillery; and finding the range to be 3350 yards, at once changed to time shrapnel with fuse 15 1/2. The enemy's position appeared to be well protected by trees; and in elevation was about on a level with our own. We, however, silenced the Boer guns after a few rounds; driving the enemy from his position and following him with our shells, which were apparently effective.

> We were soon exposed to fire from the right from field guns and pom-poms, located in a bush near a white house. Our right section, therefore changed front to the right to reply to this fire, the first range being at 3750 yards, fuse 17 3/4. They were almost immediately assisted by the left section, with the result that the enemy soon appeared to be dislodged.

We then turned our fire on the white house. No. 1 gun was at this time detached, and sent, under Captain Panet, to the right, to take a position from which one of the enemy's pom-poms could be located. No. 2 gun then changed fire to the brick building on the right of the white house, at a range of 4500 yards. The left section also changed fire at 4700 yards on artillery between the white house and brick building, the enemy quickly ceasing his fire from that direction. No. 2 gun also assisted in this work.

The artillery fire of the enemy, however was resumed, their shells still coming from the direction of the white house. Their guns were well under cover; sheltered by trees and shrubbery, and at times could not be located. As a result their fire increased for a time; and two of our men, No. 65, acting Bombardier W. Patton, No. 5 sub-division and No. 135, Gunner W. McCollum, No. 6 sub-division were slightly wounded with pieces of shell.

At this point, we received orders to change our position further east, in order to secure a shorter range and from where the effect of our fire could be observed with better advantage. We again opened fire on the white house at 3650 yards and with better results, the enemy vacating his position in great disorder, his guns having been silenced by our fire. Captain Panet rejoined us shortly after with No. 1 gun. This was the last position taken by us that day, the enemy ceasing his fire at 5:35, our last shell being fired at 5:40. The general action ceased about the same time with the exception of a few rifle shots.[5]

The battery came out of action and rejoined the column near the centre of the vacated Boer position. The plan was to bivouac and push on to Mafeking in the morning. In the meantime, the battery replaced the 180 rounds of ammunition it had fired from the reserves with Mahon's supply convoy. Shortly after, the plans changed. The column resumed the march about midnight. At 4:00 a.m. on the morning of 17 May Mahon relieved the siege of Mafeking.

There was little time to enjoy the fruits of victory. At 7:00 a.m. the battery turned out and rode into action to shell a nearby Boer laager. After half an hour and 34 rounds the Boers fled from their entrenchments, and the Canadians rode back into Mafeking. It had been a neatly handled little action. The battery diarist proudly noted that the other troops were all sounding the praise of the Canadians. It says much of C Battery's contribution that the countersign to the password on 17 May was "Canada."

Around the Empire the relief of Mafeking set off an orgy of celebrations that added a word to the English language, Maff'ick, to exult riotously. For Roberts' army at Kroonstad it was welcome news and an inspiration. On the lines of communications Drury and his gunners were doubly pleased when they learned that C Battery had arrived in time. There was no time to rest on the laurels of victory. The battery moved 16 miles north along the railway to Ramathalabama on the 18th to protect workmen repairing the railway and bridges blown up by the Boers. Scouts reported no contact with Boers anywhere in the area. It was believed the majority were near Zeerust, 40 miles east in the Transvaal. Despite this, it was decided to prepare defences.

The digging took three days to complete, relieved only by the arrival of mail on the 22nd. On the 25th Lieutenant Irving and the rest of the battery, less a small party shepherding sick horses, arrived by train from Bulawayo to join their comrades at the aptly named Fort Desolation.

The battery soon moved into the Transvaal to Zeerust. On 14 June the battery rode into Rustenburg, 50 miles west of Pretoria. The Boers seemed to be withdrawing everywhere. On the 20th Charles Drury and his brigade division staff joined the battery. Drury, his staff and C Battery were destined to spend the remainder of their tour in the western Transvaal between Pretoria and Mafeking. This area was never really secure and there were constant alarms and several actions. Despite the drudgery and boredom, C Battery seems to have kept its edge. Much of the time the battery was based on Rustenburg. Here, one section was in the town itself, while four guns were in Fort Canada on a nearby kopje. (The four gun bastions were named Kingston, Toronto, Hamilton and Winnipeg.)

On 19 August Lord Roberts inspected the battery. He made a particular point of congratulating Hudon on his battery's part in the relief of Mafeking. Drury reported Hudon was thrilled. Hudon got a thrill of a different sort the next day. The battery had marched with a column a few miles north of Pretoria. The right section galloped forward and came into action under rifle fire to cover the withdrawal of two squadrons of the Rhodesia Regiment. The two guns fired 29 rounds at ranges varying from 800 to 1300 yards, well within effective rifle range of the Boers. It was a tight corner, but the men escaped unhurt.

The column was in more or less constant contact over the next few days. It was a successful action that headed off De Wet and resulted in the capture of several prisoners. In guerilla war, such are the measures of success. At this stage of the war the Boers had not yet abandoned their guns and transport. As a result British mounted columns, even when encumbered with their own transport and guns, could often make and keep contact.

The artillery was out of the spotlight for much of its tour. Even the relief of Mafeking was a well-publicized sideshow. However both C and D Battery saw considerable action, and E Battery does not suffer badly in comparison. The 12-pounder was inferior to the Boer guns in both range and rate of fire. That the batteries did as well as they did is a tribute to the high standards demanded in training, not to their equipment. It also does not hurt to be lucky. Hudon's battery was the only Canadian unit that did not lose a man to bullet or disease. The last word may be left to Major General Baden-Powell. He was fond of telling the tale of a British battery attempting to measure the range to some Boers on a ridge. He mimicked the cries of "On, on" from the rangefinders. Suddenly there was the bang of a Canadian 12-pounder. C Battery had galloped forward, come into action, "eye-balled" the range, and landed its first round squarely on the Boer position.[6]

Chapter

10 We're Marching to Pretoria

too many names to keep track of

THE BOERS COULD field no more than about 30 000 men, although their deployment allowed them to concentrate forces on interior lines. It was a masterful example of the military science of making the best of a bad situation. Working west to east, there were 2000 Boers in the area of Fourteen Springs guarding Methuen's approach from Boshof and White's advance up the western line from Kimberley; perhaps 5000 in a line from Brandfort north of Karee Siding and to the southeast, together with another 1500 in reserve; 6000 in the hill country east of Thabanchu and Hout Nek, with a further 8000 in the Biggarsberg north of Ladybrand. A further 3000 were en route from Natal while Prinsloo retained 1500 to hold Van Reenan's Pass against the desultory advance of Sir Redvers Buller's Natal Field Force. The Boers, therefore, could concentrate three-quarters of their forces against Roberts.[1]

On paper Roberts had overwhelming strength. He planned to use more than 100 000 men for mobile operations throughout South Africa while about another 70 000 manned garrisons, guarded the lines of communications, or followed up the main advance. Perhaps a third of the army was already tied up on the lines of communications and local security duties in the two colonies and the southern OFS. Between 10 and 15 percent would be non-effective because of illness or injury at any time. As the advance progressed and more and more territory was occupied, the available fighting force would gradually be diluted.

Lord Roberts planned to strike for the gold city of Johannesburg and the Transvaal capital of Pretoria. Possession of Pretoria meant control of the rail lines that radiated out from the Transvaal capital. If the enemy attempted to prolong the war, their only supply line would be by the Delagoa Bay line from Lourenço Marques on the sea in Portuguese East Africa. The British, however, would enjoy full use of the vast railway network to supply their forces and to rush troops about the country. The advance north would be on two fronts. Lord Roberts' main column, consisting of 7th and 11th Divisions and a mounted infantry brigade, would advance via Kroonstad. Hamilton's column of two infantry brigades, a cavalry brigade, and a mounted infantry brigade would march on his right via Winburg, followed closely by the depleted 9th Division, which had detached 19th Brigade to Hamilton. As soon as he could assemble his scattered mounted units French would join Roberts to screen the main column's left flank with his cavalry division. There were subsidiary operations to tie down Boers and to cut off avenues of retreat.

names

In the far north of the Cape Colony, Colonel Bryan Mahon would lead a column detached from the main army to link up with the Rhodesian Field Force and raise the siege of Mafeking, and Sir Charles Warren was marching through Griqualand. At Kimberley Sir Archibald Hunter would strike up the western line through Fourteen Springs, while Lord Methuen would march cross country from the area of Boshof towards the Vaal and Kroonstad. In Natal Sir Redvers Buller would push through the Drakenberg and march on Pretoria from the southeast.

As Roberts moved away from the Basutoland frontier, Rundle's 8th, Brabant's Colonial and Chermside's 3rd Divisions would form successive barriers to any forays into the southeastern OFS.[2]

Before we take to the road with Roberts, we must turn back the clock a few days to follow the progress of the Canadian mounted troops. After the unscheduled delay in Canada and the sea voyage aboard the SS *Milwaukee* 1 CMR and C Battery were eager for action on their arrival at Table Bay on 22 March 1900. There were eight transports anchored in an impatient queue waiting to off-load, so it was not until 26 March that the *Milwaukee* was able to unload. She was then pre-empted to carry a different cargo and remained tied up blocking valuable dock space. Men captured at Paardeberg were waiting to be sailed into captivity abroad. The battalion escorted one group to the dock, where they were loaded on ships for the voyage to the remote South Atlantic island of St Helena. Ironically, for some of the Boers, their surrender had been forced by Canadians, their escort to the dock was Canadian, and their transport to prison had last been used by Canadians.[3]

Lessard knew full well that there were better places than Green Point Common to prepare for battle. Supported by Major Joseph Hudon of C Battery, he was able to persuade the authorities that both units should forsake the blowing dust of the common for the more pleasant conditions at Stellenbosch to rebuild the strength of their horses, weak and tired after the long sea voyage. Accordingly, on 4 April the Canadians headed up the line and camped in more pleasant surroundings. The stay for 1 CMR was not to be long. Originally the unit was scheduled to spend a month training, but when Lessard assured the authorities that his unit had made good use of the unscheduled month in Canada, plans were changed.[4]

Whatever the state of the battalion, Lessard found one thing seriously wrong with his command, its name. Both the artillery and the infantry perpetuated the permanent force— Royal Canadian Field Artillery and Royal Canadian Regiment of Infantry—while the link between the Royal Canadian Dragoons and the First Battalion of the Canadian Mounted Rifles was more tenuous. Lessard launched appeals to Lord Roberts and the Department of Militia and Defence, and before the end of the tour the battalion would be retitled the Royal Canadian Dragoons. We will anticipate the change in title. From now on the First Battalion will be the Royal Canadian Dragoons (RCD), while the Second Battalion will be the Canadian Mounted Rifles (CMR). Whatever Lessard's feelings, the change was not received with a universal wave of enthusiasm. At least one officer in the battalion told him that the change was unnecessary, and General Hutton called Lessard a "foolish fellow" and dragoons "outmoded" in a letter to Minto. It probably made little difference to most of the rank and file, especially as the change was not made official until August, well into the tour.[5]

Roberts had formed two large mounted infantry brigades, the first commanded by none other than Major General E.T.H. Hutton, and the second commanded by Ridley. The 1st Brigade had four mounted infantry corps (at the time "corps" could signify an organization such as a regiment, as well as a branch of the service as in Army Service Corps, and a grouping of divisions), each with one British regular mounted infantry battalion and a number of colonial units. Hutton had arranged for the transfer of Lieutenant Charlie Ross from Roberts' Horse to the brigade's small troop of scouts, noting to Minto that "[Ross] has a great reputation in Indian warfare as a scout, & I believe him to be first rate." Army Order 60 of 7 April 1900 allotted the RCD, CMR and Strathcona's Horse, still on the high seas, to Brevet

Lieutenant Colonel E.A. Alderson's 1st Mounted Infantry Corps. The brigade never fought together as the Fourth and Eighth Mounted Infantry Corps were detached from his command. See Table 10.1.[6]

Table 10.1 First Mounted Infantry Brigade (as eventually fielded)
Major General E.T.H. Hutton

1st Corps M.I.	3rd Corps M.I.
Lt.-Col. E.A.H. Alderson	Lt.-Col. T.D. Pilcher
RCD	Queensland M.I.
CMR	New Zealand M.I.
1st Bn M.I.	3rd Bn M.I.
	New South Wales M.I.
"G" Battery RHA	"C" Section pom-poms

Detached under Henry's command to Roberts' Column

4th Corps M.I.	8th Corps M.I.
Col. St G.C. Henry	Lt.-Col. W.C. Ross
South Australian M.I.	Loch's Horse
Tasmanian M.I.	Lumsden's Horse
Victorian Mounted Rifles	8th Bn M.I.
4th Bn M.I.	1st W. Riding M.I. Coy
	1st Oxford L.I. M.I. Coy

While the commander-in-chief had other plans for C Battery, his staff ordered the RCD forward as soon as transport could be arranged. First to move was Major Williams's B Squadron on 8 April, followed the next day by A Squadron and the headquarters. The RCD would be followed into the OFS by the CMR squadrons when they arrived at De Aar from the trek through the Karroo. The Canadian squadrons, in turn, were detailed to march up the line through the OFS, escorting convoys of vitally needed remounts and supplies.[7]

B Squadron RCD joined Roberts' army at Bloemfontein just as the counterstroke was getting under way and was ordered to join Alderson in the area of Leeuw Kop. Arriving there on the 22nd, the same day that Smith-Dorrien's brigade was transferred to Hamilton's command, B Squadron was posted on the extreme right of the British line with Roberts' Horse and two batteries. The enemy were occupying a line of kopjes running away to their left. In mid-afternoon Williams was ordered to move around the kop, cross a stream, and move forward to contact the enemy.

Scouts found a ford, and the squadron advanced in column of troops with Lieutenant Van Straubenzie's first troop leading. Once across the river the squadron advanced towards a farmhouse that was displaying a white flag. It was common knowledge that the Boers often

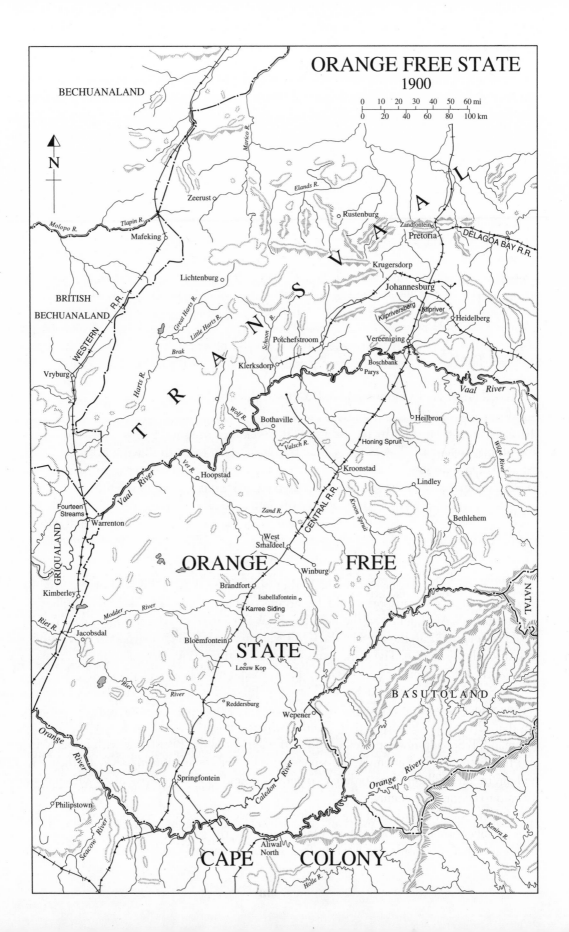

used a white flag to lure the British into an ambush. However, families would also fly a white flag on the approach of the British to signify their peaceful intent. It was a judgement call for Van Straubenzie. There were no signs of life in the area of the farmhouse and its outbuildings. Somewhat naively he decided to risk a closer look and, taking part of the troop, warily approached the farm along a track leading up from the drift. When the party reached a point about 700 yards from the farm, it came under rapid rifle fire from the buildings. Van Straubenzie ordered his men to dismount and take cover, losing his horse to a Boer bullet in the process. As horse holders led the horses into a safer position, the dismounted troopers took cover and opened fire on the farm.

Williams could see First Troop a short distance to his front exchanging rifle fire with the farm, still flying a white flag. By the volume of the fire and the size and layout of the farm he could estimate the enemy's strength. We can surmise that he appreciated that any threat to their line of retreat could encourage the Boers to withdraw. If not, at the least it would allow him to extract First Troop. Williams ordered Second Troop to engage the farm which would allow him to withdraw the forward troop. Lieutenant Young's Manitobans dismounted and advanced into a position from where they could bring the farm under accurate fire, and threaten the Boer retreat. As soon as Second Troop's fire began to take effect, First Troop was ordered to withdraw.

With the troop safe it was time for Williams to consider his next step. He concentrated B Squadron about 1000 yards from the farm while he reviewed his options. In their inexperience the Canadians formed up by troops just as they had practised in Halifax. It was too good an opportunity to let pass. The Boers opened fire again, this time with rifle fire from the farm and artillery from hills about a mile away. After frantic shouts by an officer from Roberts' Horse jolted them into action, the squadron scattered and rode handily out of the fire.

From the perspective of the Boers in the farm, the situation was beginning to go bad. B Squadron could be the advanced guard of a much larger force. The khaki-clad riders had extended their line and showed signs of enveloping the flanks. Last, it would soon be dark. There was nothing to be gained by staying in the farm when there were other places nearby to lay a trap. The Boers abandoned the farm and rode away. Williams followed up by pushing out troops, in extended order, on the far side of the farmhouse. Once this was done, Canadians moved forward to the farm and searched it for contraband, a term interpreted liberally whenever anything edible was concerned. There was only one possible response to the abuse of the white flag. The farm buildings were burned to the ground.

B Squadron, and especially First Troop, were lucky. The trap had been sprung while the Canadians were still some distance from the farm. If the troop had been allowed to approach much closer, within 200 yards or less, a number of saddles almost certainly would have been emptied. Once First Troop had been successfully withdrawn, the folly of forming ranks in close order while in contact with the enemy had been demonstrated, without cost. As for being lured into a trap by the white flag, we can smile at contemporary author T.G. Marquis's apologia, "It was hard for an Anglo-Saxon to think any man capable of such depravity." Apparently he included men named Lessard, Van Luven, and Van Straubenzie in the Anglo-Saxon category. The Canadians would be unlikely to fall for the old white-flag trick again, although there are far too many instances of even experienced troops being fooled. We should take statements such as "no mistake seems to have been committed" with a very large grain of salt. To envelop the flanks of the farm and threaten the enemy's escape route before investigating the flag would have been a wiser course. Forming up in parade formation after First Troop had been extracted was probably a legacy of a bad training habit where the squadron would form up for a debriefing after an exercise. In one afternoon the squadron learned more about war than in all the time spent training in Halifax—for the loss of three horses.[8]

For the next few days the squadron pressed the Boers, who steadily fell back. There were daily scraps with the Boers who occupied the kopjes. When threatened by troops working around behind them, the enemy withdrew to another kopje and both sides went through the whole thing again. Finally, the squadron rode back to Fischer's Farm, where the rest of the battalion had replaced the Iniskilling Dragoons.[9]

The regiment was not to spend much time together at the farm. Joined by headquarters and C Squadron of the CMR, the RCD were to lead the march north on 1 May, the same day that 19th Brigade cleared the Hout Nek position. Hutton's mounted infantry would operate to the west of the main column advancing up the railway. In the weeks to come the presence of a large body of mounted troops on their flank and the threat of being cut off would force the Boers out of defensive position after defensive position without a hard fight. At the same time the mounted troops would also provide security for the flank and lines of communication of the main army.

Before the advance Hutton felt compelled to deal with the command problems of the CMR. Hutton had expressed doubts about the training and experience of the CMR officers before the battalion had joined his command and the situation was not improved by a shortage of senior officers. Lieutenant Colonel Herchmer, the CO, had been sent back from Carnarvon to Cape Town for medical reasons on 20 March and Major Gilbert Sanders had yet to join the battalion after his bout with pneumonia. It was by no means certain that Herchmer would resume his command. Hutton had appointed Evans, the second in command of the RCD, to temporary command of the CMR from 1 May and recommended this move be made permanent.[10]

The concentration of the Winburg column was one of the last of the preliminaries to the advance to Pretoria. It totaled 7500 infantry, 4000 mounted troops, and 32 guns. General Hamilton would command something larger than a division, and not quite a corps. It is indicative of the confidence Roberts had in Hamilton, who was a relatively junior officer, that he was trusted with a large independent command, while Colvile, with only the Highland Brigade and two Cow guns (heavy guns drawn by oxen) under his command, was to follow ten miles to the rear. Hamilton grouped 19th and 21st Brigades into an ad hoc infantry division under the command of Smith-Dorrien, who had been a battalion commander in Malta at the start of the war. Lieutenant Colonel James Spens of the KSLI succeeded to temporary command of 19th Brigade.

On 4 May Roberts was ready to march through Brandfort and on towards Smaldeel, while Hamilton would drive towards Winburg. The Boers contested passage of the column, but 19th Brigade were spectators to most of the day's events as the Boer defences were forced. Next stop: Winburg! For the Canadians, by now reduced to less than half strength, there soon would be some relief. The reinforcement draft had reached Bloemfontein and was marching hard to join the battalion. Despite its reduced numbers the battalion was in good shape, and morale was high.

As the column moved north it left the hilly eastern OFS and entered well-watered grazing land. On the 5th, as the column neared the town for which it was named, large bodies of men and wagons could be seen trekking north and east. Hamilton halted his forces before Winburg and convinced the burghers to surrender the town, despite a forceful intervention from Philip Botha, a hard-nosed Boer commander.

The column did not make its usual early start on the next day. Instead, Hamilton collected three days' supplies before pushing on for the Zand River, 20 miles to the north. From intelligence reports and dust clouds it was apparent that Boer columns were heading north on both sides of, and even behind, the British. The slight delay allowed the reinforcements to catch up to the battalion. The draft had spent a month at sea and then undergone a long train journey to Bloemfontein. Unfit after the physical inactivity and forced to make a series of hard marches, the reinforcements were pretty well done in when they wheeled into the RCR lines. Even so, they were welcome—even if they did little more than make up for a fraction of the losses of the past few weeks. A number were unable to continue the march. The correspondent of the Montreal *Herald* was kind enough to point out through the medium of his paper that it was unfortunate that better care had not been used in the selection of reinforcements.[11]

No sooner had the draft arrived than the column set out on a short moonlight march to Dankboarsfontein. Here Roberts rested the column for two days to allow the left column to come up. On 9 May Hamilton's column marched on to Bloemsplaats, a splendid estate belonging to de la Plaats. The general rode across to confer with Roberts, leaving Smith-Dorrien in command. The farm was close to the Zand River, and Boers could be seen on the far side preparing defences on the kopjes overlooking the drifts. Passage of the Zand would be contested.

Hamilton returned that evening with dramatic news. A major battle would be fought at the Zand River on 10 May. The infantry would force a crossing to allow Broadwood's and Ridley's brigades to hook towards Venetersburg Siding on the railroad. Tucker's 7th Division would attack next to Hamilton, while the remainder of Roberts' column would drive straight up the railway. On the left, French's cavalry and Hutton's mounted infantry would swing towards Venetersburg Siding, to link up with Broadwood and envelop the enemy.

French, Tucker, and Smith-Dorrien wisely secured crossings over the river the night before the attack. Smith-Dorrien's action probably forestalled an attempt by 800 Boers to contest the passage. Instead, the enemy moved upstream to a position where they hoped to enfilade the column as it approached the drift.

The RCR had a busy, if varied, day. A and H Companies were detailed as escorts for the 5-inch guns, while C and G Companies had the same duty with the field guns. The remainder of the battalion, four companies of about 50 or 60 men each, formed the advanced guard of 19th Brigade. The battalion marched at 5:45 a.m. with orders to secure the right flank of the army's crossing of the Zand River. Captain Burstall with two sections of B Company advanced to within 250 yards of the river before being halted by extremely heavy rifle fire from the Boers in the river bed. Major Buchan reinforced him with the rest of his company as well as D Company, while E and F Companies remained in reserve. The enemy outnumbered the

Canadians, and the rest of 19th Brigade was in action a mile and a half away on the left. In a heavy fire fight lasting several hours, the western Ontario boys gave as good as they received.

Preoccupied with clearing a way for the horsemen, Smith-Dorrien, as he later admitted, believed that The RCR were faced with "a few snipers." The Canadians were on their own. The Boers did not necessarily see it that way. The progress made by the British in crossing the river and advancing to their right rear unnerved them. The process was completed by the arrival of C and G Companies at noon followed by two field guns by 2:00 p.m. Boers began to creep away and soon the fight for the river bed was over. The RCR, despite being outnumbered by better than ten to one at some stages, had more than held their own against an enemy fighting from behind cover. For the third time in as many battles B Company had played a key role. The choice of Burstall to command the company had been one of Otter's wiser moves.

Despite the intensity of the day's action, the division's casualties amounted to 7 killed, 11 wounded and 1 missing: total, 19. The Canadians' share was Privates F.G.W. Floyd and G.W. Leonard killed and Privates A. McLean and E. Armstrong wounded. In addition, Stanley McKeown Brown, the correspondent of the Toronto *Mail and Empire*, had been wounded and evacuated.[12]

Roberts now sent Hamilton marching first to Lindley and then on to Heilbron in search of the government and temporary capital of the OFS, while the main force moved on to occupy Kroonstad. The next two weeks brought a series of marches for the infantry, although the cavalry and mounted infantry had some contact with the enemy, and at least one stiff engagement. At Heilbron, on the 24th, the cavalry bumped the enemy and, after a running fight, eventually captured some prisoners and transport from a commando caught napping by the British. By the time word had filtered through the ranks rumour inflated the few wagons to "over 200."[13]

From Heilbron Hamilton's column marched back to the main railway line to become the left column of the army, halting at Kromelboog Spruit on the Queen's birthday to wait for supplies. The supplies did not arrive, and the column pushed on. Meanwhile, the Boers swooped down upon Heilbron after the British had marched on, temporarily capturing a number of prisoners, including Surgeon-Captain Fiset, left behind sick, and his batman. Fiset later reported that De Wet had questioned him on the place of French Canadians in Canada. At about this time the Boers decided to leave the OFS commandos in their own territory to operate behind the British lines, while the Transvaal forces opposed the enemy from the front. It was an ominous portent of things to come and the best possible use of the limited forces available, even if a tacit admission of the Boers' inability to meet the army head on.[14]

On 26 May the Canadians waded the 75-yard-wide Vaal River and entered the Transvaal, the first infantry battalion in the army to do so. The Vaal was a major river by South African standards, although one Canadian described it as the biggest stream he had seen in South Africa. Earlier in the day Otter had rejoined the battalion, bringing with him winter uniforms, fresh underwear, and boots.[15]

Alderson's corps was detailed to lead the advance past Karee Siding, the scene of an inconclusive engagement on 29 March. On 3 May the main army advanced north following the line of the railway. The enemy were unable to more than delay by engaging the advanced guard and forcing the British to prepare for an attack on a kopje or ridge that would be abandoned at the last minute.

The first engagement came shortly past Karee Siding, when Hutton's brigade was ordered to sweep around Brandfort to cut the railway and envelop any Boers still in the town. Hutton felt at the time that his brigade was not strong enough for the task and that the advance should have been delayed until French's cavalry joined the main army. Events support his assessment. By the time he completed the sweep much of his brigade, including both the RCD and CMR, were engaged with Boers retreating northwards, and he had only an RHA Battery and one company not yet committed. As night fell on 3 May a frustrated Hutton could only watch from a distance as a convoy of transport wagons and a strong rearguard passed out of sight.

Earlier in the day Alderson's Corps had come up against the Heidelberg commando and an Irish-American brigade holding two groups of kopjes three miles west of the railway. At noon First and Second Troops of B Squadron led the advance on the positions until they came under heavy, if inaccurate, small arms fire and hurriedly galloped out of range with one man slightly wounded. The RCD and the First Mounted Infantry Battalion, supported by artillery, pom-poms and machine-gun fire, soon were engaged in a fire fight with the enemy. For the first time the Canadians experienced heavy shell fire and the unpleasant sound of rounds passing through the air. The British, perhaps because they instinctively huddled together suffered some 20 casualties, while the Canadians escaped with the loss of four horses. The enemy held the kopjes until their transport had escaped and then abandoned the position and galloped away as dusk fell. Alderson reported to Hutton that both battalions had made a good start. The brigade commander noted that the men were full of zeal and eager to match the fine reputation earned by The RCR.[16]

From Brandfort the brigade forced the drifts over the Vet River on 5 May, then hooked towards the railroad and telegraph. The Canadians had their first real fight as mounted infantry. In the first phase the RCD were ordered to seize a crossing at Coetzee's Drift. B Squadron dismounted and advanced 2000 yards in open order towards the river, halting 500 yards from the banks while scouts moved forward cautiously. A burst of rifle fire and scouts returning much more quickly than they had advanced confirmed that the river was held by the enemy. Later in the afternoon, finding that the river was deep and unfordable and consequently not held in strength, small parties of dragoons led by Lieutenants Richard Turner and Harold Borden swam the river and pushed forward on foot until they encountered a party of the enemy estimated to be some 50 strong. While the Canadians were eventually forced to withdraw, the foray distracted the Boers while a proper crossing was seized in a mounted rush by the remainder of B Squadron, who followed up the advantage by pushing on to capture a gun whose crew had been killed by shell fire. The day earned Turner the RCD's first gallantry decoration, a well-deserved DSO. A Squadron, detailed as gun escort that day, was not so fortunate. The guns and the dragoons came under heavy shell fire and Captain C.St.A. Pearse and Lieutenant R.M. Van Luven were wounded.[17]

Hutton pushed a strong force across and drove the enemy off the river and two successive positions on ridges to the north. This in turn levered a large force commanded by De Wet and de la Rey out of a strong position astride the railway. The comparatively light casualties suffered by the mounted infantry prevented a potentially serious battle and consequently heavy casualties. To seize the crossing and push the enemy back from the river took much of the day, but Hutton had not played all his cards. Immediately after sundown Captain Macdonnell led two CMR troops augmented by some pioneers and native guides on a long hook through the enemy lines and across their line of retreat to cut the railway and telegraph line. By 1:30 a.m. on 6 May the westerners had reached their objective. Daylight would put the squadron in an unenviable position, deep in country swarming with angry Boers and with no immediate hope of relief. Before dawn Macdonnell took his men into hiding among some kopjes.[18]

Early the next morning the main body advanced and relieved Macdonnell's force, and then pushed to reach Smaldeel Station by early afternoon. Hutton was electrified to learn that the Boer rearguard was only 15 miles away and retreating slowly northwards. He resolved to overtake them, but first it would be necessary to rest and water the horses for a few hours. In the meantime, Roberts visited Hutton at 3:30 p.m. and ordered him to rest his horses overnight. Throughout the campaign Roberts would allow the enemy to escape on a number of occasions, usually in order to avoid British casualties. His objective was always the capture of Pretoria, not the destruction of the enemy army. Whatever the reason, Hutton was thoroughly disgusted.[19]

What were the chances of success if Hutton had pushed on? Could he have caught the Boers before they crossed the river? The Boers could move no faster than their slowest element, their wagons, which probably moved at 2 miles per hour, while Hutton's men could ride at a combination of a walk and a trot at eight miles per hour, so that he gained six miles each hour. If he had ridden at 3:30 he could not have caught the rear guard before darkness, but he would have been near enough to almost certainly guarantee a fight the next day. The next river, with the drifts that channeled and slowed movement, was less than a day's ride north. If the brigade had pushed on for a few hours and then rested while the scouts made for the drifts, Hutton might have been able to catch at least part of the enemy on the wrong side of the river. It would not have been another Paardeberg, but it could have been a major coup.

The next morning (7 May) the brigade marched to Wilgelagen Station 15 miles away, reaching it about 2:00 p.m. A rest was ordered, horses unsaddled, and men collapsed to sleep the sleep of the truly tired. Suddenly scouts reported that Boer transport was still south of the Zand River. The brigade was hastily roused and in 15 minutes was riding towards the river. Even with the quick start, by the time the men had ridden the six miles to the river the enemy had been able to complete the crossing.

Hutton shoved the New South Wales Mounted Rifles and both Canadian battalions down to the river. What Hutton called a "merry musketry fight" ensued between Boers on the north bank and colonials on the south. The fight became a little less merry when two Boer heavy guns joined in from positions 8000 yards away, well out of range of the British 12-pounders. Their fire was accurate and rounds burst all among the Canadians, fortunately with little material effect. The shelling was loud, but two guns firing on men and horses well spread out and making use of cover can achieve little. The fire appears to have been designed to cover the withdrawal of the Boers from a delaying position on the Vet to a better defensive position on the Riet, where they planned to make a stand. Hutton's comment, that he had made "the whole Boer force about 6000, show themselves—open fire with their guns—& withdraw" puts the operations in a more favourable light than was warranted. He had managed to catch the rearguard but the combination of river and Boer artillery allowed the enemy to make a clean break again.[20]

French's cavalry, less Broadwood's brigade with Ian Hamilton's Winburg Column, in the meantime, hurried north from Bloemfontein to join the main army. The march of 60 miles was completed in two days, a creditable achievement, but one that immobilized a high proportion of the horses. Like the Duke of Wellington nearly a century earlier, Roberts distrusted his cavalry. For war on the veldt he preferred mounted infantry. This was heresy to the cavalry, who in turn blamed the commander-in-chief for all their troubles.[21]

The Boers had resolved to make a fight on the main line of the Zand all along the front. On the right, as we have seen, The RCR had had a fierce little fight with a superior enemy force covering the approach to the crossing site. On the left of the British line both French and Hutton led their men in a hook around the Boer right. French's leading brigade seems to have ridden straight into an ambush, and Hutton ordered Alderson forward to the rescue. The Canadian and British mounted riflemen dismounted behind a ridge and advanced in skirmish order to drive the Boers back. It was a classic example of what mounted men equipped with rifles and trained to fight on foot could accomplish.

While the cavalry had launched their advance to the north, leaving the trapped brigade to be rescued by Hutton, the mounted infantry attacked the Boer flank and rear five miles north of Venetersburg Road Station. The presence of mounted troops, in unknown but obviously substantial numbers, on their right had the desired effect. Rumour and imagination did what numbers could not. Hutton's 2500 and French's 2000 became 20 000 riders working around the Boer flank to cut their escape. The Boers fled, despite the exhortations of their commanders, from "the vision of their imagination," not from any real threat from the British. By 4:00 p.m. Hutton found himself with the Boer army retiring to the east on his right flank, but he was unable to do more than snap at the heels of the rear guard.

By the 12th the turning movement on the west and the advance along the front had levered the Boers out of Kroonstad. The main army closed up and occupied the city, a major station on the line to Pretoria. It was a classic bit of mounted infantry work, described by Hutton as an operation that "worked out absolutely like clock work," except that once again the Boers had been able to escape.[22]

A rumour soon spread that a number of Boer leaders were hiding out on their farms in the area. At last light on 16 May Alderson led a sweep of 50 RCD, 50 CMR, and 150 British mounted infantry on a ride through the night and most of the next day. Late on the 17th the force began to raid farmhouses. As each farm was reached the column would surround the buildings and a small party would rush in. By the time the little force returned to base on the 19th they had collected 24 prisoners including a commandant, several field cornets, and four ZARPs.[23]

Herchmer arrived at Kroonstad and asserted his right to resume command of the CMR on the 18th. He was 60 years old, and his health had broken down in March after less than a week in the field. Hutton was appalled to see that "he [Herchmer] looked pale and haggard & spoke excitedly & as a man under suppressed mental worry—He walked like an old & infirm man" and sought the advice of the battalion medical officer, who advised that Herchmer was physically and mentally unequal to the strain of active service, let alone the responsibility of command in action. This opinion was confirmed by the Primary Medical Officer of Hutton's

Brigade, but the decision was Hutton's alone. Herchmer was not that much older than Otter, who was in his fifty-seventh year, or "Gat" Howard, who was 54, so age was not necessarily a factor. Hutton had already concluded that too many of the CMR officers were weak and having difficulty finding their way. From his point of view, to reinstate Herchmer would not improve the situation. On the other hand, he knew that Herchmer was disliked by Laurier and his government, who would welcome the opportunity to retire him.

Both Hutton and Herchmer were brusque and tactless to a fault, and their meeting could not have been a pleasant one. According to Hutton's version of the events, he offered Herchmer an opportunity to remain in command of the brigade depot at Kroonstad with the possibility of resuming his command after the fall of Pretoria. The alternative was a medical board that would almost certainly declare him unfit for service. Herchmer, understandably devastated and under a great deal of strain, demanded a medical board. The result was a foregone conclusion. When the advance resumed both Herchmer and Major Howe, who had requested to be relieved, were left behind at Kroonstad. Herchmer returned to Cape Town and left South Africa on 31 May.[24]

Smarting under the decision of the board and perhaps not fully recovered from his ordeal, Herchmer believed that his removal had been arranged by Hutton for malicious reasons and demanded redress from the Canadian government. Herchmer, like the other members of the NWMP seconded to the militia, should have resumed his duties in the force once his secondment ceased. The Liberals, glad of the opportunity to be rid of Herchmer and coincidentally to drag his and Hutton's names through the mud, released Herchmer's letter to the press and summarily retired him on 1 August. It was a shabby bit of work.

On the morning of 20 May the brigade massed for a mounted church parade, a cape wagon doubling for an altar. With matters spiritual attended to, the march to Johannesburg resumed. It was late autumn and the weather was chilly on the high veldt, especially at night. For the first few days the march was more of an endurance contest than an advance. The Boers had made a clean break, and the British were striving mightily to catch up. There was a certain rivalry to be the first to enter the Transvaal, a race ultimately won by the cavalry. Even so, the mounted infantry came very close, bivouacking on the night of the Queen's birthday within sight of the republic and outstripping their transport wagons in the process.[25]

On the 25th Hutton's men crossed the Vaal at Lindeque Drift without encountering a solitary Boer. Three days' advance without opposition brought the brigade to the ridges south of the Klip River. On the 28th wary scouts peered over the ridge and across the valley of the Klip at the long line of the Klipriversberg Range. The range was held in strength, although this was not apparent at the time. Even so, it was appreciated that the range, as the last obstacle before Johannesberg, would undoubtedly be defended.

The British guns came into action on the ridge and opened fire. The ridge on the far side of the valley was out of range, so the first troops into the valley would be on their own until the advance had progressed far enough to allow the guns to move forward.

The first step would be to seize the bridge at Olifants Vlei and to expand the bridgehead line onto some intermediate kopjes. Australian mounted riflemen moved forward across the bridge and swung left towards a low ridge. The enemy opened fire with artillery, pom-poms, and small arms, and the men galloped into cover, dismounted, and took up a hasty position along the crest.

Next over were the RCD, who, under heavy fire, swarmed up onto a low ridge covering the bridge. The CMR, some New Zealanders, and an RHA battery followed them across the bridge and seized two kopjes connected by a low ridge that dominated the crossing. The troops put in a long, unpleasant day and night as the focus of attention of the Boer gunners. In the meantime the rest of Hutton's force had crossed, but Lord Roberts appreciated that there was an alternative to the frontal attack that the Boers so obviously expected. To mount an attack on the flank of the Boers he had to march Hamilton's column across the front of the Boers. Hutton would cover the manoeuvre by keeping the enemy off the low ridge immediately north of the river.

It was vital that the kopjes and ridge continue to be held until the flank march was completed. Reinforced by the RCD in the morning, the CMR held on under heavy fire for three hours until the remainder of the force had crossed back to the south bank and ridden away to join the start of another left hook around the enemy's flank. The CMR then withdrew, leaving the RCD on the ridge. Finally, it was the turn of Lessard's men to creep off the rocky, shell-swept hill and ride away at the gallop. The Canadians had been entrusted with a key part in the battle and had succeeded, fortunately with only light casualties.[26]

The flank march took French and Hamilton's men towards the right of the Boers dug-in on the Doornkop Feature south of Johannesburg at the Klip River. As Hamilton's column approached the river the cavalry forced their way across the Klip and seized three kopjes to cover the crossing site. It would be up to 19th and 21st Brigades to pass through the cavalry and seize the formidable line of ridges lying 3000 to 4000 yards to the north. The enemy were in strength, supported by artillery, including heavy guns that outranged the British artillery. To assault the position the troops had to advance across coverless, long, smooth slopes and then climb the heights. The enemy had fired the grass for 1000 to 1500 yards in front of their positions, which would make khaki uniforms stand out against the blackened turf. It was one of those situations, wrote Hart-McHarg, "when no words are necessary to inform the infantryman that it is 'up to him' to do some fighting."[27]

The plan was Crimean with little subtlety or depth and no attempt to outflank the position. Hamilton's two infantry brigades would attack in line with 19th Brigade on the right. Spens decided to attack with three battalions in line: the DCLI left, the Gordons centre, and the Canadians right, while the KSLI remained as baggage guard. Each battalion would advance on a two-company frontage in four lines 150 yards apart with up to 30 paces between men. The Canadians deployed with F and G companies leading, followed by H and A, B and C, and last, D and E. As the companies crested the low ridge behind which they had sheltered, they were faced with the prospect of a long advance under fire. The situation was not improved by the smoke from the grass fires, which obscured friendly artillery fire, and, as Smith-Dorrien noted, slowness in deploying on the part of the gunners this day. Part of the way across the plain the advance met the burning grass, and the troops had to run through the flames, suffering burns and singed hair and beards in the process. The battalion came under 5-inch and small-arms fire and soon was threatened by some Boers in positions near a kraal on the right flank. Well-directed fire from Lieutenant Hodgins' Maxim section soon drove the enemy back, and the Canadians advanced to the foot of the ridge where they rushed a native hut surrounded by a stone wall, suffering three casualties in the process. Meanwhile both the City Imperial Volunteers (CIV) in 21st Brigade and the Gordons assaulted the main positions to their front. While the CIV were fortunate and suffered few casualties, the Gordons had a very tough fight, losing nearly 100 men, including 18 killed. While inflexible tactics played a part, the battalion faced a position held in depth that required three successive assaults. Whatever the reason, their advance relieved the pressure on The RCR, who successfully stormed their part of the objective at a cost of eight wounded for the day, only to see the enemy "scampering away on their horses." The ridge had been held in such strength that, when Smith-Dorrien saw the enemy withdrawing, he first thought it was French's cavalry division. A gap four and one half miles wide had been punched through the last defences south of Johannesburg for a loss of 26 killed and 115 wounded.[28]

The Canadians linked up with the Gordons and prepared to spend a cold, rationless night. In the morning the hungry battalion paraded at 4:30. The brigade, less the Gordons who stayed to bury their dead, moved off in mid-morning for Florida, a suburb of Johannesburg. By now the troops were pretty well played out. Florida itself was a small mining suburb of a small hotel, a few houses, and a store, set among mine buildings that stretched away to the east as far as the eye could see. Incongruously, there was even a small artificial lake and some large groves of planted trees.

The Canadians moved off the road to the right, leaving room for the Gordons, who were still on the road. After about an hour the Gordons appeared, headed by their pipe band. What happened next would moisten the eyes of a tax auditor. As the Gordons neared camp, the pipes began to play, and the Scots began the Highland swagger that stirs hearts and weakens maidens' resolve. Relations with the Gordons had always been good, and the Canadians had witnessed their bloody assault on the ridge. Spontaneously, the Royal Canadians jumped to their feet and cheered themselves hoarse to let the Gordons know just what they thought of them.[29]

By now the turning movement was beginning to have the desired effect, and the Boers, ever fearful of encirclement, fell back towards Johannesburg. The advance continued for another ten miles to the northwest. That night the march crossed the rough and difficult region of the Doornkop where the ill-fated Jameson Raid had come to grief.

When morning broke, the mines and mills of Johannesburg lay before them. In the distance a Boer wagon convoy could be seen making its best speed in an effort to escape. Lieutenant Borden with 12 men galloped in pursuit and managed to cut off and capture three wagons. Counterattacked by a party of Boers that outnumbered them two to one, Borden and his Maritimers had a sharp little fight, but were able to return with their prize. Hutton sent for Borden and congratulated the son of one of his least favourite people in front of Alderson and Lessard.[30]

The brigade advanced past the gold city on towards Pretoria. It was fully understood that the long march was near an end, and both the commander-in-chief and the editorial board of the Toronto *Globe*, were sure the end of the war was near. In the meantime it was expected that the army must fight for the Transvaal capital.

On 3 June the cavalry bumped the Boers, once more in strength on a ridge line, and a general engagement seemed certain. The CMR were hurried forward to help clear the way into Pretoria. Evans and his men galloped forward under fire towards a line of enemy-held kopjes, dismounted and, dodging from cover to cover, advanced to the foot of the kopjes. The battalion paused while the British artillery pounded the crests. At 4:00 p.m., as the Canadians scrambled up the hill, the Boers abandoned the position and escaped to join the last line of defence around Pretoria.[31]

The infantry columns paused for two days about Johannesburg. The city was a typical mining boom town putting on airs: untidy and pretentious, rowdy and tawdry, and plentifully stocked with bars and brothels. It had always been somewhat embarrassing to the Boers, but the revenue from the mines made Sodom on the veldt somewhat more acceptable. Access to the city was tightly controlled, although a few Canadians were granted passes to enter the town to purchase supplies. Fortunately the stay was not longer and 19th Brigade marched on the 3rd.

To the collective relief of the army the Boers chose not to defend Pretoria, and withdrew to collect themselves and prepare for the next phase of the war. The mounted troops screened the city over the next two days, while Roberts and his infantry prepared for a triumphal entry and occupation of the Transvaal capital, a city that had taken on an almost mystical value in the eyes of the army and the public. While Private George Bellamy of the RCD had made his way into the city several days earlier after having been separated from his comrades, his comrades did not enter Pretoria until the 6th when they rode through the city, collected Bellamy, and then rode on to Silverton to rest themselves and their horses, 40 percent of which were temporarily unfit for further service.[32]

On 4 June the army had pushed back the Boers past Pretoria; evidently the Boers had decided not to make a fight for it. The RCR paused for the night at Six Mile Spruit south of the city. At sunrise on 5 June The RCR moved off leading the column. The route led through the hills, and then, finally, the battalion emerged from a pass, and Pretoria lay across the plain three miles off. The division halted to await the formal surrender of the city to Roberts, whose column was a short distance to the east.

By noon the column had moved into a position just outside the city. Pretoria would be occupied by the infantry that had marched the long, hard miles from Bloemfontein. Meanwhile, the cavalry and mounted infantry were put to work clearing the surrounding countryside. At 2:00 p.m. the order came to move. The long line of infantry—Guards, Warwicks, Yorks, Essex, Welsh and all the rest—marched into the city. Then, it was the turn of 19th Brigade, followed by 21st Brigade, to trudge along the western road into Pretoria, past Paul Kruger's house and around a corner to where Roberts and his staff waited. A deeply moved Corporal Hart-McHarg wrote that the greatest occasion of his life was "when I marched past Lord Roberts in Pretoria, June 5th, 1900 with the Royal Canadian Regiment."[33]

Hart-McHarg spoke for many in the battalion, and for many more absent comrades scattered in lonely graves or crowded hospitals and rest camps along the way. Others had been invalided out of the ranks and sent to the United Kingdom to recover and a few had even returned to Canada. The numbers say more of the inefficiency of the army's administration than the ferocity of the Boer defence. Smith-Dorrien's 19th Brigade was widely believed to be the best infantry brigade in the army, and the battalion had earned a reputation as second to none in the brigade. As the Canadians marched through Pretoria, tattered, dirty men in the ranks heard a British voice say "There goes the finest battalion in South Africa."[34]

Smith-Dorrien summed up the campaign succinctly in the following message on the same day, no doubt aware of the effect the capture of Pretoria would have on the future of 19th Brigade:

The 19th Brigade has achieved a record of which any infantry might be proud. Since it was formed, [12 February 1900] it has marched 620 miles, often on short rations, and seldom on full. It has taken part in the capture of ten towns. Fought in ten general engagements, and on 27 other days. In one period of 30 days, it fought on 21 of them, and marched 327 miles.[35]

Chapter

11   After Pretoria

AFTER THE CAPTURE of Pretoria the end of war seemed near. However, Roberts' army controlled little more than its garrisons, and the advance had temporarily emptied Roberts' supply wagons and dismounted his cavalry. Until Roberts could refill his stores and remount his army, he had to pause at the Transvaal capital. Botha and 6000 Transvaalers lurked scant miles north and east of Pretoria, while 8000 energetic Free Staters in the eastern and northeastern OFS were a constant threat under the able leadership of De Wet, Prinsloo, and Olivier.

The fall of Pretoria provided a welcome pause for the Canadians. All three units were filthy, tired, and sadly depleted in numbers. Furthermore, many of the RCD and CMR were temporarily dismounted. Men had not bathed in three months and were covered in lice. Many had not had a haircut since they arrived in South Africa. The brigade sported a variety of facial hair ranging from Old Testament-prophet beards to riverboat-gambler goatees and moustaches. The short halt near Pretoria let the men boil their clothes, clean up, and be blessedly louse free for a few days.[1]

The army wasted no time resting on its laurels in Pretoria. On 6 June 1900 Lord Kitchener visited Smith-Dorrien to give him his orders for the next phase of the war. Nineteenth Brigade would be disbanded. Smith-Dorrien would command the Johannesburg garrison with 15th Brigade, two batteries, and a mounted infantry corps. The RCR and the Gordons would garrison Pretoria. The Shropshires were ordered to Vereeniging south of Johannesburg on the railway, and the Cornwalls would move west of Pretoria to guard the Delagoa Bay line as the British pushed along it.[2]

The next day brought a return to peacetime routine, what regulars call "real soldiering." The day started with reveille at 6:00, followed by breakfast at 7:00, muster parade at 9:00, and so on. Before 10:00 orders came to reconstitute 19th Brigade at Irene Station on the southern outskirts of Pretoria. Within 12 hours Smith-Dorrien mustered his troops—the hastily reformed 19th Brigade (with the Suffolks replacing the Shropshires), two batteries, and some mounted infantry. He was to join Roberts' forces for the attack on Botha at Diamond Hill. The third set of orders in as many days came on 8 June. On the 7th De Wet had struck the railway at Rhenoster Crossing, Vredefort Road Station, and Roodewal and badly shaken the confidence of the high command. The reconstituted 19th Brigade and Ross's mounted infantry would now guard 70 miles of railway from Pretoria south to Vereeniging. This was soon extended south to Kroonstad.[3]

Smith-Dorrien established posts of 200 infantry, two guns, and 50 mounted infantry about every eight miles. The mounted troops were to scout wide of the line and piquet commanding heights by day. Each night the infantry would send small patrols of six to eight men south to the next station at irregular hours throughout the night, returning by train the next day. His arrangements were later adopted by the army as a whole.[4]

On 11 June the Cavalry Division and the 1st Mounted Infantry Brigade advanced towards Kameelfontein to turn the enemy's right as part of the Battle of Diamond Hill. The mounted troops failed, in part because of a shortage of horses that had dismounted much of their strength. Both battalions seized and held kopjes within easy rifle range of the enemy, but could do no more. The battle saw the death of Private W. Frost and the wounding of Captain A.C. Macdonnell, Corporal H.H. Baines, and Private F. Greenall, all of the CMR. Frost's was the first death in battle for Hutton's Canadians. Macdonnell survived a bullet through his liver and one lung, in part because of his physical condition and physique, but he was evacuated to the United Kingdom. It was a serious blow to a unit plagued by some weak officers.[5]

The CMR returned from Kameelfontein on 14 June and entrained for duty on the lines of communication between Kroonstad and Vereeniging. This was in direct response to the threat of De Wet. In accordance with Smith-Dorrien's policy, the unit operated as four half squadrons, each of three officers and about 50 men, at Wolvehoek, Vredefort, Roodewal, and Honing (Honey) Spruit for nearly a month. There were a number of minor clashes, certainly too many to recount, and Lieutenant Thomas Chalmers and Corporal "Casey" Callaghan were singled out by Smith-Dorrien for "smart and aggressive scouting."[6]

One of the actions, however, merits special mention. De Wet was active in the area during this period. He directed Commandant Froneman to wreck the railway line at America Siding, while he would do the same at Serfontein Siding. Commandant Olivier would attack the station at Honing Spruit, which lay between the other two objectives. All three parties would attack at daybreak on 22 June. While the first two attacks were successful, the third failed. De Wet, never one to waste a kind word on the British, felt Olivier's inability to attack at daybreak caused the failure.

The defenders of Honing Spruit included two KSLI companies and two CMR troops. The fighting, or at least the casualties, fell to the CMR. The (fairly reliable) South African Field Force (SAFF) Casualty List includes 11 Canadian casualties but none from the Shropshires. Evans's report does not include the five men taken prisoner, who were soon released. De Wet reinforced Olivier during the day, which may account for Evans's report that the enemy numbered "1,000 men and several guns." Conan Doyle put the Boer strength at 700 with three guns. De Wet had 700 men and five guns during the attack on Roodewal on 6 June. His memoirs, which are precise, make no mention of reinforcement. Boer strength could vary from day to day, but Conan Doyle seems closer than Evans. Both estimates were probably high.[7]

The country was gently rolling prairie with a prominent, horse-shaped wooded kopje about four miles from camp. In other words, the Boers could approach the camp and railway under cover, were it not for patrols and posts. In accordance with Smith-Dorrien's orders, mounted troops were to patrol the railway and piquet the commanding heights by day. These piquets, called "cossack posts," were usually manned by a section of four men, the smallest organization that could provide continuous early warning and security. Each morning the CMR set up a cossack post at each end of the kopje, as well as posts two miles north and south of the camp along the railway track. After stand-to on 22 June Lieutenant W.M. Inglis led a party of eight men out of camp to set up the two posts on the kopje, while Lieutenant H.J.A. Davidson first placed four men two miles north of the camp, and then dropped off another party of four commanded by Corporal James Morden at the southern post. Morden and his section were all from Pincher Creek in the foothills of the Rockies.

As Inglis and his party approached the kopje they were surprised by several hundred Boers. As the kopje was four miles from camp and Inglis had left at 6:30, this must have been after 7:00 a.m. Olivier and his commando had probably taken cover here to consider their next move when they realized they would not be able to attack at dawn. From cover they would have seen Inglis approaching from the railway. The Boers may have attempted to surround and capture the Canadians without firing a shot. If so, their plan failed. A running fight ensued as the Canadians rode for their lives. Inglis and two men were wounded and five men were run down and captured, as a result of the poor condition of their horses. The Boers had wiped out the party in a few minutes fighting. The mounted rifles, however, had done their job—the Boers now attacked an alerted camp.

While the main attack was mounted from the east, 50 or 60 Boers began to circle around to the south to take the camp under fire from the flank. As the Boers approached, Morden and his men opened fire from the scanty protection of the two-foot-high railway bed. Private Henry Miles was wounded in the hand almost immediately. Morden sent him back with the horses and a message that the post would hold out. By the time help arrived eight hours later, the fight was over. Morden and Private Robert Kerr were dead and Acting Corporal Thomas Miles, Henry Miles's brother, lay wounded with a shattered shoulder. Two Boer bodies and patches of blood on the veldt showed the fight had not been one sided. Even after the post had been reduced to one man, the Boers had been reluctant to approach it, although they had more to worry about than a small post that did not pose a threat to them. That is not meant to disparage the fight put up by the cossack post. Morden and his men could have escaped, or they could have laid low. They also had the option of surrender. Far too many troops would have surrendered in similar circumstances. The Boers would collect their weapons, horses and equipment and release them after a few days. The high command believed the incident was noteworthy because Morden and his men did not surrender.[8]

The RCR occupied Springs, on a branch line 18 miles east of Johannesburg. Besides the village, Otter was responsible for the line from Springs to Elandsfontein. Within a few days the five coalmines in the village were supplying Johannesburg, Pretoria, and the Imperial Military Railway, and the Army Service Corps soon established a supply depot to support columns chasing Boers on the veldt to the north. Later, a "sick horse" depot also graced Springs.[9]

Observation posts were sited on the coal dumps, the highest points in the area. Companies dug trenches at key points; as time passed the trench system was improved. Otter had taken over buildings as sleeping accommodation. Given the size of the area to defend, at any time as many as half the troops were on duty as guards and outposts. All ranks stood to under arms before daybreak to guard against a surprise attack. Patrols pumped handcars along the line to Boksburg and Elandsfontein each night. Mounted patrols visited the local settlers to confiscate arms and administer a neutrality oath. If a farm was uninhabited, the mounted infantry (MI) confiscated the livestock and drove the animals into camp. Otter despatched Captain Stairs and H Company to augment the garrison of Boksburg. G Company under Lieutenant Jones followed H down the line to man an armoured train.[10]

Boers were in the area, and they often exchanged shots with outposts. As they came and went on forays, or just confused the Intelligence Department, estimates of their strength ranged from 150 to 800. It is tempting to think that the Boers were not strong enough to seize Springs. Nothing could be farther from the truth. If vigilance lagged, a surprise attack could overrun the station. There were a number of false alarms and about 600 Boers tested the defences on 28 June, but rode off after experiencing RCR volleys and some well-aimed shells from the resident section of field guns.[11]

Meanwhile Smith-Dorrien, with the Shropshires and the Gordons, had marched off to chase Boers west of Pretoria. The men of The RCR concluded that they stayed behind because the battalion was too small to take to the field. In fact, they were left behind because there were no troops available to replace them, and they were out at the end of the line. Numbers had slowly risen as men recovered from wounds and disease returned to the battalion. By the time the battalion left Springs, it numbered 548, an increase of 25 percent in two months.[12]

On 12 July the CMR returned to Irene Station near Pretoria to draw remounts and replace badly worn clothing. On the 15th Evans led his tanned, hardy riders to Rietvlei to rejoin Hutton's command. In the meantime the RCD had spent a month in camp at Derdepoort, about seven miles east of Pretoria. Victims of boredom and ennui, 70 men succumbed to the lure of safer and more lucrative employment on the railways and other lines of communications duties. The army is not an organization that encourages freedom of movement. However, the authorities, believing that the war was over except for mopping up, actively sought men with any sort of useful civilian experience. It could not have been a pleasant time for Lessard as his regiment dwindled away, without hope of rebuilding its ranks.[13]

Baden-Powell had advanced from Mafeking through Zeerust and threatened Rustenburg. The latter town controlled a pass through the formidable obstacle of the Magaliesberg Range which stretched like a giant python west, then north of Pretoria. If the British controlled the passes, the range would become a formidable barrier on which to trap and batter Boers. On 16 June Hutton led a column of mounted infantry, artillery, and infantry from Derdepoort to Rustenburg through "a thickly populated district" which lay in very difficult, bush-covered country quite different from the open veldt. The regiment could muster enough fit horses for Major Victor Williams to lead 150 men, a strong squadron for the time. On the 18th Hutton learned that a party of Boers with two guns was laagered at Klip Kop about six miles away. It was late in the day and the horses were in no condition to attempt a further march. Instead he sent out three scouts followed by a RCD patrol led by Lieutenant F.V. Young.

Young decided to lead his men on a wide loop around the defences to take the enemy from the rear and exploit the combination of rumour, confusion, and panic caused by the presence of even a small party in the rear areas. This had the added advantage of delaying his arrival until the Boers, who did not like night fighting, relaxed their vigilance. Young's 12 men followed a small river for two or three miles, then crossed a small drift. As they progressed, the patrol came across a number of farms. Each was searched in turn and prisoners and weapons were collected. The scouts located the two guns sited to counter any thrust from the front. Young organized a cutting-out party, collecting some oxen to draw the guns in the process. Audacity reaps its own rewards. The guns were sent on their way back to the British lines despite a last-ditch effort from some outraged Boers and the patrol returned without casualties by 3:00 a.m. Besides the two guns, enough prisoners and weapons were captured to ensure, in Hutton's ambiguous words, that "between 40 and 50 men were thus rendered powerless to make further resistance." Hutton was delighted and waxed eloquent in his official despatch as well as in a letter to Minto. He made particular mention of Young and Sergeants Purdon and Ryan and two South African scouts. Hutton went so far as to suggest to Roberts that he might wish to present one of the captured guns to the Canadian government.[14]

The interlude at Derdepoort was marked by an incident that dirtied the regiment's reputation and deeply hurt Lessard. During the march from Johannesburg to Pretoria, in an incredibly stupid stunt, two dragoons, both regular soldiers, turned some captured burghers free, with their horses and rifles returned, in return for their available cash. The plan went awry when the Boers were soon recaptured and demanded a refund. On 20 June the two Canadians were sentenced to ten years penal servitude. The men were later returned to Canada and dismissed from the service. The consensus in the ranks was that a firing squad would have been in order.[15]

To block any attack on Pretoria from the northwest, Lessard commanded a force of 100 regular mounted infantry, 50 Kiwis and 50 RCD near the kopjes known as "the Pyramids" about seven miles west of Waterval on 30 June. On 3 July Lessard withdrew his force back to Derdepoort. The next day the British went back on the offensive. Alderson's 1st Mounted Infantry Corps rode southeast onto the high veldt as part of an effort to crush Botha's forces lurking near Pretoria. Joining up with Mahon's column at Rietvleifontein, Lessard's men advanced along the Standerton Road, joining Hutton at Rietfontein on 6 July. Hutton commanded 7000 men, "2/3 mounted Troops [sic] & 1/3 infantry with a powerful artillery." Boers were active in the area and sometimes could be seen watching the column from nearby kopjes. A section of field guns, escorted by A Squadron, sortied out to shell some Boers who had fired on the flank guard from a nearby ridge. The next day Alderson took to the Standerton Road towards Oliphantsfontein. Once again it was the turn of the RCD to escort the guns, and this was not a sinecure. In their worst day of the war to date the dragoons suffered eight, or nine, casualties.[16]

The Boers took the British advance seriously and reinforced their forces. Hutton's force fought several general engagements in the next week. At Leewberg on the 7th the RCD machine-gun section ably led by Gat Howard and Sergeant Eddy Holland reinforced the 1st MI Battalion. When the battalion retired, Howard, because his own horse, Holland's horse, and the gun horse had all been hit, carried the Colt away under his arm. The Maxim team were able to withdraw the gun without incident even though "the bullets were coming as thick as black flies when we go up the brook fishing." Howard and his men later collected the carriage and brought in two wounded men all within 100 yards of the Boers. In the process Gat potted a burgher who was drawing a bead on him.[17]

On the same day Otter had led an unsuccessful sortie to assist Hutton against these same Boers. He contacted Hutton's right flank guard and heard firing about five miles ahead, no more than two hours' march. However, the firing soon ceased and there was no contact with the enemy. Otter, never one to trust his own or anyone else's initiative, turned his column about and marched back to Springs. The sound of battle could be plainly heard by The RCR for the next two days, as Otter sat tight. One can only wonder what effect 650 fresh troops appearing in their rear would have had on the mercurial Boers if Otter had persevered.[18]

Part of French's cavalry division reinforced Hutton on 12 July. With the additional strength, the British turned the Boers out of their position in a range of hills called Wittpoort, Koffyspruit, and Oliphantsfontein. French, taking Mahon's force with him, returned to Pretoria, while Hutton held the erstwhile Boer position. The RCD, soon joined by the CMR, took their share of outpost duty. Hutton's force was none too large, "as I had been weakened on account of the threatened attacks upon Pretoria from the North [sic] & the organized rising in Johannesburg & the Capital [sic], my position was a very critical one." He was left with 700 MI, 1000 cavalry, 600 infantry, and 18 field and two 5-inch guns to hold a wide front. The weakness of the position begged for a Boer attack.[19]

The Boers concentrated what Hutton estimated as 2500 men and at least eight guns on the night of 15 July without his knowledge. The enemy commander, Ben Viljoen, in his first fight as a general disposed the Germiston and Johannesburg commandos with a Krupp and some pom-poms on his right, the Krugersdorp commando and the Johannesburg ZARPs with a captured 15-pounder in the centre, and the Boksburg and Middleburg commandos with a Krupp and a Creusot on the left. At daylight they mounted an attack that lasted all day.

Initially Viljoen feinted upon Hutton's centre and then followed with attacks on his left and right while still applying pressure to the centre. On the British right about 900 Boers "with three [sic] guns" attacked the 1st Cavalry Brigade, reinforced with an infantry company and one 5-inch and six RHA guns. The situation was confused for much of the day and it was not until about 2:00 p.m. that the brigade commander reported he could hold the position. On the left the attack fell upon three companies of the 2nd Battalion, Royal Irish Fusiliers, B Squadron RCD, and the NZMI at Witpoort. The defenders were heavily outnumbered and the situation begged for reinforcement. However, Hutton dared not commit his reserve until he was sure that the right was secure. Once he received this assurance, he wasted no time in sending "all my available Mounted Troops & Artillery to the relief of Witpoort." By 2:45 the reserve had got well into the enemy on the left flank.

While B Squadron RCD had fought a delaying action A Squadron and the CMR had formed part of Hutton's reserve. By early afternoon the situation at Witpoort was still in doubt. The Boers had overrun a NZMI post and then launched an assault on the Irish that had resulted in hand-to-hand fighting in the trenches before it was repulsed. This position was still threatened by a large body of enemy in the dead ground immediately under the ridge. The arrival of the reserve began to decide the issue. Lessard, who commanded the reserve, sent the CMR to secure the left flank before dealing with the enemy lurking beneath the ridge. A Squadron and two guns were pushed up onto the ridge itself to the chagrin of the Boers. Viljoen wrote, "We made a few prisoners and took a pom-pom, which, to my deep regret, on reinforcements with guns coming up to the enemy, we had to abandon, with a loss of five men." Major Munn, the Irish commander, asked Lessard to attack the enemy from the flank.

Lessard sent three dismounted troops of B Squadron "clambering over the rocks round the shoulders of the ridge." The Canadians suddenly came upon a large party of Boers at short range. RCD officers led from the front and Lieutenants Borden and Burch were shot and killed. Their men were not to be denied and charged through the Boer position, routing the defenders with the further loss of two Canadians, Privates Brown and Mulloy, wounded. The latter was blinded by a Boer who was in turn killed by another Canadian just after he had shot Mulloy. Mulloy was awarded the Distinguished Conduct Medal and later completed university and became a prominent lawyer in Eastern Ontario.[20]

This ended Hutton's operations southeast of Pretoria. Roberts was ready to clear the Boers from the Delagoa Bay railway. The first objective was Middleburg, 50 miles northeast of the camp at Rietvlei. At 6:00 a.m. on 23 July, the 1st Mounted Infantry Brigade began its advance. The advance took five days against very light resistance. As the army advanced the Canadians moved from post to post along the railway. In late August the two regiments moved into the Belfast region where they would see out their service.

In late July the British had cornered several thousand Boers in the Wittenbergen region of the northeastern OFS. Several columns penned them in and captured all but a couple of thousand. However, it was less of a success than it seemed. De Wet, Olivier, and OFS President Steyn escaped to fight on, unleashing what came to be known as the first De Wet hunt. Otter was ordered to pack up his battalion, the field guns, the mounted infantry, the supply depot, and the sick horses and abandon Springs. At 9:00 a.m. on 3 August the Canadians detrained at Wolvehoek in the northern OFS.[21]

De Wet lurked with his back to the Vaal at Vredefort 30 miles to the west across the veldt. The RCR, less G Company with the armoured train, would join Ridley's MI column and attack De Wet. The next morning the Canadians and Ross's 8th MI Battalion marched southwest away from the railway. On the afternoon of 5 August, after two 12-mile marches, the small column opened heliograph communications with Ridley. Evening saw De Lisle and Legge join with their MI, and Ridley linked up on the 6th. Ridley's column included P Battery RHA, several pom-poms, five MI battalions and The RCR. On the morning of 7 August the column could hear firing from the west, apparently where Lord Methuen's column was attacking De Wet. During the day large parties of Boers were seen in the distance moving rapidly to the north, still south of Vaal. De Wet was in a trap. His only escape lay a day's march to the northeast. The unanswered question is why Ridley did not either immediately pursue De Wet or try to cut a corner by driving an MI battalion and a section of guns towards both Old Viljoen's Drift and Lindeque Drift, the only two possible crossings.[22]

Ridley resumed the chase on the morning of 8 August and his advance guard briefly caught De Wet's rearguard at Lindeque Drift the next afternoon. Ridley seemed to have maintained a pace worthy of the leisurely Buller, as The RCR, escorting the large and cumbersome baggage train, had no problem matching the pace of the mounted infantry.

The column halted for the night at Lindeque Drift. During the night General Hart's column, largely marching infantry, closed up to the drift. The RCR joined this column, which included Marshall's Horse, a field battery, 2 Naval 4.7-inch guns, and four regular infantry battalions. At 7:30 a.m. Hart crossed the Vaal and continued the pursuit, making 11 miles that day under very trying conditions.[23]

For the next few days the column forced march northwards, trailed by small parties of Boers. Several columns were converging on De Wet who was being forced up against the Magaliesberg Range. By one of those errors that plague war, the force guarding the pass at Olifant's Nek withdrew just in time to allow De Wet unopposed passage. Hart's frustrated column halted, was ordered in several directions more or less at the same time, and then returned to Pretoria. It is unlikely that the Canadians had very much good to say about this period. There is nothing like hardship and adversity to pull a unit together, though. Otter had allowed the men to sing on the march and this had done much for morale. The battalion performed well during marches which averaged 17 miles a day and the men seemed satisfied with their lot.[24]

On 25 August the battalion moved to Eerste Fabriken and Silverton on the Delagoa Bay line east of Pretoria. Major Pelletier with E, F, and H Companies replaced three companies of the Cornwalls at Silverton while Otter and A, B, C, and D Companies did the same at Eerste Fabriken. On 2 September the battalion took over responsibility for Olifants River. Otter sent Pelletier there with C, E, and F Companies and reinforced Silverton with D Company. He gave command of the latter place to Captain Stairs. The disposition of the battalion was: A and B Companies at Eerste Fabriken; C, E, and F Companies at Olifants River; D and H Companies at Silverton; and G Company manning the armoured train.[25]

Inactivity breeds boredom and rumours swirled as the volunteers counted the days to their return home. The men had enlisted for six months' service, or, if required, for one year. This meant that their terms of service would end between 13 and 30 October. On 13 July Otter had written Ottawa for instructions regarding the possibility of enlistment for further service, if the men agreed, and the British required their service. His letter arrived in Ottawa on 20 August and was referred to the Department of Justice on the 24th. On 13 August Otter had brought the matter to the attention of General Hart and asked him to forward a letter explaining the situation to headquarters. In the letter Otter had made the point that the majority of the battalion had temporarily left their civilian careers and requested that the battalion be returned to Canada by 15 October. Otter relaxed his reserve enough to tell his men on the 14th that he had reminded the authorities that the Canadians' period of service ended on 15 October. He added, "I have no doubt the Chief of Staff will take the necessary steps to have the matter attended to when we get back to the railway." He failed to mention that he had raised the possibility of extensions of service with Ottawa. On 22 August, when The RCR were returning to the railroad, Otter learned that Hart had not yet forwarded the letter. He retrieved the letter and sent it to the military secretary, at the same time telegraphing a précis of it to him. On 29 August the British government wired the governor general for a recommendation. Minto replied, without consulting the Militia Department, that the "men may claim discharges after the expiration of their period of service, unless they voluntarily agreed to an extension." The Canadian government had failed to inform Otter of its position. The War Office, however, wired Roberts in early September, supporting Minto's position.[26]

Roberts still believed that the war must end soon and had expressed a desire to see the Canadians, and the other colonials, share in the triumph. He was a regular soldier and could not fathom the attitudes and aspirations of civilian soldiers. However, he had had no trouble agreeing to return the Victorian yuppies in the City Imperial Volunteers to England, while dragging his heels over honouring the terms of enlistment of the overseas colonials. The Canadians and Australians were resentful and made no efforts to hide their feelings. On 8 September Roberts wired Otter requesting the Canadians to extend their service to the end of the war, which he considered imminent. The obvious thing for Otter to have done was to canvas the men and pass on their wishes to the commander-in-chief. Instead Otter discussed

Roberts' proposal with the officers at Eerste Fabriken. No effort was made to consult the six companies not at Eerste Fabriken. The next day he replied that the commander-in-chief's "wishes will gladly be complied with—would ask your permission for one or two officers and a few men whose cases are urgent to be given leave to return at once." Otter then published a regimental order repeating both telegrams and informing the men that their service was being extended for the duration of the war. Roberts was delighted by the reply and magnanimously gave permission for "one or two officers and a few men whose cases are urgent to return at once." In his zeal to do the right thing, Otter had completely ignored the practical and legal realities of the situation.[27]

The same day, Colonel Barker, the officer commanding Line of Communication Pretoria-Middleburg, telegraphed directly to all the stations where The RCR were stationed that "all men of Canadian regiment engaged to serve one year whose services expire in October, and who do not voluntarily extend their services, are to be sent to Canada as soon as possible." The wire also requested the numbers of officers and men at each location who wished to return home as well as the number of those who would volunteer to extend their tour. This telegram arrived at about the same time as Otter's order announcing the extension of service. To Otter the telegram could only confuse the situation, and he probably would have replied that the battalion would extend its service, if the query had not gone directly to the various stations.[28]

On 10 September Roberts arrived on his way back to Pretoria from Belfast and personally thanked Otter, adding that, had the regiment not agreed to extend its service, this would likely have caused the other colonial corps to withdraw. Otter then showed Roberts Barker's telegram, which he warned "was likely to confuse and might upset his wishes." Roberts immediately took action to quash the telegram. Otter also wired Ottawa to inform the minister and GOC of Roberts' request and his response, and requested, after the event, direction. Ottawa agreed with his actions, based on his description of the events. The damage, however, had been done. The men at the other stations had seen Barker's message concerning their return to Canada, as well as Otter's order extending their service. It did not take giant leaps in logic to realize the colonel had extended their services without their consent and contrary to direction from the War Office. Messages soon arrived from the outlying companies informing Otter that the men were opposed to any extension and were determined to return to civilian life in Canada. Otter had no recourse to do anything but send a carefully worded message informing the commander-in-chief that "the large majority of officers and men of Royal Canadian Regiment feel they cannot, with justice to themselves or families, re-engage for further service in this country, and desire their discharge in Canada on Oct. 15 next, in accordance with terms of engagement." He also apologized for misleading Roberts but shifted some of the blame to his officers and men who, he inferred, did not share his zeal for soldiering.[29]

Roberts was furious, but managed to conceal his anger when he replied, "I much regret the decision which the officers and men of the R.C. Regt. have come to. It is unlikely that their services would be required much longer, and their going away now will prevent them taking part in the annexation ceremony I hope to hold at Pretoria, and being present at the parade I understand Her Majesty contemplates honouring by her presence on the return of the troops that have taken part in this war. If, on receipt of this you inform me that officers and men still wish to return to Canada, the necessary transport arrangements will be made."

Otter canvassed the stations and found that, except for A and B Companies at Eerste Fabriken, who may not have been aware of the Barker message, the other officers and men were almost unanimously opposed to any extension in their service. He gerrymandered the total willing to stay in South Africa up to about 300 by decreeing that the permanent force members as well as the reinforcement draft were liable to serve beyond October.[30]

On 1 October Major Pelletier with 16 other officers and 385 men embarked on the S.S. *Idaho* and sailed directly to Canada. The severely reduced remainder, A, B, and I Companies (the last was made up of permanent force members and reinforcements as well as the few others who had extended) served in South Africa for a few more weeks. On 7 November the battalion sailed on the *Hawarden Castle* along with the Composite Regiment Household Cavalry and A Battery, Royal Horse Artillery. On arrival in Portsmouth on 29 November the Canadians were immediately transported to London. The British wasted no effort in fêting the colonials. Queen Victoria, in one of her last public appearances, reviewed the battalion and there were a number of official and private events for the officers and men. It was a pretty well done-in lot that sailed for Canada on 12 December. After a difficult passage the battalion arrived at Halifax on the 23rd. On Christmas Day, 1900 the 2nd (Special Service) Battalion, The Royal Canadian Regiment of Infantry passed into history.[31]

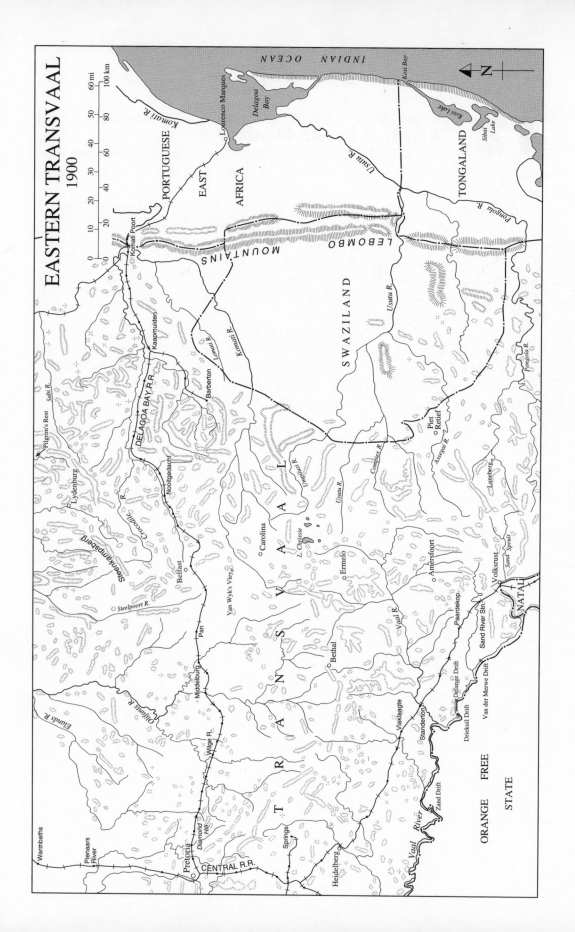

Chapter

12 Their Finest Hours

WITH THE OCCUPATION of Middleburg the RCD and CMR turned to defending the railway against an active and determined foe. They were soon joined by D Battery, who had chased De Wet and then marched with Ian Hamilton's column on the left of the British advance east along the railway. By mid-August the advance was nearing Belfast, 40 miles east of Middleburg. While Strathcona's Horse fought in the prolonged action south and east of Belfast, the RCD and D Battery arrived too late to see any action. After the battle of Belfast, D Battery was deployed with Van Tuyl's centre section at the unhealthy Crocodile Poort, McCrae's right section at Machadodorp, and Morrison's left section at Belfast.[1]

The two mounted regiments had frequent contacts, usually involving a four-man cossack post trading a few shots with the enemy. On 19 August Corporal Taylor was killed and Private Flynn was wounded in separate clashes three to three-and-a-half miles north and northeast of C Squadron's camp at Doornkop. Flynn's wound was treated by the dapper little Boer who had shot him. The Canadians later captured his assailant, a doctor from Middleburg, who had joined his friends for a few days' shooting in the country.

As well, disease continued to take its deadly toll, including Private Smith from the CMR under the most unusual circumstances. He had fallen ill on the march and reported to the ambulance, only to find that the doctor was absent. The medical supplies were carried in a large wicker chest. On the inside of the lid was a printed sheet with a list of diseases, followed by a diagnosis for each as well as a remedy which had a number. Thus, if a soldier was constipated, he should take a number nine pill. Smith read the sheet carefully and decided he needed a number seven pill. Alas, the number seven bottle was empty. Instead, he decided to take a number two and a number five. In the words of Private Griesbach, "Mathematically he seemed to be deadright, but ... we buried him that night.[2]

For the remainder of its tour the CMR operated in detachments. A typical day, 25 September, saw Evans with his headquarters and two troops of D Squadron at Middleburg, another D Squadron troop at Aasvogel Krantz five miles to the north, and C Squadron at Oliphant's Nek 10 miles west of Middleburg. In contrast, the RCD would soon concentrate at Belfast with two troops detached at Wonderfontein, the next station west along the railway.[3]

The RCD Colt was sent with a composite force of mounted infantry under Hutton's command east of Belfast. The dragoons had a trying and exciting time ranging the ridges and valleys where the high veldt began its irregular drop to the coast. By mid-September the section was reunited with Lessard at Belfast. It would be difficult to find machine-gunners in South Africa to match the RCD section, with Gat Howard and Sergeant Eddie Holland in command.[4]

The Nooitegedacht (pronounced, according to Private Anderson, "night attack") garrison, including four officers and 100 men from the CMR and the RCD Maxim, narrowly averted a humiliating defeat on 5 September when 250 Boers led by Commandant Dirksen crept past the outposts and seized a post from the rear, capturing six men. After a few hours' fighting, some at close range, the enemy was beaten off, earning kudos for the garrison commanded by Major Gilbert Sanders of the CMR. Dirksen later volunteered the information that his men had approached the post from the rear. This still did not explain how the enemy had entered the Canadian lines. Further investigation revealed that a sentry had been sleeping. The culprit was court-martialed and spent eight weeks at hard labour.[5]

The westerners of the CMR operated in patrols of one or two sections, sweeping the country, ambushing and being ambushed. Particularly active were the battalion scouts under Corporal "Casey" Callaghan. It was a case of fighting to control what the next generation would term "no man's land." The only casualty was one of the scouts, Private Weaver, missing and presumed dead after a surprise contact on 22 October near Wonderfontein. Evans was ever ready to send his scouts out by day or night to locate laagers, provide early warning, or to ambush unwary Boers. When the occasion demanded, the CMR would take the battle to the enemy. In response to intelligence, Evans and a troop of CMR rode from Pan Station at 5:30 a.m. on 11 October. At 8:00 a.m. he rendezvoused at Sharkstrom with 175 men, including 40 from C Squadron from Middleburg. The combined force, 200 men and four guns, advanced with Callaghan and his scouts riding a mile ahead of the advance guard. The scouts came in contact with 100 enemy who made for some abandoned trenches at Bankfontein. The scouts beat them there and, dismounting, opened fire from the trenches. First Troop of C Squadron soon joined the scouts, and together they drove the Boers back over the next ridge line. Evans forced the enemy, who were steadily reinforced by small parties riding in from the northeast and northwest, back over three successive ridges. Finally, Evans neared a large laager located on the north side of a large kopje near Wouverkraal on the edge of the bush veldt. He was outnumbered, but his four guns made the difference. Shelling forced the Boers to break laager and retreat into the bush veldt. With the enemy driven away, at least for a few days, the column returned to camp.[6]

On 24 September khaki-clad Boers lured four dragoons into a trap and shot three of them down when they tried to fight their way out. Privates Spence and Radcliffe died because of what their comrades considered treachery. By a neat twist of fate, Villamon, the Boer who had led the ambush, later lost a shootout with "Casey" Callaghan and Jefferson Davis, the Métis scout. Villamon, who was alone, had tried to ambush the Canadians, but failed. The two CMR scouts chased him until he bogged his horse in some low ground and fled on foot through a marsh. They hit him with three shots out of five at 500 yards, the last, in the back of his head, "scattering his thoughts upon the grass."[7]

At Belfast, Lessard chaffed under the restraint exercised by the garrison commander, Lieutenant Colonel J.W. Godfray of the King's Own Scottish Borderers, who believed in "defence, not defiance." This strategy allowed Boers to range freely in the rolling country about Belfast and to snipe at the cossack posts. On 1 October Lessard with a party of 65 dragoons and two machine-guns had a series of sharp scraps with several parties of five to 15 Boers a few miles from camp.[8]

Lessard got his chance on 4 October when the command of Belfast temporarily passed to him. The next day saw a Canadian sortie towards the broad, fertile Steelpoort Valley. The valley, 6 miles wide and 25 miles long, was a hotbed of resistance. It ran roughly a bit west of north from Belfast into the rolling country. A series of ridges and kopjes ran diagonally across the route from Belfast to the valley, providing a series of opportunities for the Boers to delay the advance. On the skyline the Canadians could see the prominent ridge that overlooked the valley, whose inhabitants threatened the railroad between Wonderfontein and Belfast. There was another reason to take the war to the valley - it was home base for the Boers who had killed Radcliffe and Spence.[9]

As the Canadians passed through the outpost line, Boers began to "pop up on every kopje to have a look at us." There is absolutely no reason to signal one's position and strength, but that is what the Boers did. Perhaps their carelessness says less about their use of ground than their contempt for their enemies. Lessard resolutely pushed forward against sustained resistance. As each potential enemy position was neared, a troop of dragoons would smoothly prove it free of enemy. Proving was done by one rider who cautiously approached the crest with the rest of his section 300 to 400 yards behind. The remainder of the troop remained another quarter mile to the rear. If there was no opposition, the lead dragoon would check the crest and wave his comrades forward. As Morrison observed, the procedure was preferable to marching infantry battalions in quarter column onto unscouted kopjes. Howard's machine-gun rushed from position to position covering the advance, ever ready to "dust up" any suspicious areas. When enemy were encountered, Morrison's gun would chase them out of their position with a few well-placed shrapnel rounds. It was a textbook demonstration of minor tactics and the skilful use of ground. As the day progressed, and more and more Boers appeared, it was evident there were more than small parties of the enemy in the area. Since there were no attempts to cut the line of retreat, it seems the Boers were trying to draw the Canadians into a trap.[10]

By 3:00 p.m. the column of 60 dragoons and one gun had pushed deep into the valley. (Morrison could either field one gun organized as horse artillery, where all the men were mounted, or two guns organized as field artillery, where the gunners rode on the guns. In this case, he opted for mobility over firepower.) The advance halted on a ridge overlooking a wide valley speckled with grazing cattle. As Lessard was satisfied about the strength and position of the enemy, he decided to return to Belfast. It would be dark in a few hours, and he was deep in enemy country without possibility of reinforcement. Still, all seemed in order, and he ordered Morrison to start his gun back to camp without an escort. The RCD would follow and catch up as soon as Howard's machine-gun section returned. Morrison and his men, who were unarmed except for a few pistols and two carbines, skulked their way back to camp. Meanwhile, Lessard's plans for the withdrawal had come unstuck. The machine-gun section had become heavily engaged, and Lessard had to mount an attack to enable the 54-year-old lieutenant and his men to escape. The section fought its way back, frequently halting to loose off bursts of .303 rounds whenever the enemy presented a favourable target.[11]

Lessard commanded the Belfast garrison for 14 days during, in Lessard's words, "very exciting times." Louis Botha with a 400- to 500-man commando with three guns and a pom-pom lurked north of Belfast, while Commandant Prinsloo with 1000 men, three field guns, and a pom-pom waited in the hills south of the railway. A report by an American settler resulted in a fruitless search on the 12th for 300 Boers by 30 dragoons, the machine-gun section, and one gun. Lessard credited the report of the Boer force to Yankee exaggeration, but on the next day the Boers drove a 500-man British force back from the reported location of the 300 Boers to Delamantua, east of Belfast. Just as well that Lessard had not found them.[12]

On 17 October, "The force under command of Major General E.T.H. Hutton, C.B., A.D.C., [was] broken up in consequence of the conclusion of operations in the Elands Valley, Eastern Transvaal and upon the conclusion of active hostilities in South Africa." Lessard was succeeded in command of Belfast by none other than Major General Horace Smith-Dorrien. Lord Kitchener made a point of telling him to take the offensive to the Boers, and he was glad to oblige. Smith-Dorrien brought the Shropshires (KSLI) and the Gordons as well as a CMR Squadron with him to Belfast. The increased strength of the garrison enabled him to take to the field, although his expeditions would be unable to catch the fleet commandos.

In the late afternoon of a rainy 1 November the British left Belfast for the treacherous rolling hills south of Belfast. This was not a reconnaissance—this time the objective was the laager of the Carolina commando near Witkloof, 18 to 20 miles due south of Belfast. Smith-Dorrien decided to aim for surprise by a night march. Furthermore, there would be two columns, not one. The general led the left column made up of two CMR troops under Major Sanders, D Squadron of the 5th Lancers, the Gordons, a section of 84th Battery, and a cow gun, through Bergendal and Frishgewaadgt. Lieutenant Colonel James Spens of the KSLI commanded the RCD, the left section of D Battery, his own battalion, a section of 84th Battery, two pom-poms, and a cow gun. Spens's route took his column through Leeuwbank to Van Wyks Vlei. The baggage column was to follow along and join both columns south of Van Wyks Vlei. At daybreak the columns would sweep the area north of the Komati River, burning farms, gathering prisoners, confiscating weapons and livestock, and eventually attacking the laager.[13]

Things started badly, and they rapidly got worse. Rain fell in sheets, and the temperature plummeted as a bitterly cold wind blew. Visibility was no more than 60 yards in thick mist, and there was constant thunder and lightning. The mounted troops scrunched down in their saddles as their shivering horses laboured through the black night, while the infantry in their soaked uniforms and sodden boots plodded miserably over uneven, muddy ground. To make matters worse, both columns experienced great difficulty finding their way, although the trails had been marked by the guides with small pieces of glowing phosphorus. The only solace was that the weather would keep the Boers at home. The columns halted for the night with strict orders against smoking and fires. It was, in Smith-Dorrien's words, "the most abominable twenty-four hours imaginable."[14]

Daybreak brought the prospect of action, but no break in the weather. Spens's column pushed on against light resistance. After coming under fire, Lieutenant Turner's troop skirmished forward and secured a farmhouse on the right of the line of advance. As the enemy had fired from a clump of trees rather than the farmhouse itself, Lessard decided not to destroy it. Instead, he pushed forward to the next ridge from where the Komati River and the hills beyond were visible. Lieutenant King's troop from southwestern Ontario skirmished across a long plain and towards a hill. The hill was held in strength, and the Canadians came under heavy fire. In the melee Private Angus McDonald was shot in the head, and another Canadian's horse was killed.

The RCD retired under pressure, closely followed by the Boers. Morrison prepared to gallop forward onto the plain to support the withdrawal but, as orders had been received from the general to return to Belfast, he was ordered into action on a ridge about 600 yards to the rear. Some good shooting forced the Boers to break contact. Using a long range "blue" fuse, Morrison dropped a shrapnel round into a gulch at the end of the plain. Boers burst out in twos and threes and swarmed back over the hills, pursued by two or three more rounds for good measure.[15]

Heavy firing to the left rear seemed to indicate that Smith-Dorrien had found the Boers. In fact, the firing came from beyond the main column, where the CMR were heavily engaged. During the night their guide had led the CMR astray, and the advanced guard found itself two miles away out to the left of the axis of the column. Lieutenant Chalmers's troop encountered Boers (at 4:30 which appears in Evan's report, and seems too early) on a kopje marked with trenches dug by Buller's army in August. The troop, although heavily outnumbered, held its ground for half an hour while it waited for support from the main body. However, in response to an order from Smith-Dorrien to rejoin the column, the troop withdrew to join Major Sanders and the other CMR troop a few hundred yards to the rear. As Chalmers's troop reached their comrades, Corporal Schell's ankle was injured when his horse was shot and fell on him. Major Sanders and Sergeant Tryon rode back to rescue Schell. The sergeant dismounted and aided Schell onto his own horse, sending him on his way to safety. Sanders then helped Tryon up on the withers of his horse and galloped to the rear. Before they rejoined their comrades, the saddle on Sanders's horse turned, spilling both men to the ground. Sanders, partially stunned by the fall and a wound in the side he suffered at about the same time, lay out in the open. An attempt to rescue the major was aborted because of heavy rifle fire. Chalmers began to organize a further rescue attempt, this time, dismounted. Before the attempt could be mounted, Corporal Herchmer appeared with a message from Smith-Dorrien. In the open and unaware of the situation, Herchmer was a sitting duck. Chalmers ran out, shouting at the corporal to take cover, and was almost immediately shot through the body and died a few minutes later. Meanwhile, the guns of 84th Battery with the main column had come into action 3000 yards away, perhaps to cover the withdrawal of Spens's advanced guard. Someone noticed the Boers pressing the CMR and the guns opened fire, forcing the enemy to retire. It was 7:30 by the time the Canadians, with Chalmers's body slung over a horse, rejoined the column.[16]

Smith-Dorrien had already assessed the situation. He could see Spens's column on the far side of Van Wyks Vlei. The ponderous baggage column, which had followed along the main road, was three miles to the rear. His objective, the laager at Witkloof, was still three or four miles away. If he persevered and attacked the laager, his troops would spend another night in the open. There was no sign of any break in the weather. The men were wet, cold, and tired. Three horses had died. There was nothing to be gained by prolonging the ordeal.[17]

Smith-Dorrien ordered the baggage column back to Belfast and despatched a message to Spens to follow by the main road. His own column would bring up the rear, with a rearguard made up of the 5th Lancers, two companies of the Gordons and a section of 84th Battery. At first all went well, and the combined column retired according to plan. The Boers soon concentrated against the rearguard and drove the Lancers, armed with short-range carbines, swords, and lances, back through the Gordons. As the Gordons retired under fire, they closed up to the main body, where the artillery was making a slow crossing of a spruit. The Boers, always quick to exploit an advantage, galloped forward to rake the spruit at close range.

Lessard's foresight saved the situation. He had realized that a nearby ridge controlled the crossing over the spruit and sent King's troop and the machine-gun to occupy it. The Canadians checked the rush by the Boers, the Colt being particularly effective because of its mobility and rate of fire. Smith-Dorrien's guns soon joined in and drove off the Boers.[18]

Attempts to interfere with the retreat had been halted and the column was back in Belfast by 5:00 that afternoon. The weather had been as miserable during the trip back as on the advance. Smith-Dorrien had been wise to cancel the operation when he did. Morrison noted that his section had gone 22 hours with "no sleep, one hard-tack and a piece of bully beef, had marched nearly forty miles and fought a small fight, soaked to the skin and shivering with cold all the time." He had wisely sent a rider ahead to camp, and by the time the men had cared for their horses, a hot drink was waiting for them. That, combined with a meal, a rum ration, and a good night's sleep, did the trick. Morning found his men (except for two sick and one injured) and the horses frisky.[19]

The overnight excursion into an icy hell had resulted in Lieutenant Chalmers dead and 15 wounded in the column. Most of the casualties (eight, not 13, as reported by Lessard) were suffered by the two companies of Gordons in the rearguard. The number of sick men and dead or sick horses are not available, although both must have been significant. The RCD alone reported 40 men suffering from rheumatism.

There was one bright spot on 3 November when Private McDonald staggered into camp. He had been left behind unnoticed on the morning of the 2nd when a Boer bullet struck him behind the ear. The bullet had glanced off his skull and ran around his head under the skin, coming out at the eyebrow. His eye and the side of his head were black, and he looked like he had been beaten with a club. The enemy had found him lying stunned and brought him to a farm. After questioning, they lodged him in a sheep kraal. His guard decided he was too used up to escape and went off in search of coffee. McDonald stole a horse and escaped. Aided by the weather, he cautiously felt his way across the battlefield, thick with Boers. To cap what surely was the worst day of his young life, his horse broke a leg while still some distance from Belfast and McDonald completed his trip on foot.[20]

The next few days provided a breathing space for the men and horses, but a number were still too sick to ride. Four men from Morrison's section, including two NCOs, had been sentenced to hard labour for attempted theft of supplies. The culprits were lodged in the Belfast guardroom.[21]

On 6 November, with the return of good weather, Smith-Dorrien took the battle to the Boers again. This time he organized a single column, including a baggage train six miles long that earned the comment that "some corps travel with a wagon train like a circus procession, even if they were supposed to be travelling light." On 1 November, he had opted for two columns and a separate baggage train. As a result he had been forced to provide two sets of advanced, flank and rearguards. Coordination had been difficult and the rearguard of British cavalry and infantry with his column had been unable to hold off the Boers during the withdrawal. This time he opted for a single force organized as shown in Table 12.1.[22]

Table 12.1 Organization of the Column

Royal Canadian Dragoons	Advanced	
D Squadron, 5th Lancers	troops under	Advanced Guard
2 Pom-Poms	Lt.Col	under Lt.Col
2 Guns, D Battery	Lessard	Spens
4 Companies KSLI		
Canadian Mounted Rifles		
4 Guns, 84th Battery		
2 5-inch guns		
Section, Royal Engineers	Main column	
4 Companies KSLI		
2 Companies Suffolks		
Bearer Company		
Baggage[23]		
2 Companies Suffolks	Rearguard	
20 NCOs and men, 5th Lancers		

The advanced guard moved off at 3:30 a.m., which provided about two hours of darkness. Because of heavy fog the column experienced some difficulty keeping contact between its various elements. The sun soon burned off the fog, however, and the weather was pleasant for the rest of the expedition. Boers appeared as the weather cleared at about 7:40 a.m near Eersterlingfontein, but the advanced guard steadily forced them back from successive ridges and past Van Wyks Vlei. The clear air enabled the left section of D Battery to engage Boers at three miles and more, well beyond the maximum range on the sights. All of this took time, however, which the Boers used to take up a strong position along the rocky, broken escarpment from Witkloof to Leliefontein.[24]

In the meantime, a CMR troop had been burning farms and collecting livestock. At one stage, it was noticed that one farm had missed their attention, and Lieutenant Begin's troop was sent back to complete the deed. Evans noticed Boers gathering on a ridge about two miles from the farm and sent Lieutenant Bliss to warn Begin. Bliss missed Begin's troop and arrived at the burning farm just before the Boers. He rode for his life until his horse was killed and then took off on foot. The Boers finally rode him down and captured him. As Evans later wrote, "They took his revolver, spurs and cigarettes and endeavoured to secure information from him with regard to the strength and object of our column, and the owner of the farm which was being burned appeared anxious to have him shot. The remainder of the party treated him civilly and he was allowed to go. He rejoined the battalion on foot about an hour later."[25]

The advance neared the Witkloof Feature overlooking the Komati River and paused to allow the main body to catch up. A general movement of troops towards the left front and firing by a section of 84th Battery at a grove of trees in the distance signalled that the war had resumed. The Shropshires moved forward in line towards the river with some RCD, still mounted, extending their line to their left. Morrison's section followed behind the Shropshires, 84th Battery was in action to the rear, and the baggage had gaggled onto a ridge behind the guns. Suddenly the Colt began to pepper away, and Mauser bullets began to sing through the air like a swarm of deadly bees. Lessard shouted, "Morrison—the rocks" and pointed to a low, ugly kopje about 1700 yards in front.

The guns wheeled half-left and then half-right and galloped through the gap between the Shropshires and the dragoons and forward into the open. Once clear, Morrison ordered a "crash action" and sweating, swearing gunners swung the 12-pounders about under heavy fire. The infantry lay down, and the RCD dismounted and sent their horses back. The gunners were on their own. In the excitement, Morrison badly misjudged the range, and his first rounds whistled over the kopje to burst in the Komati valley. William Hare, senior, the lead driver of Number 6 gun was hit and pitched from his horse, but his son William Hare, junior, took his place without a word. When the guns finally got on the target, timed shrapnel began to keep the enemy's heads down. The two guns and Sergeant Holland's Colt were doing all the fighting except for three volleys from the infantry.[26]

A section of 84th Battery came into action to the left rear and a 5-inch gun began to fire from the right. Under the cover of the fire, four companies of Shropshires closed to within 500 yards of the Boers and held their ground for three hours under very heavy fire.

At 2:00 p.m. Smith-Dorrien ordered Lessard to take his regiment, the left section, the pom-poms, and two companies of Suffolks on a wide turning movement to the right. The manoeuvre was not completed until 4:00 p.m., when the Suffolks outflanked the left of the Boers. With their line of retreat threatened, and their wagons safely away down the Carolina Road, the Boers scampered away to the south in small bodies.

Although personally fearless, Smith-Dorrien was neither foolhardy nor given to wishful thinking. Casualties were heavy for this stage of the war. The Shropshires companies had borne the brunt of the fighting and had lost six killed and 15 wounded; 84th Battery had three men wounded, and the Suffolks one. Driver Hare, with a bullet in the shoulder, was the lone Canadian casualty. The Boers were in a fighting mood and, by the number of signal fires that sprang up on hills around the horizon, it appeared they would be reinforced overnight. The general decided to return to Belfast rather than prolong the expedition. First, to mislead the enemy, he feinted towards the river and camped on three sites, one near the site of the commando's headquarters at Leliefontein and two on a neighbouring farm, Goedehoop.[27]

During the night the British had sent their wounded back to Belfast and organized the return march. Morrison noted, without apparent concern, that he had less than 150 rounds of 12-pounder ammunition remaining for his two guns. As this included 16 rounds of case shot (in effect a giant shot-gun shell effective out to 400 yards), he had less than 70 rounds of shrapnel per gun for the rearguard action.

Smith-Dorrien realized he would not escape without a fight. While he planned to get the jump on his foes, they had the advantage in speed and knowledge of the ground. His greatest concern was the cumbersome baggage train. It could probably make no more than three miles per hour on level ground, and less on the rolling plain between the Komati River and Belfast. He had to commit a large proportion of his infantry to guard the wagons. Smith-Dorrien detailed Spens with the 5th Lancers Squadron, a section of 84th Battery, and (probably) four companies of Shropshires for the advance guard. The remainder of the infantry, four companies each of Shropshires and Suffolks, and the cow guns would move with the main body, although the general had disposed part of the Shropshires to support the rearguard. The RCD and Morrison's guns would form the rearguard, just as they had led the way on 6 November. Smith-Dorrien retained the CMR with an 84th Battery section as a mobile reserve. While some Canadian writers have described it as a vote of confidence in his best troops, Smith-Dorrien had little choice. His only other mounted troops, the 5th Lancers Squadron, were at a disadvantage because they were armed with short range carbines.[28]

Before the Boers discovered the British intentions, the advanced guard had started back along the Belfast Road to Van Wyks Vlei. The main body trudged along behind them, with the baggage convoy last to move. Lessard had already given his orders to his officers. First, he put out a cordon of scouts. As the rearguard had a clear view across the valley and along the Carolina Road, the scouts covered approaches where the ground allowed burghers to approach undetected. There was little else he could do except deploy a screen across the rear of the convoy—and wait. He had three troops each about 30 strong, one Colt, and two 12-pounder field guns. Lessard disposed the troops in an arc one and a half miles wide across the rear of the column. The troops from east to west were commanded by Lieutenants Cockburn, Turner, and Sutton. Each troop was split into two groups, in effect small troops 12-to 15-men strong, that took up positions about 500 yards apart. The Colt commanded by Sergeant Holland and Lieutenant Morrison's section were posted in the centre with the guns moved forward of the dragoons to gain every possible bit of range.[29]

Rearguard tactics were fairly simple, on paper. As the baggage column inched towards the next ridge to the rear, the rearguard held the enemy back. When the tail of convoy had passed over the ridge, the guns dropped back in turn and then covered the dragoons as they fell back. It would be at least four hours from the time the advance guard marched (7:00 a.m.) before the tail of the baggage train was past the height of the escarpment three miles back, and another three hours until it crossed the Witkloof Spruit and reached the next ridge. The Canadians had to hold the Boers at bay for six or seven hours on an open forward slope.

During the afternoon and evening burghers had ridden into the laagers from their outlying farms in response to the signal fires. Not only was the Carolina commando reinforced, but a contingent from the Ermelo commando had also arrived. After midday on 7 November, riders from the Middleburg commando would also get a taste of battle. It is impossible to fix the strength of the Boers with any accuracy. The United States military attache with the Boer forces had reported the number of men "registered for the field" on the outbreak of war as Carolina commando 427; Ermelo commando 963; and Middleburg commando 1550. While by no means all the registered men would have reported, about two-thirds of the Carolina commando were present. Probably at least 100 from Ermelo and perhaps nearly as many from Middleburg were also present. This would have resulted in a force of about 500 mounted men, all armed with rifles. The British fielded 12 infantry companies, or nearly 1000 men, plus at most 250 mounted men, six field and two 5-inch guns, two pom-poms, and the RCD machine-gun. Despite the disparity in numbers the Boers could achieve local superiority.[30]

The leaders of the Carolina and Ermelo commandos held a council of war in the evening to consider their options for the next day. General J.C. Fourie and Commandant H.R. Prinsloo of the Carolina commando and General H. Grobler of Ermelo concluded that the British would continue their advance to Carolina in the morning. They decided to attack the British from three sides to pre-empt any attack on Carolina. The Carolina men would make a frontal attack up over the escarpment, while Grobler and his burghers hit the camp from the left or western flank. A third, smaller party would harass the right flank and menace any retreat. The attack was planned to coincide with the confusion of breaking camp, or, if that failed, when the column was stretched out crossing the Komati River and toiling up the long, open rise on the east bank.[31]

The burghers, shivering in the morning chill, were in the saddle before dawn riding north towards the camps near Leliefontein. Fourie was taken aback to find the British returning to Belfast. Smith-Dorrien's ruse had gained valuable time and forced the Boers to improvise a plan of attack. General Fourie realized that, if he could seize yesterday's defensive position, he would cut the British line of retreat and put them in a very difficult position. His 200 men were soon pounding down the hill towards the Komati River and the Witpoort Escarpment overlooking its far bank while "Boers began to crop up on the hills in a semi-circle of three miles round our position." In accordance with the plan, the right-hand force began to ride north along the river bed to cut the line of retreat.[32]

Fourie's men charged down the Carolina Road and galloped across the valley towards the low, ugly-looking kopje they had defended so ably the day before. As they crossed the plain the guns pitched a few rounds of shrapnel at them to little avail. Smith-Dorrien ordered Evans to take the kopje. The 35 Canadians (Lieutenant Begin's troop was on patrol) raced the Boers for what was the key to the position. The reserve, followed by the two guns of 84th Battery, had two miles to go. As they neared the kopje, the first Boers had already dismounted and begun to scramble up the steep, far side. Evans won the race for the top of the kopje. Smith-Dorrien sent three companies of Shropshires to support Evans, but these troops played little part in the battle. Never prone to sit still under fire, the Boers soon retired to protected positions in rocky ground on the other side of the valley, encouraged on their way by shells from the Canadian guns 5000 yards away. Smith-Dorrien had realized other Boers were working east and north down the valley and ordered Lieutenant Colonel Spens to seize the high ground at Van Wyks Vlei with the advance guard. The squadron of Lancers and the other section of 84th Battery easily won the race and secured a firm base to retire through.[33]

Parties of the Ermelo commando were steadily working their way forward, appearing and disappearing behind the kopjes as they sought to outflank the convoy to the west. The situation was deteriorating. Lessard sent word back to the general for reinforcements. Shortly after, Evans asked Lessard if he could spare some men, probably to take over the kopje as the CMR and guns moved along the flank of the convoy. The guns hammered away, but as fast as they drove the Boers off one ridge, they popped up on another. In an inspired move, Morrison transferred the remaining ammunition from his wagons to the gun limbers and sent the two empty ammunition wagons to join the column. A limber held only 44 rounds, while four rounds were carried on the gun carriage. The 12-pounders, which provided much of the rearguard's punch, were in danger of running out of ammunition.[34]

The Boers began to press the rearguard, testing the defences and occupying the dragoons' attention. After the main body passed the ridge the CMR and guns abandoned their position and hurried north to cover the right flank. It was now somewhere between 10:30 and 11:00. The rearguard had been fighting for three hours, and the baggage convoy had yet to cross the ridge. The abandonment of the kopje by Evans relieved the pressure on the Carolina commando across the valley, while Grobler's burghers continued to work towards the left rear of the dragoons.

The rearguard was isolated, except for three companies of Shropshires who were too far away to provide any meaningful support. The baggage train was approaching the ridge, but it was still vulnerable. Lessard began to withdraw the rearguard. One gun would limber up and gallop back to the next position. Once it was in action, the other gun would hurry back to join it. With both guns in action, the men would mount up and ride to the new position.

A Boer on a ridge on the right rear flashed signals across the Canadian position towards its other flank. In response, the Carolina commandos began to swarm onto the escarpment and threaten to roll up Lieutenant Cockburn's men. The lieutenant requested help from Lessard, who sent Morrison with Number 5 gun to his assistance while the other gun supported the western flank. The neat line had broken down, and the rearguard was in two groups, covering the left and right rear, with a few men in the centre.[35]

Morrison and Number 5 gun galloped across the front, a distance of about a mile and a half. By the time they arrived the gun's horses, which had been worked hard on the previous day, were tiring badly. As soon as the gun halted and began to come into action, the mounted Boers concentrated rifle fire on it. However, shell fire forced the Boers to dismount and continue their advance on foot, dodging from cover to cover. Cockburn extended some men forward to keep the Boers at bay, while Morrison "put the fear of the Lord in them" with shrapnel. If this rush could be held the baggage train could make the ridge unscathed.

The gun had only been with Cockburn long enough to fire less than a dozen rounds when Lessard galloped across from the western flank. "For God's sake, Morrison," he shouted, "Save your guns!" Gesturing to the rear, he added a more useful, "Limber up! They're coming down on our flank to cut us off!" Boers, reinforced by the Middleburg contingent, were flooding over the hills from the west, threatening the left of the rearguard commanded by Lieutenant Sutton. Cockburn dismounted his men and took cover in the grass to buy time for the guns. Lessard rode back to the west, picking up men to reinforce the left flank as he went.[36]

Number 6 gun had already begun its withdrawal to the ridge and Numbered 5 limbered up and took off at a gallop. It immediately came under heavy Mauser fire. To Morrison's practiced ear, the fire was coming from an unexpected direction. Turning in the saddle, he saw a long line of Boers 1500 yards away galloping towards him, firing from the saddle as they came. The Boers had forced Lessard to empty his centre and were now exploiting the gap. Meanwhile, the burghers on the right rushed forward to catch the gun. Cockburn's men were overrun, and the Boers accepted their surrender. However, the delay allowed the gun to make its escape. In return the RCD strength was reduced by a third, and the Boers were charging from the south, opposed only by Holland's Colt machine gun and a few men.

On the west flank dragoons desperately tried to hold off the Boers as they slowly retired under heavy fire. Excited horses broke loose and galloped in all directions, forcing Lessard to order some of his men to recover them. On the extreme flank a party of Boers had suddenly appeared on the crest of a hill a half mile from Sutton's troop. The heavy fire stampeded the led horses, including that of Corporal P.R. Price. Price, left to retire on foot, ran to the protection of an anthill. Private W.A. Knisley rode back and helped Price mount behind him, despite heavy fire from Boers estimated to be as close as 50 yards. They escaped although Knisley was severely wounded.[37]

Number 5 gun galloped across the plain towards the safety of the ridge and the three supporting infantry companies. It was too much to expect tired horses to maintain the pace drawing a gun uphill. The horses slowed to a trot and then faltered to an exhausted walk. A rifle bullet hit one of the gun horses but it managed to keep on its feet and pulling. The Boers were rapidly closing the distance, and Morrison resolved to hold them off with case shot as a last resort. The first shrapnel round, set at 1200, burst 100 yards behind the riders. The next, at 800, blew a wide gap in the line. (Despite his intention, there is no indication Morrison fired any case shot during the battle. However, Number 6 gun fired at least one round of case at a party of Boers, downing three riders.) Undeterred, the Boers on both sides of the gap came on firing wildly from the saddle.

Lieutenant Turner, who had been wounded in the arm, gamely tried to hold off the Boers with the few men remaining in the centre. When the gun halted Turner posted a scratch force from both squadrons in a shallow depression near Holland's machine-gun. He was wounded again, this time in the neck, and bleeding heavily. Realizing that his force was too small to hold the burghers off and that the infantry had abandoned the rearguard, Turner rode off to seek help from Lessard.

Earlier Lessard had requested reinforcements from Smith-Dorrien. The general, who had been watching the desperate struggle from the ridge, ordered Evans to return and cover the dragoons' withdrawal. The ridge itself was hardly a safe haven. The CMR arrived just before the Boers began their last effort to capture the guns.[38]

Meanwhile, the Middleburg and Ermelo commandos continued to force the left of the rearguard back towards the ridge while some Boers attempted to gain the ridge and attack the convoy. In the centre General Fourie decided that this was the last chance to capture the guns. It was now about 1:30 p.m., and both sides had been fighting for several hours. Fourie rallied about 100 Boers and led a charge on the guns. The Boers failed to see the dismounted dragoons until it was too late. Fourie was the first to spot the men lying in the grass and dismounted hurriedly. He had time to fire only one shot before he was hit in the mouth by a bullet and killed instantly. Meanwhile, Commandant Prinsloo was shouting to warn his comrades when he was hit in the head and dropped to the ground. The other Boers, intent on capturing the guns and the Colt, rode over and past the Canadians. On the far side, they realized what had happened and began firing on the Canadians from behind.

Sergeant Holland had been blazing away with the Colt all morning, but it suddenly jammed. The Boers would overrun the gun before he could clear it. He unfastened the little machine-gun from its two-wheeled carriage and carrying the hot gun, despite burns to his hands, ran to the nearest group of led horses. He mounted, a difficult feat when encumbered with a machine-gun and under fire, and rode off. He was able to join Number 6 gun and transfer the jammed Colt to the gun's limber. The Boers captured the carriage and attempted to turn it on the guns. If the machine-gun itself had been captured, it would have been disastrous. The other Canadians were taking casualties, and their ammunition was nearly exhausted. Reluctantly, they surrendered.[39]

Morrison saw the Colt carriage overrun and realized that he could not hold the Boers off as they would eventually envelop him from both flanks. The gun limbered up and resumed its climb up the ridge, the exhausted horses staggering at a fast walk, and the gunners dismounted and pulling on the traces. As they neared the supporting infantry, the Canadians were horrified to see them turn and start for the ridge. The Boers had closed to within 300 yards of the guns, opposed only by a few mounted dragoons fighting desperately. Morrison sent Private Maycock, who had been with Number 5 gun as an escort, to see if Lessard could spare some men from the left to help hold off the Boers. The dragoon met Turner, who again managed to find a few men to delay the Boers. This, combined with the loss of Fourie and Prinsloo and the delay caused by the prisoners, stalled the last serious attack.[40]

Morrison caught up to the infantry who were marching along like automatons. He asked their senior officer to turn and engage the Boers, but the officer refused. The three companies, more men than all the Canadians engaged that day, disappeared over the ridge without firing a shot. The CMR, however, had arrived and sailed into the Boers. The surviving dragoons, meanwhile, began to straggle to the ridge and extend the firing line. While the main body of the Carolina commando had halted near the Colt carriage, other groups worked their way onto the ridge on both sides of the Canadians.

Morrison moved over the crest and halted. Both his guns had got away, but the horses were staggering, and his men were sprawled over the gun seats, completely exhausted. The general rode up and asked him about his casualties. He replied that he had none. Smith-Dorrien then asked Morrison to move back to the next ridge and stop the enemy, who were moving along the left flank. Somehow the section managed to cross the spruit, and, when the horses could go no farther, got into action. The Canadian guns, assisted by a section of 84th Battery, forced back groups of Boers who had worked up on the ridge from the left and right and were firing at the baggage train bunched at a ford. Other Boers streamed along the left flank, crossing the spruit in an attempt to cut off the line of retreat. The guns forced them back over the ridge. The two ammunition wagons came up, and the tired gun teams were exchanged for the fresher wagon teams.[41]

That was the end of the serious fighting. The column camped near Blyvooruitsicht at 5:00 p.m. and was back in Belfast the next day. In two days the column had "burned 13 farms, captured one prisoner, 14 cattle, 350 sheep, 19 horses and killed a lot of Boers." The latter was optimistic. A young Boer told a Canadian prisoner that his brother had been killed on 6 November, but the total casualties are unknown. Two Boers, Fourie and Prinsloo, were killed on the 7th, and others were wounded. On the British side the column had lost 6 killed and 20 wounded on the 6th while the RCD losses of 3 killed, 11 wounded and 16 prisoners were the only casualties on the 7th. (The prisoners were released during the night of 8 November.) The guns had fired 563 rounds, 240 by Morrison's section. This was an astounding figure for the time and reflects the intensity of the fighting.[42]

Two attempts to take the battle down the Carolina Road had failed. Much of the failure could be laid at the immobility of the British troops. Foot infantry could not contribute to mobile operations. The Boers could concentrate and gain local superiority. As a result of the two forays, Smith-Dorrien concluded that he could not cross the Komati except with two strong columns, each having at least 500 mounted riflemen.[43]

The decorations awarded to the rearguard should not be taken purely as an attempt to disguise defeat. The conduct of the rearguard action speaks for itself. Turner, Cockburn, and Holland would all be awarded the Victoria Cross, Morrison the Distinguished Service Order and Knisley, who was recommended for the Victoria Cross, the Distinguished Conduct Medal. It was fitting that a decoration went to each element of the rearguard: the three RCD troops, the machine gun section and the guns.

What about the conduct of the battle? The commanders and troops, on both sides, fought bravely and well. The Boers treated the wounded and other prisoners admirably and were thanked for their courtesy. The Boer plan and tactics were sound, and once they gained the initiative, they did not relinquish it until they broke off the battle. Their plan, improvised or not, nearly succeeded. Both Smith-Dorrien and Lessard were surprised by the new Boer tactics and reacted as best they could. One could question whether Lessard should not have put his guns farther back up the hill. This would have sacrificed hitting Boers across the river but would have gained valuable time when the withdrawal of the rearguard began. Both options were justifiable. More seriously, Lessard, without a reserve, denuded his centre to reinforce the flanks, although he knew, or should have remembered, that a large number of Boers lurked beyond the escarpment. It is unclear if he realized the loss of Cockburn's men turned the position. His galloping about the battlefield coupled with his shouts to Morrison leave the impression, perhaps unjustified, that he did not have a grip on the battle. Evans does not escape unscathed. His decision to leave the kopje nearly doomed the dragoons. The major criticism, however, is reserved for Smith-Dorrien. His plan was too ambitious, and the baggage train was far too large and cumbersome. The Shropshires companies supporting the withdrawal, perhaps because of a lack of clear orders, achieved nothing. As a result the rearguard ended up out on a limb, and the price was paid in Canadian blood.

At Pretoria, officers were hard at work resolving the myriad of details required to return the Canadians home, while others tracked down individuals who had been sucked into the giant line-of-communications black hole. The more footloose or adventurous were accepting offers of employment or seeking transfers to units such as the corps of scouts that was to be formed by Gat Howard at the end of November.

Lieutenant Begin's troop was sent on a night march to burn a farm on 9 November and returned without incident at noon. This was a continuation of the process of denying the Boers their commissary. War is brutal, and none more so than guerilla war. All during October and early November the British had warned the Boers that if the men did not surrender, their families would be driven from the villages and farms to join their men on trek. Morrison, who disliked but accepted the policy of burning farms, rationalized that fair warning had been given, and that "if farm houses were to be used as barracks and villages as laagers, they would have to be destroyed as laagers when captured."[44]

Even with the tour nearly over, there was no difficulty with men shirking duty. When word came of the last expedition, the four imprisoned men from Morrison's section requested permission to go on it. They had also demanded to be released to join their comrades when word of the rearguard action reached Belfast on the 7th. Morrison paraded himself to Smith-Dorrien to plead their case. This provided the general with the solution to a dilemma—the four miscreants would not finish their sentences until after their comrades had sailed for home. After a suitable interval to consider the matter, he commuted the sentences "as a mark of his appreciation of the magnificent work and gallant conduct of the section under your command."

On 13 November the Canadians left Belfast on their last operation of the war. As usual the Canadians formed the advance guard with the 5th Lancers and the pom-poms. Lessard was in Pretoria, attending to details of the return, so Lieutenant Arthur King commanded the sadly depleted unit. The route led through the Steelpoort Valley, scene of the October excursions, and on to Witpoort and Dullstroom. The advance guard had no sooner entered the hills than the Boers came out as usual to oppose them. The burghers were steadily driven back by the advance guard on the right and the main body on the left. By night, despite a heavy rain, the column was in the valley and closed up in a secure camp.[45]

The expedition slowly made its brutal way, destroying farms and collecting stock. It was not a happy time, and the men did not enjoy it. About noon on the 14th the RCD with Howard's two Colts (he had received a second Colt since Leliefontein) were advancing towards a line of kopjes with the guns a short distance to the rear. Morrison stopped to water his horses at a spruit. He invariably put his guns in action at every halt and this time was no different. The horses had just been led away when rifles crashed all along the ridge line for a quarter mile. The dragoons wheeled and rode for their lives. The two guns began to reply to cover their retreat. When Morrison had time to look around, he saw a handful of dragoons galloping in, while riderless horses milled about the slope. It looked bad for the Canadians.

Two troops of mounted infantry came up, followed by the pom-poms, the Gordons' Maxim, and a section of 84th Battery. The general arrived with the cow guns. All the guns were pounding away, and Boer rifle fire was cracking back. Suddenly, during a lull came the "rat-tat-tat" of a Colt. Gat and his men were still alive and fighting. A careful search with glasses revealed khaki-clad figures within 400 yards of the enemy. The general called for the infantry who, supported by the guns, drove off the Boers. As soon as the position was secure Morrison took the ambulances forward to sort out the carnage. Miraculously only one Canadian had been wounded. When the Boers opened fire, the dragoons had rolled off their horses into cover.[46]

The rest of the expedition saw more farms and villages burned, but rather less resistance. That the operation was less brutal than seemed at first sight was proven when the column burned Dullstroom. A handsome Boer woman raised the pity of the troops moving her possessions out of her home before it was burned. The pity soon dissipated when the ammunition concealed in the walls of the burning house exploded, nearly killing some of the men.[47]

The column was back in Belfast on 17 November and the Canadians were soon on their way to Pretoria. Soon the three units had concentrated and begun to move to Cape Town to embark. All the horses and wagons were left behind, as were C Battery's six guns. Where three ships were needed for the trip out, one sufficed for the return voyage. Unlike The RCR, the second contingent returned directly to Halifax. Again unlike The RCR, the units came home united and cohesive with bonds of mutual confidence between officers and men and between the units. Morrison expressed a popular sentiment when he wrote that in the next war the Canadian troops should be formed in a division. When he arrived in snowy Ottawa a little boy asked him, "Mr Morrison, did you have a nice time at the war?" He laughed, but on reflection decided that indeed he "had a nice time at the war." He was not in the minority in the second contingent.[48]

Chapter

13   The Queen's Cowboys

THE SS *MONTEREY* carried Strathcona's Horse (SH) into Table Bay on 10 April 1900. The next day the regiment disembarked and set up camp at Green Point Camp. A staff officer met Steele when he landed to tell him the corps would be off to the front in ten days. Because the regiment had sailed with 10 percent extra horses, only about 100 remounts were required to replace shipboard losses. By the 13th the regiment was training in the country around Green Point in preparation for the move to the front. It was not to be. On the 21st the British veterinary staff diagnosed glanders, a contagious disease of the respiratory system, in the Canadian horses. The only treatment for glanders is to quarantine the suspect animals until three weeks have passed without any further cases appearing. Altogether 44 horses, or 10 percent of the animals landed, were destroyed because of the disease. Despite the handicaps, Steele maintained a rigorous training program. He also was astute enough to not restrict the men to camp. As a result, while there were incidents of men getting in trouble downtown, it also allowed an outlet for frustration. By the end of April C Squadron moved to Maitland Camp, eight miles from Green Point, where the squadron drew Argentinian ponies to remount the regiment.[1]

While Lord Roberts had originally allocated the Strathconas to Alderson's 1st Mounted Infantry Corps in Hutton's brigade, he advised Colonel Steele on 13 April that he had a "special" mission for the regiment and that Steele must not be disappointed at not being ordered to Bloemfontein. The British had decided to cut the Delagoa Bay rail line, the Boers' last link with the outside world. Steele with a reinforced B Squadron would travel by ship to Kosi Bay in Amtonga Land near the border with Portuguese East Africa. Here they would disembark and ride overland through the difficult Lebomba mountains to destroy the railway bridge at Komati Poort. The remainder of the regiment led by Major Belcher, the second in command, would ride from Eshowe in Zululand to Lebomba to reinforce Steele. The plan depended on secrecy, boldness and luck. If Steele had reservations, there is no sign of it in his correspondence. The venture was risky, but the risk and the glory appealed to a Victorian soldier. Steele must have appreciated that if the Boers were taken by surprise, he could make the dash, destroy the bridge, and get away without heavy loss.[2]

Steele and B Squadron sailed in convoy on 29 May while Belcher had led the remainder of the regiment to Eshowe on 24 May. The ships arrived at Kosi Bay on the 2nd and prepared to disembark the troops the next morning. However, during the afternoon a despatch boat arrived from Lourenço Marques with word that the Boers had learned of the venture and 1500 burghers were waiting to fall on the Strathconas. The plan was scrubbed, and the regiment received orders to join Sir Redvers Buller at Laing's Nek. Steele submitted a proposal to Roberts and the high commissioner for an overland dash to the bridge from Eshowe. This was approved and the order to join Buller countermanded on the 7th. By the 8th the regiment was reunited on the Lower Tugela and arrived at Eshowe three days later. The next morning the scheme was cancelled once and for all. Too much of the venture was based on wishful thinking, compromise, and beating long odds, like Dieppe.[3]

Once again the regiment was ordered to join General Buller's Natal Field Force probing its way carefully forward towards Standerton in the southern Transvaal. Strathcona's Horse wasted no time in marching back to Durban through the picturesque Natal countryside. From there they moved north by rail past the scenes of the humiliating defeats that had shattered Buller's reputation, arriving at Newcastle on 18 June. From Newcastle the Canadians would ride to Zand Spruit in the Transvaal to join Major General the Earl of Dundonald's 3rd Mounted Brigade. On Wednesday, 20 June 1900 the regimental diarist penned:

Very warm. Marched at 7. Passed Majuba Hill and went over Laing's Nek about noon. Halted at Charlestown 3 miles from the nek for an hour, then proceeding entered Transvaal at Volksrust. Found Lt Gen. Hillyard's division here. Marched rapidly N.E. from this point over the Volksrust plain and joined Sir Redvers Buller's army at Zand Spruit about 8.30. Bivouacked between Thorneycroft's Mounted Infantry and "A" Battery Royal Horse Artillery. In to-nights orders the Regt was taken on the strength of the Brigade. Major Sangmeister, Border Mounted Rifles attached to the Regt for duty.

Buller's army was poised to open the Natal railway line to Pretoria, thus easing Roberts' precarious supply system. He could also strike north to cut the Delagoa Bay railway, cutting the Boers off from the sea. While the advance through Natal has been criticized for its pace, he had been advancing through, in the words of a Boer commander, "very difficult mountainous country." Another Boer wrote that Buller "had no chance to outflank the same as Lord Roberts had on the flats right through to Pretoria." The Boers had known where the danger lay and had concentrated against Roberts. A small force of burghers fought a delaying action through the hills and passes of northeastern Natal and into the Transvaal.[4]

At 7:00 a.m. the next morning, three months after leaving Canada, the SH were finally at the front. Dundonald's brigade was a mixture of imperial and colonial forces. It now included the Composite Regiment Mounted Infantry; the South African Light Horse (SALH), commanded by Lieutenant Colonel Julian Byng, a future governor general of Canada; Thorneycroft's Mounted Infantry; Strathcona's Horse; and A Battery, Royal Horse Artillery (RHA). Buller, like Steele a veteran of the Red River expedition, rode with the regiment for a time reminiscing about the northwest. On 22 June, after a long day's march of 27 miles, the British entered Standerton at 4:00 p.m. to find that the railway bridge over the Vaal had been destroyed, and the railway stores set afire. With Standerton in British hands, Buller paused while the railway was repaired. To the Canadians the country resembled the prairies. As the area was about a mile above sea level, water left in buckets often would freeze during the night. After all the trials, the horses were bearing up to the long marches and poor rations remarkably well.[5]

The army spent a relatively quiet time at Standerton except for the strain of patrols and outposts and a few incidents of enemy sniping. It was not until 29 June that the railway line from the south was finally put in operation. Finally, on 30 June Lieutenant General Sir C.F. Cleary led a force made up of his 2nd Division and Dundonald's brigade north to open a line of communications with Heidelberg. On 1 July 1900 the SH had its baptism of fire. The regiment was detailed for the scouts, advance, and flank guards. The advance had progressed several miles when the B Squadron troops commanded by Lieutenants Tobin and Kirkpatrick came under fire from a rocky kopje and a house flying a white flag. Private Jenkins died when he was hit in the abdomen by a shot from the farmhouse. Clearly, this was more than a few local Boers taking pot-shots. Thorneycroft's Mounted Infantry and some artillery joined the Canadians, and the combined force obliged the Boers to retire. The enemy, who lost at least four men, was identified as the commando led by General Viljoen. However, Ben Viljoen was near Balmoral on the Delagoa Bay line at the time. Canadian casualties were light: Private Jenkins killed and Captain Howard and Private Hobson captured on an ill-advised reconnaissance. Later A Squadron also came under fire while on outpost duty, but held their ground without loss until relieved.[6]

Boers were active along the axis, but seemed content to trade shots at long range. Steele was ordered to detach a squadron to assist the 2nd Battalion, Devonshire Regiment, in protecting the railway bridge at Waterval, halfway back to Standerton. Accordingly, C Squadron retraced its steps to the bridge. The squadron remained detached for nearly a month and was reinforced by Lieutenant Harper's troop from A Squadron on 5 July. The British Columbians were in contact nearly every day, losing two men killed and one who later died of his wounds. Two of the casualties occurred when a party commanded by Lieutenant White-Fraser was lured into a trap. A party of Boers had sent word that they wished to surrender, but preferred that their comrades believe they had been taken prisoner. The Boers were at a farmhouse at Washout Spruit about seven miles from camp. When Sergeant Parker, an ex-Imperial officer, and two black scouts approached the house which was flying at least one white flag, they were shot dead. Private Arnold was dangerously wounded and later died of his wounds. A large party of Boers burst from cover and chased the Canadians towards a kopje. The Strathconas galloped over the ridge and then quickly dismounted and lay down. When the Boers rode over the ridge they were met with a burst of rifle fire that emptied saddles and sent the survivors fleeing for their lives.[7]

Harper's troop had been escorted back to Waterval Bridge from Vlaakfontein by the rest of A Squadron commanded by Major Snyder. On its return Snyder's squadron joined the escort of a convoy proceeding north from Greylingstad. The Boers first fired on the convoy from kopjes near Greylingstad. The squadron Maxim gun detachment led by Lieutenant Benyon did "very efficient work . . . firing on the Boers at short range" from a concealed position in a farmhouse. After the first engagement, the convoy commander, Major Rycroft of the 10th Hussars, attempted to hurry the convoy. As a result, there was not enough time to prove the ground. The burghers continually harassed the escort, which was hard pressed to keep the Boers outside rifle range of the convoy. Escorting a convoy through rolling country is a difficult business. The escort must secure the commanding ground to the front and flanks, hold it while the convoy approaches and passes, and finally abandon it after the convoy has moved out of range. The process is repeated over and over again. Six men from Lieutenant H.D.B. Ketchen's troop were unable to break contact and were posted as missing. One of the men was later found to have been killed in action. The others were prisoners. The convoy, reinforced by Thorneycroft's mounted infantry and a detachment of B Squadron, finally made its way into camp, having been sniped at from all sides along the route.[8]

After the regiment had sailed from Halifax, Strathcona decided to raise one officer and 50 men as reinforcements. The men were easily recruited and Lieutenant Agar Adamson of the Governor General's Foot Guards was selected to command the draft. They arrived at Durban on 20 June and began to make their way north to join the regiment. By early July the draft had reached Standerton and was temporarily attached to the SALH. On the 5th the troop accompanied Byng's men on a sweep to the north and west. At Wolve Spruit, about 15 miles north of Standerton, the Canadians, who were the advanced guard, encountered the enemy. Adamson decided to draw the Boers into a trap by feigning a retreat, while the SALH waited in ambush to take the Boers in each flank. Unfortunately, the plan went awry when the Boers dropped back and Adamson chose to pursue them. The situation went bad very quickly, the Boers began to press the troops from three sides, and three men were wounded. One of the wounded men, Private McArthur, whose horse had been killed, was in imminent danger of being captured. Sergeant Arthur Richardson rode back under heavy fire and rescued McArthur, covered by the fire of another wounded Strathcona, Private Sparks. Richardson's gallantry earned him the first Canadian Victoria Cross of the war.[9]

The regiment spent July in the area between Standerton and Heidelberg with squadrons and troops frequently on detachment at various points along the railway. Steele was unable to concentrate more than his headquarters and A Squadron, less the troop attached to C Squadron, for the operation mounted by Lieutenant General Clery on 12 July to drive a marauding commando away from the railroad between Greylingstad and Vlaklaagte Station. The commando was said to have been led by Ben Viljoen, who, however, was fighting Hutton at the time. B Squadron remained at Greylingstad, partly because of a shortage of fit horses.

On 13 July the Strathconas were the advance guard for the force. The guide with the advance guard had taken a route too far to the left. As a result, Major Sangmeister, the Border Mounted Rifles officer attached to the regiment, led his right flank guard troop towards One Tree Hill, a high, rocky feature which "rose abruptly from the plain" and was believed to be held by the enemy. The Strathconas were proceeding more or less carefully when an alert trooper spotted two men on the hill about a mile ahead. The proper course would have been to scout the hill, but the major decided to ride straight ahead. The men rode up a gentle slope until they were within about 100 yards of the crest. Suddenly a heavy volley emptied three or four saddles in the centre of the Canadian line. Sangmeister and six men, two of them seriously wounded, were taken prisoner. Later the two wounded men were returned. The guide's error was discovered at about the same time that Sangmeister had ridden into the ambush. To correct the error the regiment was required to make an oblique movement. In doing so the Canadians came under flanking fire from an enemy position well-sited in a ravine. Steele dismounted the regiment and advanced to within 600 yards of the enemy. The Boers soon crept away down the ravine and retired. The British chased them until dark, inflicting a number of casualties including eight killed. Steele attributed the lack of Canadian casualties to the speed with which the regiment had moved into cover.[10]

The force cleared the country as far as Lieu Spruit, eight miles north of Standerton, and then returned to Greylingstad. By that time the reinforcements joined the regiment and B Squadron had drawn its remounts. The regiment then rode west to Zwickerbosch Spruit near Heidelburg where it halted until 30 July. In the meantime, Sir Redvers Buller prepared to advance through rolling ground to cut the Delagoa Bay railway near Belfast, while Roberts advanced east from Middleburg, after a detour to chase De Wet. On 3 August, with the regiment together for the first time in a month, Strathcona's Horse moved to Paardekop, the starting point for the advance. Here the westerners strutted their stuff by rounding up 500 remounts that had stampeded across the veldt. As a reward, Steele enjoyed first pick of the remounts.[11]

Buller commanded a small corps—a cavalry brigade, Dundonald's brigade, and Lieutenant General Lyttleton's 4th Division, plus some corps artillery and supply and remount units. His two mounted brigades were both understrength, the cavalry brigade having only seven and one half squadrons, while Dundonald's brigade consisted of A Battery, the SALH, and Strathcona's Horse. His plan involved a march potentially as arduous as Roberts' march from the western railway to Bloemfontein. The country was difficult, devoid of supplies and swarming with enemy.

At 8:00 a.m. on 7 August Buller's column marched north from Paardekop with the two mounted brigades leading. The SH led the 3rd Mounted Brigade on the left. The column marched due north, passing Mierzitch on the right. By 9:00 a.m. the first contact was made with the enemy four miles from Paardekop. The SH had a very trying day as the country forced the column to change direction several times. As a result the advance guard squadron would become the flank guard, and the flank guard squadron would find itself in the lead. The infantry marched on Christiaan Botha holding the Roi kopjes southeast of Amersfoort, while Dundonald's brigade moved to lever the Boers out of their position. After an all day fight B Squadron galloped into the village under heavy fire. They were soon reinforced by the 1st Battalion, King's Royal Rifle Corps, and moved up onto the heights beyond the village. For the cost of 31 casualties, one in the SH, Buller's corps had taken its first objective on the march into eastern Transvaal. The column spent a cold, hungry night as the transport was delayed by grass fires. In a widespread breakdown in discipline, "the stores of the town were looted by the troops, everything was taken or destroyed."

The column remained in Amersfoort the next day because of heavy fog, which delayed the arrival of the transport until 11:00 a.m. In the meantime the Boers attacked the outposts north of the town. The infantry reinforced the outposts and the Boers were driven off. The advance resumed on August 9. The SH saw little action over the next few days, although the pom-pom section under Lieutenant Magee killed four burghers on 9 August. On the 11th the regiment sent one squadron ahead in a dash to seize the town of Ermelo. B Squadron occupied the telegraph and other public offices and established posts throughout the town. A quantity of arms and ammunition was seized. The rest of the column halted four miles from town for the night, then entered it on the next day. Meanwhile, the enemy retired northeast towards Lake Chrissie.[12]

Monday, 13 August, was spent near the source of the Vaal River. Tuesday the regiment led the advance and once again made good progress despite being forced to shift around a veldt fire. At noon Lord Dundonald ordered Steele to seize and hold Carolina, while an intelligence officer searched public buildings, an addition to the regiment's primary objective for the day of seizing Witbank. Steele ordered Major Belcher to take C Squadron and Lieutenant Harper's troop from A Squadron on the mission. As the force approached the town, it came under fire from enemy behind stone walls and in houses on the outskirts of town. The Canadians dismounted and advanced in skirmishing order, driving the enemy out of the town at the cost of one man wounded. Belcher held the town, while the intelligence officer searched it and blew up the magazine. The force then left town to rejoin the main body at Witbank. Three men had become separated from their comrades while scouting and arrived in Carolina after Belcher had left. Because their horses were exhausted, they were forced to remain in town overnight. The scouts convinced the largely hostile inhabitants that they were part of a superior force surrounding the town. In the morning they wasted no time in making their way back to the regiment.

Steele had seized Witbank by 3:00 p.m. and the rest of the force followed it into camp. At 4:00 p.m. a rider arrived with an oral message from Belcher that he was heavily engaged and required assistance. Dundonald ordered Steele to ride out with the regiment at once. When the SH arrived on the heights overlooking Carolina at dusk, all appeared quiet. Steele soon encountered Lieutenant Pooley's troop which reported that the task had been successfully completed. Belcher later explained that he had told the messenger to report that he was meeting considerable opposition, but had said nothing about needing assistance.

On 15 August the column reached Twyfelaar on the Komati River. That day something happened which remains unexplained. As the legend goes, a party of SALH were shot down by fire from a farm flying a white flag. Unfortunately for the Boers, a troop of C Squadron witnessed the incident and quickly surrounded the farm, capturing the six men responsible. A drumhead court martial was hastily convened, and the Boers were lynched. One version has the Strathconas threatening to lynch an officer who attempted to intervene. While Steele always denied that the incident happened, it was widely believed at the time. All the evidence is either circumstantial or hearsay. Two members of the SALH died of wounds apparently suffered at Twyfelaar. C Squadron had lost Sergeant Parker and Private Arnold to fire from a farm flying a white flag on 30 July. The regimental diary for 15 August reported "The cavalry encountered a force of the enemy on the south bank of the Komati River, being fired upon from a house flying a white flag. Burnt the place and proceeding crossed the river and bivouacked on the N. bank at Twyfelaar." Private R.P. Rooke of the regiment, who did not witness the incident, repeated the story in a memoir he produced in 1908. Private A.S. McCormick of 2 RCR included a version in a manuscript he wrote 50 years after the event. Lieutenant George Whitton of the Bushveldt Carbineers included a poem from *The Navy Illustrated* in his book *Scapegoats of the Empire*. The last verse reads:

Twas thus Strathcona's Horse left Vengeance sitting by her shrine,
Where six accursed corpses broke the grey horizon line,
Their flesh to feed the vultures, and their bones to be a sign.

Whitton, who had been sentenced to death with Breaker Morant for murdering prisoners, was pardoned and returned to Australia. In his book he claimed Morant had testified at his court martial that his commanding officer had justified an order to not take prisoners by citing the actions of Strathcona's Horse.[13]

On 21 August the advance finally resumed. While there was heavy fighting, the SH were not engaged. The 2nd Battalion, Gordon Highlanders and the cavalry brigade bore the brunt of the firing and suffered accordingly in the early stages of what came to be known as the Battle of Bergendal. Altogether Buller had 44 casualties before camp was made at Van Wyks Vlei. The advance resumed on the 23rd, and once again the SH missed most of the action.

The fighting had been all on the British right flank, but on the 24th the pressure shifted to the centre. Lieutenant General Pole-Carew had concentrated his division at Wonderfontein and now advanced along the railway to Belfast, screened by mounted infantry on both flanks. By evening the town was firmly in British hands. The next day Roberts issued orders for his favourite tactic, a double envelopment. French's cavalry would loop wide through the Steelpoort Valley, turn right and come down on the railway near Machadodorp. Meanwhile, Buller was to march around the Boer's left flank to join hands with French on the railway. Buller, instead of a right hook, opted for a straight jab.

Before first light on the 26th, B and C Squadrons relieved some British infantry entrenched on a forward slope 600 yards away from dominating Boer trenches. The squadrons were ordered to withdraw from the positions at 2:30 p.m. Despite the heavy fire only four men were wounded in the regiment on the day. From the Boer point of view the British were being held despite the severe disparity in numbers. This, however, was not the case. On the 27th an enemy position at Bergendal Farm held by ZARPs was carried by an attack by two battalions of 8th Brigade. That effectively decided the battle. The Boers began to stream away to the east all along the line. The British failed to exploit the opportunity and the majority of the Boers made a clean escape by nightfall. Despite the numbers involved, 20 000 British and 5000 Boers, the battle was decided by an attack by two battalions on 74 men.[14]

The next day the SALH led the brigade advance for Delamantua. The only Boer response was sporadic shell fire that continued during the day. A short distance past the station the advance guard contacted the enemy, and the SH were ordered up in support. Heavy fire was coming from an enemy-held farmhouse on the left flank. Two squadrons under Major Belcher were quickly sent to the left to eliminate that threat. The enemy ousted from the farm, Belcher rejoined the regiment, which advanced to a rise overlooking Machadodorp. This was the signal for the enemy to concentrate shell fire on the Canadian position. Shortly after, Captain Cartwright's A Squadron led the brigade into the town. With the town secure the Strathconas halted for the night on the heights to the north of the town.[15]

The next morning B Squadron led the column forward over the mountains and pushed on for two miles past Helvetia, a few miles north of the railroad. The regiment then swung right and rode south to Waterval Boven on the railroad. Lieutenant McDonald's 2nd Troop of C Squadron succeeded in working forward very close to the town despite heavy fire. When French's cavalry arrived the regiment returned to Helvetia. On 30 August, while French struck south of the railway, Buller arced southeast to capture Nooitegedacht, about 12 miles from Helvetia. The country was extremely rough, in places resembling untimbered parts of British Columbia. From the heights overlooking the town the British could see a dramatic sight—a large, khaki mob straggling along the railway. It was the 2000 occupants of the prisoner-of-war camp at Nooitegedacht, some of whom had spent ten months behind bars. As Pole-Carew and French were advancing along the railway, the brigade turned back north and halted at Vluichfontein. Before leaving the heights Steele ordered Lieutenant J.E. Leckie with six men to reconnoitre the town and to make contact with French to inform him of Buller's location. The patrol made its way into the valley, leading its horses down a steep, narrow trail which showed sign of recent use. After meeting a friendly native, the patrol laid up under cover while Leckie and one man cautiously made their way forward on foot to a vantage point. After observing the town and station for several hours, the two Strathconas rejoined the patrol at dusk. The Canadians took refuge in a farmhouse overnight, then in the morning rode west along the railway to Waterval Onder where they contacted French's division. After making his report, Leckie and his patrol rode back to camp, arriving about 7:00 p.m.[16]

Roberts' army was concentrated astride the railway, while the Boer army had slipped to the sides. He ordered French to strike southeast towards Barberton and Buller to capture Lydenburg north of the line, while Pole-Carew would continue his advance along the railway towards Komati Poort. The ground over which Buller was to advance belied the popular image of South Africa as open veldt and rocky kopjes. The road from Helvetia climbs steadily for ten miles across a series of ridges between mountain peaks until it crests at Schoeman's Nek, where the Crocodile River suddenly erupts into view a few miles ahead. Beyond the river an apparently impassable mountain range rises abruptly from its banks. The few roads then were rocky trails winding their way through the labyrinth. To make matters worse, the Boers had been allowed time to prepare defences unimpeded by British pursuit. Buller, realistic and cautious, proposed that while he marched from Helvetia through Badfontein, another column should parallel his march on the road from Belfast via Dullstroom. Roberts agreed with his logic, but would only despatch the second column if Buller met heavy opposition.

On 1 September the SH advance guard contacted Boer piquets at the Crocodile River where a new iron bridge crossed. The regiment's pom-pom and A Battery came up and shelled the Boers until they withdrew from a conical kopje that commanded the crossing. With the bridge seized intact, the column pushed on and camped at Badfontein eight miles from Lydenburg.

Lydenburg appeared ripe for the taking as intelligence indicated the enemy were not defending the Lydenburg Road in strength. It was not to be. A semicircle of mountains completely dominates the ground and all possible approaches from the south. During the night information was received that Louis Botha's men held a strong position on a rugged ridge stretching across the valley. Steele later wrote that "a frontal attack would be suicidal and the nature of the country was such as to make a flanking movement impossible." The 3rd Mounted Brigade and the 4th Division's mounted infantry battalion advanced to reconnoitre the position. Fortunately, the Boers disclosed their position prematurely by shelling the advance guard at long range. Once again, the ammunition was defective, and most rounds failed to explode, "otherwise there would have been many casualties." The mounted troops took cover behind some stone walls and held their positions throughout the day. That evening Buller, who had concluded that the nut was too hard to crack, pulled the troops back into camp and wired Roberts for assistance.[17]

Ian Hamilton left Belfast in the morning and by the next evening had reached a point 15 miles to the southwest of Buller. Buller was content to wait. The Strathconas took their turn providing outposts for protection of the camp. The unit's staff diary implies that security arrangements left much to be desired. As a result the regiment suffered its heaviest one-day loss of the war on 3 September in a futile attempt to prevent the enemy from gaining a tactical advantage. On that day the regiment was providing the screen around the camp, although a high rocky ridge on the right of the camp had been left unguarded. Sergeant Nelles, who commanded the regimental scouts, reported the enemy were attempting to move a gun onto the feature. Steele ordered Lieutenant Leckie to establish an observation post on the hill, while Sergeant Logan was ordered to site a cossack post further forward. When he approached the hill, Leckie found the Boers were already on it in considerable strength. When he received Leckie's report, Steele realized the implications and immediately reported the matter to Dundonald. The brigade commander "advised" Steele to reinforce Leckie with two more troops.

Meanwhile, Sergeant Logan's party had encountered a superior force at close range, and Logan together with Privates West, Jones and Wiggins were killed after refusing to surrender. There was only one survivor, Private Albert Garner, who was severely wounded. Steele had ordered Lieutenants Kirkpatrick and Tobin to reinforce Leckie. In doing so, Kirkpatrick rode further to the right than was intended. His troop became entangled with the enemy near where Logan's men had fallen. Sergeant Brothers and Private Cruickshanks were killed in the melee and the troop fell back to camp. Six Canadians had died and another was wounded to no avail. The Boers were left in possession of the ridge. For want of taking elementary security precautions, the British could expect a great deal of trouble on the next day.

True to expectations, the Boers began to shell the camp in the morning. It took an attack by two infantry battalions to force the Boers off the top of the ridge, although it was not until the following day that the feature was secured and the Canadian bodies recovered. Hamilton had meanwhile continued to advance through the hills and ridges west of Buller. On the 6th his column turned the Boer position, freeing Buller to advance and sealing the fate of Lydenburg.[18]

On 7 September the SH reached the outskirts of the town by noon, then pushed a squadron towards Paardeplaats. The enemy had retired to a precipitous ridge which loomed 1800 feet above the valley. It would take more than a few score of mounted men to dislodge the burghers, who could shell the town with relative impunity. Steele, anticipating more of the same in the morning, ordered a 4:30 reveille so as to have the unit saddled and ready to move at dawn. The Boer fire resumed at dawn, and the SH took cover in a donga until the brigade moved off at 9:30 to screen the left flank of an attack on Paardeplaats. The infantry steadily climbed up the difficult slopes, while the British guns silenced the Boer guns.

Buller's column set off on an advance east across the grain of the mountains to Spitz Kop on the 9th. The going was very difficult, especially for mounted troops. The regiment found itself in contact with the enemy rearguard all day, being able to employ the Maxims twice. In late afternoon the Canadians arrived at the 8900-foot-tall Mauchberg, where they could see enemy transport, just out of rifle range, but several miles away by road as the trail wound around the mountain. Prominent at the rear of the escaping transport were several ambulances, placed there to deter artillery fire. The next morning the regiment descended from the mountain and set out across the Sabi River valley. Despite the country the advance was hot on the enemy's heels. Lieutenant Tobin's troop discovered several tons of supplies abandoned in a donga to the right of the route. Within a few miles the regiment came under fire from a 6-inch gun posted on the road four miles ahead. Buller aborted a dash to capture the gun by the regiment as "the Boers had it well protected and as no support was available." In their haste to save the gun the Boer gunners abandoned the gun's sight and derrick as well as a wagon load of ammunition. The next day the regiment continued the pursuit, while the rest of the brigade swung north up the Sabi Valley in an attempt to cut the line of retreat. The SH pressed hard again all day and captured 150 loaded supply wagons and a large quantity of ammunition at Spitz Kop.[19]

Buller remained at Spitz Kop until 25 September. Roberts had withdrawn Hamilton back to the railway, and many of Buller's troops were guarding his line of communications. Further south Pole-Carew was on the railroad with his division, while French was advancing from Carolina to Barberton. The enemy had Botha and 2000 men facing Buller, Ben Viljoen with 1200 men at Godwaan on the railway and another 300 prolonging his line towards Waterval Onder, Smuts and Fourie with 1000 men from the Ermelo, Bethel, and Standerton commandos between Carolina and Barberton, and 150 men at Barberton. In round numbers it was 26 500 to 4650. The Boers faced the prospect of being pinned down against the border with Portuguese East Africa. Buller effectively blocked access from the east to Lydenburg and the high veldt beyond. However, he lacked the troops to be able to block the passes 20 miles north of Spitz Kop, which would have forced the Boers to follow a long, difficult detour. Groups of burghers began to make their way around to the north to Pilgrim's Rest and Kruger's Post. From there their way was open to join Erasmus and Grobler north of Pretoria or General de la Rey near Klerksdorp.

During the halt there was a steady routine of patrols, convoy escorts, and outposts. After the rigours of the previous weeks, it was a welcome respite. The regiment's horses had suffered badly, and at least 200 remounts were required. The war seemed nearly over, and there was a stream of good news, starting with the announcement of the award of the Victoria Cross to Sergeant Richardson, followed by Kruger's departure for Europe, and Botha's resignation. Unfortunately, looting was widespread at the time. The situation was serious enough for Lord Dundonald to issue a stern reminder that "it is not war to loot the poor people or to burn their homes."[20]

Buller was able to resume the advance on 25 September. The next day his column belatedly blocked Burghers Pass just hours after Botha had crossed it. A skilful rearguard action provided enough delay for the Boer transport to escape. On the 27th, in a well-executed action, A Squadron rolled back the opposition and entered Pilgrim's Rest under heavy fire. On 1 October the regiment entered Kruger's Post, which had fallen to a thrust from Lydenburg on the 30th. The town was not yet secure, and the Boers began to shell the town shortly after Dundonald's brigade entered it. The regiment was fortunate to escape with one man wounded and a number of horses killed. During the night the enemy withdrew, ending active operations in the area.[21]

On 6 October the regiment began the return march to Machadodorp through Badfontein and Helvetia. Few would be sorry to see the last of the steep trails and commanding crests north of the railway. As the regiment neared Machadodorp orders were received to hurry, as Sir Redvers Buller wished to address the regiment before he departed for Pretoria en route to England. It was a time for kind words, and Buller made the best of it, concluding with, "I have never served with a nobler, braver or more serviceable body of men. It shall be my privilege when I meet my friend Lord Strathcona, to tell him what a magnificent body of men bear his name." In his despatch Buller referred to Colonel Steele's great influence on all ranks and his thorough knowledge of frontier work. He also recognized 21 other officers and 34 soldiers for their service in the field.[22]

The Natal Field Force was being absorbed by the South African Field Force. As part of the reorganization, Dundonald's brigade would disappear. There is, of course, more to it than a stroke of a pen. All sorts of stores had been issued to the regiment by the brigade. Some had been destroyed or lost for a variety of reasons, including enemy action. The regiment convened a board of officers to determine the losses and recommend that these be written off the books of the regiment. While this sounds like an exercise in bureaucracy, if this was not done Steele would be liable for the losses.

The war was not over. Orders were received to join French's column to march to Standerton via Carolina. This was soon countermanded, and the regiment was next warned to move to Pretoria by train. On 12 October the regiment turned its horses over to the 6th Dragoon Guards, a regular cavalry regiment. It was a difficult thing for a mounted regiment to do, even if the receiving unit complimented the Strathconas on the condition of the animals. The horses did not take kindly to the change. Steele wrote, "Several of them bucked so badly that I had, at the request of the remount officer, to send some men over to remind them that they have to behave themselves. These horses had not bucked for months, yet, strange as it may seem, no sooner did they change masters than many of them began their old tricks."[23]

Regimental headquarters and B Squadron caught the train for Pretoria on 14 October, finally arriving at 10:00 p.m. and camping on the station platform for the night. The rest of the regiment went on a memorable debauch in Machadodorp. It started when some members of C Squadron forged Belcher's signature to draw an issue of rum from the stores. The bacchanalia quickly spread to A Squadron, and things began to get out of hand. The officers and senior NCOs were, by this time, in no shape to control the junior ranks. In the end, several companies of troops surrounded the bivouac and marched C Squadron out on the veldt to sober up. The next day, very much the worse for wear, the two squadrons climbed into open-topped boxcars and jolted their way east to Pretoria. The authorities let the matter drop, perhaps because it was too hot to handle.[24]

The regiment had experienced several varieties of warfare against the Boers. First guarding the railroad, then the advance from Paardekop, the battle of Bergendal, and fighting through the mountains. Now Strathcona's Horse would chase the elusive, dangerous De Wet. On 16 October A and C Squadrons joined Steele and B Squadron in camp three miles outside of Pretoria. That day the commander-in-chief ordered the regiment to prepare for further service in the field, although other Canadian units were preparing to return home. To add insult to injury, the only remounts available were London bus horses that were in good condition but too heavy.[25]

By 23 October the regiment had moved by road and train to Welverdend, a station about 50 miles from Johannesburg. General Barton's brigade was beseiged by De Wet and Liebenberg at Frederikstad, the next major halt along the line. Roberts hastily assembled a relieving force from whatever could be made available. On the 25th the SH guarded the left of a column consisting of the Elswick Battery (six quick-firing 12-pounders originally ordered by the Japanese Navy), Brabant's Horse, a battalion of the Essex Regiment, and four companies of the Royal Dublin Fusiliers. The Strathconas provided the advance guard, and in addition posted B Squadron on the left or eastern side where the Gatsrand range paralleled the route south to Frederikstad. Good progress was made, and as the column was nearing Barton at 1:00 p.m., the general launched an attack on an enemy-held embankment northwest of his position. De Wet had ordered the place held by 200 Boers, but only 80 had actually taken up their positions. A bayonet charge from the camp by three regiments routed the Boers. (Boer casualties were reported as 30 killed and wounded and about the same number taken prisoner

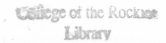

by De Wet, and shown as 24 dead, 19 wounded and 26 prisoners in the SH diary.) Barton allowed De Wet to retreat without pursuit towards Vanvurenskloof near the Vaal River. Another column surprised De Wet two days later and drove him deeper into the Orange River Colony (ORC).[26]

The Canadians remained in the western Transvaal in the general area of Frederikstad and Potchefstroom until 30 November. Heavy rain and thunderstorms were frequent. Illness struck down both Steele and Belcher as well as many men. Although the regimental diary emphasized searches for the enemy, the objectives included denying the enemy their commissary. Hundreds of cattle and sheep were collected. In addition, the purpose of at least one excursion was to move Boer women and children into town from their farms. This forced relocation included destruction of their farms and confiscation of their herds. Steele hinted at this when he wrote, "It was better for them to be brought in and cared for than to be left out at the farms suffering from want of food." There were spirited engagements and skirmishes alike. On 14 November Private Stewart, a regimental scout, was confronted by two Boers at a farmhouse. One of the Boers levelled his Mauser and took aim at him after Stewart had thrown down his rifle. The scout drew his revolver and shot the Boer at 50 yards range, a very lucky shot indeed. The other Boer then wounded Stewart and fled. Stewart survived, the Boer did not. Another Strathcona, Private Reed, was captured on the 9th but escaped when his guard fell asleep. It was a difficult time, and the already fragile discipline and alertness suffered. Tragically, two men, Privates Bull and Scott, were shot in the unit lines, the latter case more the result of negligence than accident. Scott died instantly and was buried in Pochtesfroom's cemetery on 21 November. While relations between the Strathconas and the locals were good, and at least one marriage resulted, few could have been sorry to leave the western Transvaal.[27]

De Wet, after his escape at Frederikstad, had made his way south through the ORC. On 23 November his burghers captured the British garrison at DeWetsdorp. This brought General Knox with three columns hurrying down from Pretoria in pursuit of De Wet, who was attempting to cross the Orange River into the Cape Colony. The Strathconas were ordered south to join the chase. On 2 December the two trains carrying the regiment shunted east off the central line at Springfontein towards Bethulie, just north of the border with the Cape Colony. First to arrive were the headquarters and B Squadron at 5:00 p.m., followed by A and C Squadrons four hours later. The SH marched at midnight with Laing's column and joined General Knox in the morning near "Good Hope" farm.

Knox had caught up to De Wet once again. The unmistakable sound of heavy pom-pom and gun fire could be heard from the right front. About 7:00 Steele with B Squadron moved forward to support the Irish Yeomanry and the Seaforth Highlanders. The enemy had caught the advance guard in a crossfire from kopjes on both flanks as they neared a farm. Knox decided to hold the Boers across the front with three columns, while a fourth, led by Pilcher, swung to take the enemy in the rear. Steele led his men up a donga towards the farm until a wire fence was encountered. Nine horses were lost when the squadron halted while the wire was cut. Steele called up the rest of the regiment and Major Jarvis, supported by Lieutenant Laidlaw's pom-pom, attacked and captured some sangars and kraals to the front. The effective pair of Lieutenants Tobin and Kirkpatrick once again distinguished themselves. Belcher with A and C Squadrons then galloped across to the farm and established themselves there. Captain Boyd (a reinforcement officer of The RCR who was attached to the regiment prior to joining the SAC), leading a troop of C Squadron, had a narrow escape when the artillery mistook his men for enemy after they had captured a kopje. B Squadron carried the kopjes on the left, centre, and right. It was an effective, coordinated operation, and one of the few times that Steele and his men had a chance to fight a multi-phased action.[28]

De Wet, however, got clean away once again, marching to the east for 27 hours in driving rain while Knox pursued ghosts to the north. De Wet managed to cross the rain-swollen Caledon River, but found the Orange River impassable and the bridges heavily garrisoned. He was in a difficult position in the triangle between two rivers in flood and neutral Basutoland. Knox belatedly reversed his route, and Barker's column reached the Caledon at a drift south of Carmel, where they met another column that had already crossed. The fast-rising river forced a halt before the SH could cross, but Steele wisely planted markers on the bank to gauge the water level. Once the level dropped the regiment crossed and rejoined Barker. De Wet, who had been sighted at Rouxville, was believed to be making for Commissiedrift. He had attempted to cross at the drift, but, finding it held and the river dropping, rode north along the river. Shortly before dawn on 8 December, De Wet arrived at Zevenfontein Drift, 10 or 12 miles upstream from Commissiedrift. To his "immense joy," it was unoccupied and fordable. Knox had marched towards Rouxville, not Commissiedrift. Lieutenant Christie, who was scouting towards the drift, arrived in time to see De Wet abandon an attempt to force a crossing, ride along the river and escape across it.[29]

For the remainder of the year the Strathconas pursued De Wet north up the eastern frontier of the ORC. The regiment caught De Wet on 12 December and managed to corner his convoy for a time. Knox, however, refused to send his guns forward, much to Steele's disgust. The advance continued, just far enough behind to be unable to make any serious contact. De Wet slipped through trap after trap and finally broke contact and disappeared. There is little else of tactical note to recount except for the regiment's actions on 6 and 8 January when the Strathconas fought brilliant rearguard actions covering a column that could make no more than one mile per hour. The climax saw the regiment withdraw across a bridge while in close contact with a superior force.

By the time the regiment embarked on the SS *Lake Erie* to travel to England to be presented their medals by the new monarch, it had made a name for itself. The taciturn Lord Kitchener, the new commander-in-chief, lavished praise on the regiment. Forgotten, or at least unmentioned, were the transgressions at Machadodorp and elsewhere. By arranging to march the regiment directly from the station to the waiting ship, Steele managed to avoid a repetition of the second contingent's farewell spree in Cape Town. While the regiment included a number of unruly characters, including its commanding officer and most of the officers, what should be remembered was its success in the field. The last word goes to a British artilleryman who told the recently-promoted Sergeant Hart-McHarg of The RCR that when the Strathconas were scouting, the gunners could sleep with their boots off![30]

Chapter

14   Other Canadians

THE FIRST AND SECOND contingents returned home at the end of 1900, and the third and fourth contingents did not sail until 1902. However, there was a visible Canadian presence in South Africa throughout the war. More than 2000 Canadians, including some who opted to remain in South Africa rather than return home, served outside Canadian units. There always was at least one unit in South Africa with a strong Canadian flavour.[1]

A number of Canadians came to South Africa "for instructional purposes," including Major Cartwright on the staff of Hutton's brigade, Major Boulanger in 7th Division (he later made his way to China and served in the Boxer rebellion), Lieutenant Colonel W.H. Gordon attached, initially, to 6th Division, and Major J.L. Biggar, who was a very useful Staff Officer, Canadians at headquarters. Lieutenant Layborn and a small group from The RCR's rear party had joined French's cavalry in the relief of Kimberley. Other Canadian officers held staff jobs for varying periods of time. Of these, the best known was Major S.J.A. Denison, who had engineered a posting to Roberts' staff, apparently behind Otter's back. Major Buchan commanded a convalescent depot in the closing months of the RCR tour. Nineteen-year-old Lieutenant Weldon McLean left G Company to join Colvile's staff and later became a lieutenant in the Royal Horse Artillery. Lieutenant J.H. Elmsley of the RCD was Hutton's aide-de-camp during the advance to Pretoria. More than 20 other officers filled jobs ranging from railway staff officer to cartographer. Some of these postings were due to special qualifications or aptitude. The majority were unavoidable as headquarters would order a unit to provide an officer, leaving the choice to the CO.

The two extra medical officers and eight nurses with the first and second contingents worked as hard as anyone in South Africa, especially during the enteric fever epidemic. Once the British decided that anyone could treat the sick and wounded regardless of nationality, Canadians served on an equal footing with their British counterparts. Another doctor and two nurses sailed to South Africa with the Canadian contingent of the South African Constabulary (SAC) and eight nurses served in the third contingent. Of the "extra" doctors and the nurses who served in South Africa, one doctor and five nurses served two tours. Nursing Sister Georgina Fane Pope was awarded the Royal Red Cross.

Those mentioned above, however, were only a small proportion of the Canadians who served outside the contingents. Undoubtedly, the most visible were officers in the British regular army. Of these one was in a class by himself. Lieutenant William Henry Snyder Nickerson, a medical officer, was born in New Brunswick in 1875. He served in the field with the mounted infantry from 11 October 1899 to 31 May 1902. Nickerson won the Victoria Cross at Wakkerstrom on 20 April 1900 when he saved a gravely wounded man while under heavy fire.

"Percy" Girouard, an RMC graduate serving in the Royal Engineers, had earned fame, and the patronage of Kitchener, by building the railway that supported the British forces in the Sudan. A substantive captain and brevet major on the army list, he ran the South African railways as a temporary lieutenant colonel. He became a Knight Commander of the Order of St Michael and St George on the same honours list with five generals, two colonels and two senior civil servants. Girouard made the greatest contribution of any Canadian to eventual victory in South Africa.[2]

Girouard was only one of many RMC ex-cadets in the regular army in South Africa. Two of his key assistants were Captains H.G. Joly de Lotbiniere and H.C. Nanton, both fellow Canadians and engineers. Captain D.S. MacInnes, another engineer, played a key part in the defence of Kimberley. Captain Herbert Carrington Smith, after recovering from his wound suffered at Sannah's Post, commanded Roberts' Horse until it was disbanded in January 1902. After Girouard intervened with Kitchener on his behalf, Smith then commanded the South African Light Horse. Major C.M. Dobell of the Royal Welsh Fusiliers was a successful commander of mounted infantry. Other officers included Major H.P. Leader of the Caribiniers, Captain H.N. Cory of the Royal Dublin Fusiliers, and three Van Straubenzies. One hundred and eight ex-cadets were officers in the British army in 1899 although some did not fight in South Africa. Inevitably, a few fell prey to bullet or fever: Lieutenant Christopher Wood, Captain John Laurie, Captain Charles Hensley, and Lieutenant John Osborne among them.[3]

A few were Canadian by an accident of birth or had left their homeland decades before. Lieutenant Lord Frederick Hamilton-Temple-Blackwood, the son of a former governor general, was Canadian by birth. He probably had little in common with the average Canadian officer, and even less with the men. An officer in the 9th Lancers, he won a Distinguished Service Order, and was mentioned in despatches twice. Brigadier General John Dartnell was born in London, Canada West, in 1838. After serving in the regular army he formed the Natal Mounted Police. His call for reinforcements had prompted Lord Chelmsford to split his command at Islandawana. The rest, as they say, is history. In this war he would be a successful column commander. After a narrow escape from an ambush by De Wet on 18 December 1901 he decided enough was enough. At the age of 63 he accepted the honourary rank of major general and retired.[4]

During the war Canadians were able to obtain commissions in the British army and the colonial forces. Several officers and men took advantage of the opportunity and subsequently served in South Africa and elsewhere. First among equals was Sam Hughes until his self-inflicted falling out with officialdom. We have also met Captain Mackie who commanded Warren's Scouts. Major William Hamilton Merritt of Toronto's Governor General's Body Guard fought as a squadron commander and then second in command of Brabant's Horse. He returned to Canada in a fruitless attempt to raise a corps of "Canadian Rangers." In April 1900 the British offered 24 commissions in the British army to officers and men serving in the Canadian contingents. The number was later increased. Others, such as Lance Corporal E. Molyneux took commissions in the colonial forces.

Canadians, of course, also served in the ranks of various colonial units, and a few were British regular soldiers. E.R. Burkholder of Hamilton, caught in the siege of Kimberley, joined the Kimberley Light Horse. His brothers came to South Africa and served in the Imperial

Light Horse. Gavin Wasson, late of Toronto's 48th Highlanders, was in Vancouver on his way home from the Yukon when war broke out. Unable to obtain a place in a Canadian contingent, he hopped a ship to Australia and thence to South Africa. Private Robert Lindsay of the Manchester Regiment fell at Ladysmith in January 1900. Frank Douglas, an architect from Toronto, died on 17 February 1901 while serving in the Imperial Yeomanry. Sergeant F.C.A. Douglas, another Canadian, died of wounds the same day. There is no doubt these were two completely different individuals. Both names appear in the casualty return.

A few Canadians fought on the other side. Not surprisingly there is little available data on their background or motivation. A Toronto-born prisoner of war, who claimed that he did not approve of British and Canadian methods, identified himself to a party of RCD. He later asked them to sing the national anthem as he liked the tune, if not its sentiments. Typically, no one could remember the words.

Two organizations had strong Canadian overtones. By far the greatest number of the Canadians who served outside the contingents did not serve in the army at all. By late 1900 Lord Roberts, the government, the Toronto *Globe*, the army, and the public all believed that the war was won. Roberts picked General Baden-Powell, the hero of Mafeking, to organize a mounted police force to pacify the country pending the reinstitution of civil authority. Baden-Powell and his police were to take over the theatre from the army in July 1901. The SAC began recruiting in October 1900. General Baden-Powell, based on his experiences with C Battery, felt that Canadians should be included in his corps. An attempt was made to induce Canadians serving in South Africa to enlist, rather than returning home. Major Biggar wrote Lessard highlighting the very liberal rates of pay and concluding that "Gen. Baden Powell [sic] is anxious to get as many of the Canadians in his force as possible." Similar overtures were made to the other Canadian units in South Africa, with some success.

Some Canadian officers transferred, including Sam Steele. After some leave he returned to South Africa, where he commanded B Division until 1906. The others included Otter's adjutant, Lieutenant J.H.C. Ogilvy, Lieutenant A.J. Boyd, a reinforcement officer with The RCR, and Lieutenant W.B.M. King of C Battery. Ogilvy died of wounds in December 1901, while Boyd succumbed to fever in April 1902.

In Canada recruiting for a draft for the SAC that would eventually number 28 officers and 1208 men began soon after the return of the contingents. Not surprisingly, considering the wide play given Canadian exploits, and the liberal pay scale, interest was high. Of the officers selected, four, including Henry Burstall, had been officers in The RCR. A further 14, including Queen's Scarf winner, Richard Thompson, and Edward Reading, The RCR chief clerk, had served in the ranks of the contingents. Over 100 veterans decided they were not ready to settle down in peacetime Canada, and they signed on for a three-year tour in the SAC. While the official figure for Canadians in the SAC is 28 officers and 1208 men, this does not include the officers and men who joined in South Africa.

The constabulary fought in the operations in the Orange River Colony (ORC) and Transvaal during 1901 and 1902, as the casualty returns and the honours and awards, including two Victoria Crosses, show. At least six Canadians won decorations and 57 died, including ten killed in action or died of wounds. The SAC was a military organization disguised as a police force, but there was one critical difference. The army did not accept the constabulary as a full partner in the war. The SAC occupied small posts superimposed on the system of blockhouses spread across occupied territory. Small parties and even individual troopers patrolled the surrounding countryside. This was a frustrating, dangerous business where only the tough, crafty, and bold could survive. Eventually the SAC, unlike the regular cavalry, took part in the great sweeps of the last year of the war. On at least one occasion a force of 700 members of the SAC attempted to corner a commando in the north-central ORC. As the Boers could assemble 400 men in the same region, it was none too many.

The constabulary often collaborated with irregular corps such as the native scouts commanded by Lieutenant J.F.C. Fuller of the Oxfordshire Light Infantry. In February 1902 a column commanded by Captain Reynolds of the SAC and Fuller's scouts clashed with a strong force of Boers under Harman and Kritzinger. The action degenerated into a series of confused running fights. By the time the Boers made their escape they had lost one man killed (by Lieutenant King) and several captured. The constabulary had four men wounded and nine captured. Later it was announced that 19 Boers were killed or wounded. It showed what could be done by mobile troops who were familiar with the local area. On balance, full use was not made of the potential of the SAC.[5]

There was a curious collection of irregular units in the army. It is not surprising that Gat Howard surfaced in command of one of these, the Canadian Scouts. He had made a name for himself and won a DSO commanding the RCD machine-gun section. By October 1900 he had authority to raise a Colt gun battery. This battery soon grew into a corps of scouts, including, of course, six Colt guns. Howard had marketed the Canadian reputation as scouts, although his own name must have played a part, as Kitchener agreed that his men were worth a premium. An entry in CMR orders of 22 November 1900 read:

> Lord Kitchener is anxious to form a small Corps of Canadian Scouts for a limited period in which he proposes to make all the men Corporals or Sergeants according to merit and paid at Colonial rates of Pay. Any man who would like to join the Corps or the Battery of Colt Guns being formed under Lieut. Howard RCD will hand their names in tomorrow morning.[6]

Pay at the colonial rate, with the extra rank, meant $1.75 a day instead of 40 cents for a private. There was the added bonus of serving in an elite organization under a popular and proven leader. For a young Canadian not ready to return to peacetime Canada the combination of adventure and money must have been irresistible. Lieutenant Morrison, no slouch as a fighter himself, wrote "Most of the Canadians who have made a name for themselves as scouts have been enrolled, and with the redoubtable "Gat" as major commanding it should be a hot combination."[7]

Howard selected Charlie Ross as his second in command and four NCOs from the RCD and CMR, Casey Callaghan, Alex MacMillan, Edward Hilliam, and Robert Ryan, as lieutenants. Arthur King, an ex-troop leader in the RCD, joined temporarily, pending his posting to a mounted infantry battalion. The second contingent provided most of the men, with one each from The RCR, Strathcona's Horse, and the artificers. Others came from various colonial corps including the New South Wales Lancers. Kitchener kept his word. In January 1901 the unit mustered a regimental sergeant major, two quartermaster sergeants, five sergeant majors, 92 sergeants, and five troopers.[8]

In early 1901 Sir John French commanded a drive starting east of Pretoria down to the border with Swaziland. It was the first major operation of Kitchener's command and would set the tone for the rest of the war. In all, seven columns would ultimately take part: counterclockwise, Smith-Dorrien from Wonderfontein, Campbell from Middleburg, Alderson from Eerste Fabricken, Knox from Kaalfontein, Allenby from Zuurfontein, Dartnell from Springs, and Colville (not to be confused with Colvile) from Greylingstad. The distance from Wonderfontein to Greylingstad was almost exactly 100 miles.

The scouts served in Alderson's column as a combination of scouts and advanced guard. Alderson, who had led the First Mounted Infantry Corps in Hutton's brigade, commanded a force made up of, besides the scouts, four sections of horse artillery, the 13th and 14th Mounted Infantry Battalions, and a battalion of the King's Own Yorkshire Light Infantry (KOYLI), in all about 2000 men.[9]

There were frequent contacts and some casualties. On 27 January 1900 two scouts were killed and one was wounded near Eerste Fabricken, and Lieutenant Ryan and a machine gun were captured. Ryan was soon released. On February 4 another scout was killed and three were wounded near Maraisburg. A week later two more were wounded.

In early February French sent a party made up of Callaghan, Jefferson Davis, and another scout to carry an urgent despatch to Smith-Dorrien. The distance to be covered could not have been less than 40 miles as the Aasvogel flies. The country was alive with Boers, and the party split up after burying the despatch. A party of Boers captured Davis, but he shot his way out with his revolver. Callaghan retrieved the despatch and arrived at Smith-Dorrien's camp just as a large force of Boers attacked. After the British beat off the attack, Callaghan rode into camp and coolly presented the despatch to Smith-Dorrien. He reported that a Boer had been eyeing him suspiciously during the battle. He added that, since dead men tell no tales, a rifle bullet took care of that problem. Several sources mention the exploit, one adding exasperatingly that he did not have time to record the details, but it was "wonderfully exciting."[10]

By mid-February Alderson had reached Derby, close to the Swaziland border. Other columns were eight to ten miles to the north and south. The British were slowly closing the trap. On the 17th a strong force rode east to round up 200 to 300 Boers trapped in the hills with their wagons. The force consisted of parts of the two mounted infantry battalions, four guns of J Battery Royal Horse Artillery, and the Canadian Scouts. Gat Howard, who had turned 55 the day before, commanded the force.

Howard's force was not alone. Alderson sent out another force under Captain Dick of the 13th MI. He led two guns of J Battery, 100 men each from the 13th MI and the KOYLI, and 20 men and two Colt guns from the scouts. His task was to maintain contact with Campbell and Smith-Dorrien operating to the north. The country was very difficult, with hills, valleys, and deep gorges. To make things worse, a cold drizzle was falling and mist was everywhere. The force moved off at 8:30 and rode eight miles to the east, then halted in the hills. Progress had been slow because of the country and weather. Under good conditions the column could have made no more than four miles per hour. At two miles per hour, a more realistic speed under the conditions, the column could not have covered eight miles before 12:30, and it must have been later before the rearguard closed up. The halt was probably to allow patrols to search out the enemy. At 3:00 p.m. the scouts rode off at a trot followed by a MI company in support. What happened next is unclear. Lieutenant Moeller of the 14th MI heard firing as he rode forward to join a party of scouts lining a rocky ridge. From the ridge he could see a huge bush-covered kopje across the valley. Four wagons were at the foot of the kopje. Riding forward he discovered the bodies of Gat Howard, Sergeant Richard Northway, and a native scout. Alderson's ADC was actually the first on the scene. He had a narrow escape himself when the Boers opened fire at him at 200 to 300 yards' range and killed his horse.

There is evidence the Boers had captured and then shot the three men. The Boers often would kill everyone in any party that included armed natives. Charlie Ross and most of the scouts believed this was the case and vowed to take no prisoners. However, there were no witnesses. The Boers had opened fire at point-blank range. From what we know of the man, it does not seem likely that Gat surrendered. His wounds in the arm, stomach, and jaw were not consistent with an execution. Northway had wounds from dum-dum bullets in his belly and back. Possibly the Canadians made a fight for it, and lost. Two more Canadians were wounded the same day, and one later died.[11]

What had happened? It was late in the day and would soon be dark. Gat must have decided to capture the wagons without waiting for support. Howard would not order his troops to do something he would not do himself, and his men knew it. If he had waited, troops could have advanced and flanked the wagons supported by a machine-gun. This would have sprung the trap, and the result might have been different. Perhaps it merely postponed the inevitable. Gat lived and fought on the edge. His loss was keenly felt and was lamented in several accounts at the time. If he had a fault it was his combination of almost boundless self confidence and desire to fight, preferably at close quarters. He had had a number of close calls as machine-gun officer with the RCD. If he had been present at Leliefontein, the casualty roll would probably have included one more name.

When the initial six months' enlistment period ended, many of the men returned to Canada. After a recruiting drive and some training the unit soon was back in the field again. The Canadian Scouts were now more Canadian in name than in composition. The British had decided that a corps of sergeants was a needless expense, and the rank and file were paid as troopers, not sergeants. The unit evolved into an irregular mounted corps of four squadrons, a machine-gun battery, a troop of native scouts, and a transport column, about 350 colonials and 125 native scouts and drivers in all. In September 1901 William Hare Jr., an ex-member of D Battery, had arrived in Cape Town as a wrangler with a ship load of Canadian horses. He enlisted in the Scouts and served with the unit for the rest of the war, eventually becoming the regimental quartermaster sergeant. Despite his experience at Leliefontein, Hare felt he saw more action with the Scouts than he did in the second contingent. He was not alone in holding this belief. In 1956 he noted that the Canadian Scouts were no more than 10 to 15 percent Canadian. The unit included Americans, Australians and Cape Boers, among others. The key officers were still Canadian, although a few British officers were able to meet Ross's standards. One of these was Captain Hugh Trenchard, who later would command the Royal Flying Corps and then the Royal Air Force.

The Scouts served under Rimington's command from July 1901 to the end of the war. Rimington, a British regular officer, was probably the best commander of irregular troops in the war. In early 1902 Ross left the Scouts, perhaps because of a scandal that may have involved cattle rustling. Alexander MacMillan replaced him and commanded the Scouts until the war's end. The unit's last recorded casualties were in May 1902. There was one last chore. Richard Turner VC, DSO, commanded the official Canadian contingent in King Edward's delayed coronation parade. His party were all veterans of the Canadian contingents except for one of the Burkholder brothers mentioned above. In the same parade MacMillan led a troop of hard-bitten Canadian Scouts.[12]

Chapter

15 The Third and Fourth Contingents

IN LATE 1900 and early 1901, with the war seemingly won, the main Canadian effort was devoted to recruiting for the South African Constabulary. However, in early 1901 the Canadian government had also raised the possibility of providing another contingent. The British procrastinated and then, in July, replied there was no further need of troops. Individuals continued to sail to South Africa to enlist, and influential citizens continued to urge the government to raise a third contingent. Among the more vocal was Major William Merritt of the Governor General's Body Guard, who had served in Brabant's Horse. He had pressed for authority to raise a corps of Canadian Rangers even before his return to Canada. Merritt, a staunch Conservative, remained a constant irritant to the government.

In November 1901 the British government reversed its position and requested another contingent, this time a corps of Canadian Yeomanry. The unit would be over 600 strong organized as a four-squadron regiment of Imperial Yeomanry. In a sharp departure from earlier practice, it would be recruited as part of the British army, but would be visibly Canadian. Furthermore, the British would pay all the bills while the Department of Militia and Defence raised, equipped and trained the unit. It was the answer to a Canadian politician's dream.

The dubious title Canadian Yeomanry was soon changed to the 2nd Regiment Canadian Mounted Rifles (2 CMR). This not only built on the achievements of the second contingent, but also had links with the mounted rifles squadrons authorized in June 1901. The response from the public for recruits was enthusiastic and would have been so even without the change. When the government realized there would be surplus space on the troopships, it offered to raise two more squadrons. After all, this could be done at no cost to the national treasury, and the government would reap the political benefit. The offer was gratefully accepted, and the men easily recruited. The result was a six-squadron regiment of 901 officers and men. The squadrons were slightly smaller than the second contingent's and led by a captain instead of a major, with four 32-man troops each commanded by a lieutenant. However, 2 CMR nearly matched the combined fighting strength of the RCD, CMR, and Strathconas. Altogether the three units had fielded seven squadrons, only one more than 2 CMR.

There was only one choice for commanding officer. Sam Steele had been seconded to the South African Constabulary. There were disturbing questions about Lessard's performance. Otter had been promoted. Drury was competent, but untried as a commander of mounted troops. Lieutenant Colonel T.D.B. Evans had commanded the CMR with distinction and was considered to be the best Canadian mounted officer. He was allowed a free hand in the selection of his officers, with one exception. Borden persuaded Evans to accept Merritt as his second in command, ostensibly to recognize his efforts in support of the war. Most of the officers had previous South African service, many in the ranks. With the exception of Merritt, competence, not connections, was the overriding principle. The officers included proven veterans such as Major G.W. Cameron, Frank Church (the ex-RSM of the CMR), Captain

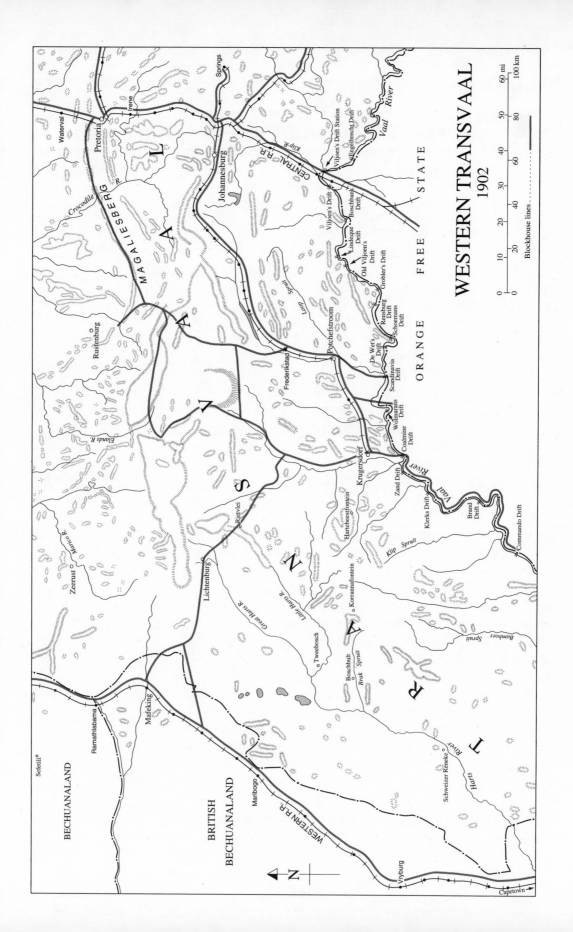

WESTERN TRANSVAAL
1902

Blockhouse lines ....

J.H. Elmsley (fully recovered from his near-fatal wound suffered at Leliefontein), and Surgeon-Majors Devine and Duff. The lieutenants included Bruce Carruthers, the ex-RCR signals sergeant, C.R. Tryon, commissioned by Evans in the field in the CMR, the formidable "Casey" Callaghan, and R.H. Ryan, who had led the RCD scouts.

The roster of the men was almost as impressive. A quarter had previous service in South Africa, most with Canadian units. These included SSM Michael Docherty, Corporal Bill Warren and Private C.K. Rorison from 2 RCR, and Corporals Albert Hilder and William Knisley, DCM, two Leliefontein veterans. A less-certain quantity, but one who passed Evans's scrutiny was Sergeant D.C.F. Bliss, who had had problems as an officer in the second contingent. Events would prove that any failings as an officer, real or imagined, did not include a lack of courage.

The unit's equipment was standard British army with one exception - the distinctive Stetson hat was retained. Pay had been a sore point, especially in the first contingent. The third contingent would be paid at the Imperial Yeomanry rate, $1.24 a day for a private against fifty cents a day in the first contingent. Against this was balanced the terms of service—twelve months or the duration of the war. This eliminated a major difficulty the Imperial authorities had experienced with previous contingents. The one-year enlistment combined with time spent training and on board ship had limited campaigning to nine months for the RCR, CMR, and D and E Batteries; seven months for the RCD and C Battery; and a bit over six months for the Strathconas.[1]

There was another component of the third contingent that has received less attention than it merited, the 10th Canadian Field Hospital (10 CFH). The minister, of course, was a medical doctor and had already formed the Army Medical Corps of six bearer companies and six field hospitals. It was a logical step for him to provide a field hospital to support 2 CMR. The commanding officer was Lieutenant Colonel A.N. Worthington, who had been mentioned in despatches for his service at Faber's Put in May 1900. With his appointment, all three unit medical officers of the second contingent returned for a second tour in South Africa.[2]

The unit was small, numbering only 61 all ranks and 29 horses. It was organized into a Hospital Staff of five officers, a Ward Section of 35 other ranks, and a Transport Section of 21 other ranks to pick up and transport the wounded. The hospital could hold patients for short periods, the more seriously sick and wounded being evacuated to a static establishment. The hospital was based on British practice, with a veneer of Canadian innovations. These included the Hubert tent, ambulances based on light transport wagons, unique water carts, and an acetylene gas lighting system. Like 2 CMR, the unit included many veterans. A number of qualified doctors and even a dentist served in its ranks. Recruiting began on 3 January 1900 and the recruits moved to Halifax on the 11th. The two weeks before embarkation were "devoted to the distribution of clothing and equipment; drill (stretcher and company) and tent pitching."[3]

As was the case with the other contingents, nurses were selected to serve with the third contingent. After some negotiation, the quota of five was raised to eight. The nurses, including four on their second tour, sailed to South Africa via London. They arrived at Cape Town on 2 March 1902, and then proceeded to Durban on a hospital ship. For 12 weeks, until the end of the war, they provided the nursing staff of Number 19 Stationary Hospital at Harrismith in the

ORC. After the ceasefire they returned to Durban and sailed home with the returning 10th Canadian Field Hospital.

The CMR spent about a month in Halifax organizing and training, although weather and a lack of equipment limited the training. Potentially more serious, several cases of measles appeared, resulting in 14 men being left behind in hospital. The unit sailed to South Africa in two lifts. First, the unit's eastern or left wing of D, E, and F squadrons and 4th Troop of A squadron along with 513 horses sailed on the SS *Manhattan* for Cape Town on 14 January. The voyage was not a happy one. While the weather was generally pleasant once out of northern climes, there were problems caused by inactivty and indiscipline. The voyage was unusually long, including a diversion to Durban caused by the appearance of a Boer commando within 40 miles of Cape Town. By the time the right wing docked, the deplorable state of the unit caused concern to the British. The blame belongs at the top—Merritt had been too concerned with his own popularity to impose the strict regime needed.

The remainder of the regiment and the field hospital along with 486 horses left Halifax on 28 January on board the SS *Victorian*. Under the capable hand of Evans, a routine that included care of the horses, drill, and weapons training occupied the time on board. While only ten cases had plagued the *Manhattan*, a mild epidemic of measles swept through the mess decks of the *Victorian*. In addition, four cases of the mild form of smallpox "prevalent throughout Canada at the time" were discovered. The sick men were quarantined, and the disease contained. It was fortunate that the smallpox was not more virulent. The (limited) supply of vaccine was marked "good only until January 28," the day the ship sailed. Twenty-two horses expired from various causes and were swung over the side to bob in the wake.[4]

On arrival at Cape Town on 21 February, the medical landing officer quickly ordered all ranks revaccinated. The smallpox cases were removed to quarantine and the other sick to Woodstock Hospital. The ship then sailed for Durban, arriving on the 24th. The next day the two units disembarked and entrained for Newcastle, about midway between Ladysmith and Standerton, where Merritt's contingent awaited their arrival. The two-day trip through the rolling hills of Natal was a new experience for all but the veterans of the Strathconas, who had made the trip 19 months before. The heat was intense and the horses, carried in iron-floored box cars and unfit after the sea voyage, suffered accordingly. The left wing was quartered close to town, while the right wing and the hospital, both still under quarantine, were isolated at Fort McCready for two weeks. The left wing, which was not under quarantine, blocked Botha's Pass through the Drakensberg during a drive and furnished convoy escorts. The isolated right wing could only prepare defences and man outposts around its camp, which was vulnerable to a surprise attack.[5]

Both the regiment and the field hospital were passed for service on 1 March by Lord Kitchener, the commander-in-chief. He was followed by Lieutenant General Lyttelton, who commanded in Natal, on the 6th and Major General Walter Kitchener on the 10th. The quarantine was lifted on the 8th, and on the 14th orders came to move to Klerksdorp, southwest of Johannesburg.

Events at Newcastle had weakened the relationship between Merritt and Evans. Merritt, in his semi-independent status, was indecisive and inconsistent. Worse, he had kept alive his dream of commanding his Canadian Rangers. At Newcastle he pressed the British to split the regiment into two smaller units, one to be renamed the Canadian Rangers and commanded by him. Fate intervened to forestall a confrontation. On 12 February Merritt was thrown from a mule and injured. Evans wasted no time in appointing his other field officer, Major George Cameron, who had won the DSO with the Strathconas, to command the left wing. When Merritt returned to duty, he was given command of a details camp at Klerksdorp. To his credit he accepted his fate like a soldier and carried out his lacklustre duties in an entirely satisfactory manner.

The war had changed dramatically. While commandos still ranged the country and even raided within 40 miles of Cape Town, the end was near. In March of 1902, less than 25 000 Boers remained in the field. These were the hard core of the resistance, the "bitter enders," proud warriors in the tradition of the Old Testament. They were reduced to the bare essentials, without artillery or the large convoys that had accompanied the commandos in the early days of the war. More than 30 000 of their comrades languished in prison camps in faraway places like St Helena, Bermuda, and Ceylon. Others had pledged allegiance to the Crown, while some had taken to the field in the British service. Meanwhile, their families sickened and died in the vile concentration camps that housed the people cleared from the veldt to deny the burghers supplies and intelligence.[6]

The drives of early 1901 had failed because the Boers still had free passage through the country. By mid-1901 small forts had sprung up along the railways about one and a half miles apart. Kitchener realized that blockhouses, in sufficient density, could neutralize the Boers' mobility. The engineers were soon erecting lines of prefabricated blockhouses, first along the Modder near Bloemfontein to the railway south of Kimberley and from Groot Olifant's River on the eastern line south across the veldt to Vaal Station on the Natal railway. By war's end more than 40 blockhouse lines, with 8000 posts garrisoned by 50 000 men, snaked across the veldt or followed the railways in the Cape Colony, Transvaal, and Orange River Colony. Each blockhouse was manned by an NCO and a few men aided by one or two native scouts. In important areas blockhouses were perhaps half a mile apart, elsewhere the interval was a mile or more. Posts were linked by a barbed-wire fence, which was being improved into an entanglement several rows thick and hung with alarms and flares. This major engineering feat was well advanced when 2 CMR rode into the Transvaal in March 1902.[7]

On first glance, the scheme seems to be a retrograde step that tied infantry to lines of tiny forts. De Wet called it a "blockhead" system, although he was prone to selective interpretation of the facts. However, mounted troops were now free to pursue the burghers, instead of patrolling the tracks. The army had about 150 000 troops in the field, with 70 000 manning blockhouses and garrisoning towns. The bulk of the remainder were mounted, pursuing Boers. The number of regular mounted infantry battalions had more than quadrupled since 1900, while the artillery had formed a number of very effective mounted rifle corps. There still were major gaps in the network of blockhouses. Key among these was the desert-like western Transvaal, an area half the size of New Brunswick. Here General Koos de la Rey with 3000 Boers had thrashed two pursuing columns and captured Lieutenant General Lord Methuen early in 1902.

Kitchener ordered a massive drive by thirteen columns, 16 000 troops in all, to catch de la Rey. The Canadians were allotted to the column commanded by Brevet Lieutenant Colonel George A. Cookson, 16th Bengal Lancers, in Walter Kitchener's division. Following two days' march and a further two days' travel by train, 2 CMR joined Cookson in sleepy Klerksdorp. Other units in Cookson's column included the 30th, 31st, and 93rd Companies, Imperial Yeomanry; Damant's Horse, an irregular unit 300 strong; two pom-poms; and two field guns. The challenge was, now that the troops had been concentrated, to use them effectively.[8]

The field hospital had accompanied their comrades on the journey to the western Transvaal, reflecting Lord Kitchener's promise that the unit would "accompany the Canadian troops in their South African operations." At Klerksdorp, the hospital was split. Worthington detailed his second in command, Major G. Carleton Jones, to lead the 17 man left section with Cookson's column, while the rest of the unit remained in situ. On 26 March, in response to a request from Brevet Colonel Robert Kekewich, another column commander, the reduced 10 CFH was ordered to Vaalbank, 40 miles away on the Lichtenberg blockhouse line. Here the unit received sick and wounded from the columns operating in the area. The hospital remained at Vaalbank until 18 June. In that time Worthington and his men treated over 1000 patients until they were returned to duty, evacuated by 10 CFH ambulance to Klerksdorp, or buried. The record is silent on the number in the last category, but the unit spent 13 June "decorating the graves of those who died in hospital (British, Boers and Natives)."[9]

In the third week of March intelligence reported that large numbers of Boers were within 30 miles of the Schoon Spruit blockhouse line that ran north from the Vaal through Klerksdorp to the Lichtenberg blockhouse line. Kitchener ordered the four columns, by a night march of 40 miles, to pass undetected to the west of the Boers. Once in position the whole force would turn east, deploy in driving formation over an arc of 90 miles and drive back to the Schoon Spruit line.[10]

Cookson's column moved off at 6:30 p.m. on 23 March, travelling without wagons or ambulances. The men left their greatcoats behind and carried only a half ration of army biscuit and tinned meat. They did, however, carry 180 rounds of ammunition per man and six pounds of oats for each horse. Visibility was generally good under a moonlight sky, and the column was able to maintain a fast trot and even a gallop at times over the undulating, bush-covered country. A number of horses came to grief in the animal burrows that dotted the ground, and others were too weak to maintain the pace. No attempt was made to pick up either men or horses. Stragglers were on their own.[11]

By 3:00 a.m. the column had reached its first objective—the ridge at Witpoort, 45 miles away. Cookson deployed Damant's Horse on the north half of the ridge while Evans, with the CMR right wing, occupied a line two-and-a-half miles in length along the rocky ridge. Cameron, with the left wing, some reinforcing mounted infantry, and the yeomanry, was held in reserve along the main road that crossed the ridge. By 4:30 the deployment was complete and at 5:00 on the 26th the eastward movement began.

There was contact on the extreme right of the line even before the advance started. Captain R.G.E. Leckie, commanding A Squadron, had deployed his four troops in line, about 300 yards apart while Casey Callaghan and his scouts took up position to the south of Lieutenant Tryon's first troop. In the darkness the column had very nearly ridden into a laager on the west side of the ridge. In the half light neither side could be sure of the situation, but the Boers prepared to withdraw to the east ahead of the drive. Meanwhile, Callaghan had sent word back along the Canadian line that enemy were in the area. Within minutes the CMR scouts, with a surprised Boer prisoner, dropped back, picking up First and then Second Troop, and took up a position on both sides of a track. A scout and the prisoner had just reported to Captain Leckie when three Boers rode into the Canadian ambush. The burst of firing killed two and drove the third into the cover of some bushes. Callaghan and his men cautiously moved forward to examine the bodies. Hearing sounds in the bushes, they opened fire, severely wounding the third. The scouts and the two CMR troops then retired with the wounded man to a position behind Third Troop.

It was apparent to Evans that the enemy party was not large. A Squadron, temporarily supported by two troops of B Squadron, could deal with the enemy, while C Squadron with the remainder of B extended across the front. As the advance got under way, Leckie observed a wagon train moving in a southeasterly direction across the south side of the kopje, while more Boers were in-spanning on the west side of the hill. It was a tempting target, but Leckie felt that the object was to trap the main body of Boers, not chase small parties. The squadron commander ordered his men to mount and move into extended line with two troops forward and two in support on the extreme right of Cookson's line.[12]

The general advance trotted into the rising sun for about seven miles. At about 7:00 a.m. Callaghan and his scouts caught up to a wagon train escorted by a party of the enemy. After an exchange of fire the Canadians captured a wounded man, six wagons, two cape carts, and 100 cattle. The advance continued for the rest of the day, with generally indifferent results. In all 2 CMR had killed two enemy and wounded two, and had taken three prisoners, six wagons with their oxen, three cape carts, 100 cattle, and six ponies. Canadian casualties were one man wounded and 22 missing, although all the latter rejoined within two days. When the advance finally halted at 5:30, the men had ridden 85 miles in 23 hours. It was a far cry from 1900, when Roberts' army was hard pressed to manage more than 10 miles a day.[13]

The British had been unable to reach the blockhouse line in one day and were equally unable to form a continuous line before nightfall. A large party of Boers were trapped in a desperate situation only a few miles from Cookson. When their scouts reported wide gaps in the cordon, the Boers slipped through the gaps and rode west to concentrate on the Harts River. The results were disappointing; eight enemy killed, 165 prisoners, and three guns and two pom-poms captured. The failure was one of execution, not planning, and can be attributed to the inexperience of three of the column commanders—Kekewich, Walter Kitchener and Rochfort—in the coordination of the movement of large bodies of troops. Less important given the circumstances, no one short of the commander-in-chief, who was notorious for refusing to delegate, was in charge.[14]

It had been a useful introduction to operations for 2 CMR. Evans could be generally satisfied with his regiment's performance, even if there had been little actual contact with the enemy. The Canadian share of the bag was respectable, although it might have been greater if Cookson, Evans or even Leckie had decided to pursue the convoy. There was, after all, a substantial reserve available to provide troops to either ride after the Boers or replace A Squadron in the line.

Shortly after the end of the drive, Kitchener's column returned to Klerksdorp. The next few days were spent recovering from the ordeal of the hard forced march. It seemed all but certain that, with the Boers driven from the eastern end of the region, the army would next move west towards Vryburg. Waiting for them in laagers on the Harts River were 2500 burghers, the largest concentration of enemy in the area for more than a year.

Lord Kitchener conferred with his four commanders on 26 March at Klerksdorp. The intelligence was worse than sketchy—it was contradictory. One report put the Boers at Barber's Pan, while others placed them farther south and east. Kitchener's plan reflected the uncertainty. Rochfort was to hold the line of the Vaal while the others marched westwards in succession. First, Kekewich, on the 28th was to march from Vaalbank to Middlebut, near the source of the Little Harts River. Next, Walter Kitchener was to move to Driekuil, close to the source of Brak Spruit. Last, on the 31st, Rawlinson was to proceed to Rhenoster Spruit, 16 miles west of Klerksdorp. All three columns were to build entrenched camps to support further operations.

Kitchener marched on the 29th, stopping for the night at Hartebeestfontein. By the 30th Kekewich had scoured the bush around Middlebut and found nothing. That day Kitchener arrived at Rietvlei and decided to search out the enemy, while still building the fortified camp at Driekuil. He decided to proceed to the latter place with Lowe's column on the 31st. Cookson, meanwhile, with a combined column of 1800 mounted men, would reconnoitre for 40 miles along the practically dry Brak Spruit to its junction with the Great Harts River. The main elements of the column were 2 CMR, Damant's Horse, RHA Mounted Rifles, 28th MI, Kitchener's Fighting Scouts, two weak yeomanry companies, four guns of 78th Battery, and two pom-poms. The Boers were known to have concentrated in strength. Despite this, Kitchener split his column and sent part of it deep into enemy territory without the prospect of immediate reinforcement. It was a reversion to the failed tactics that invited defeat in detail.[15]

Cookson started on his reconnaissance at 2:00 a.m., the men carrying two days' rations with supplies for another day in the transport wagons. The advance guard was made up of Damant's Horse reinforced by the 2 CMR scouts. Major Cameron and the CMR left wing escorted the transport. The remainder, the equivalent of four or five mounted battalions, made up the main body. By 3:00 a.m. the column was well on its way through the rolling, dusty scrubland.[16]

Callaghan and his scouts were working well to the front and right of the column. At about 10:00 a.m. two scouts on the right flank struck the fresh trail of "about 500 men and two guns" near an isolated farm. The tracks ran away to the west of north, generally towards where the Harts River meandered southwards from its junction with the Little Harts River. By the condition of the tracks, and the presence of a dust cloud hanging low in the sky, the enemy were only a few miles ahead. Cookson decided to change direction and pursue the Boers. He ordered Evans to wait for Cameron and the transport and bring the convoy up in one body as quickly as possible. Meanwhile he launched his main body in pursuit, with Damant's Horse leading. The odds looked good. Even without 2 CMR, Cookson had 1500 riders, four guns, and two pom-poms to reinforce Damant. Sixty men of the advance guard soon caught up to Callaghan and his men and continued at a gallop after the guns. The trail followed the nearly dry bed of the Brak Spruit towards its junction with the Harts River. The advance guard had ridden no more than three miles when it rode into an ambush. A strong Boer rearguard was hidden in the bush near a farmhouse, extending left and right across the trail. In a few minutes the advance guard lost two killed and nine wounded, as well as fifteen horses killed. When the British main body appeared, the Boers fell back to join a large number of Boers on the gently rising ground on both sides of the spruit near a farm called Boschbult.[17]

Cookson had advanced more than 30 miles since leaving camp at 2:00 a.m. on 31 March, the last few in contact with the enemy. In the few hours since his presence had been discovered, the Boers had been able to concentrate 2000 burghers to join the small body Cookson was pursuing. Suddenly, Cookson was faced by a superior force holding the high ground and enjoying the advantage of cover. He resolved to hold his ground around the farm and the water in pools in the river bed. In truth, he had little choice. The British stood a better chance defending the farm than trying to hold off commandos in a running fight. Walter Kitchener was no closer than Driekuil, 20 miles to the east. If Cookson sent a galloper for help now, and the rider got through, help could not arrive before dark. The first priority was to hold the Boers off until defences could be prepared. The RHA Mounted Rifles and Kitchener's Fighting Scouts under Lieutenant Colonel J.L. Keir were sent to hold the rising ground on the left. Damant with his own unit, the 28th MI, and the Yeomanry protected the front and right. Cookson had thrown his screen far enough out to keep the Boers from shelling the farm. However, the Boers could potentially achieve local superiority and drive in the screen anywhere they chose. The balance shifted back towards the British at about noon, when Evans and the convoy arrived. In the dry scrubland, the sight of a line of horsemen advancing in front of a long, wide dust cloud through which other riders were visible was sufficient to deter the Boers until the wagons entered the British perimeter.[18]

With the arrival of 2 CMR and the convoy operations entered a new phase. The wagons were laagered and wired together, while the Canadians began to prepare defences. The horses and mules were piqueted in the cover of the dry river bed. Cookson pulled Keir's force back closer to camp and sent 200 RHA Mounted Rifles with a pom-pom to hold a farmhouse about 600 yards east of Boschbult. In the north the Yeomanry and most of Damant's Horse pulled back to camp, while 28th MI and a company of Damant's men formed a reduced screen. Lieutenant Bruce Carruthers with two troops of E Squadron, 2 CMR, who had formed the rearguard of the convoy escort, halted northeast of the farm. Carruthers had realized that the two troops could usefully block an open flank here. He sent a rider to camp to report and, with his orders confirmed, kept 20 men with him, while sending Sergeant Hodgins with a smaller number a few hundred yards to his right.[19]

In the early afternoon (the time is variously reported as 1:20 or 2:00 p.m.), the Boers began to shell the camp using four of the guns and a pom-pom captured in February, while riflemen on the surrounding ridges opened plunging rifle fire on the wagons and the milling animals. Two Canadians, Privates Harry Ballard and Alex Smith, wrote that the firing started before the rearguard had arrived in camp. Without trenches or other fortifications, both men and animals were hit from all sides, causing panic among the animals and their civilian drivers and impeding the digging of trenches. Some of the drivers fled back along the trail to the east. Over the next few hours the Boers attacked the camp several times, repeating the mounted charge used at Leliefontein.

At about 3:30 Cookson ordered the screen on the north to pull back into the camp. This screen seems to have consisted of, from west to east, two companies of 28th MI, the squadron of Damant's Horse, a company plus of MI, Carruthers's men, and part of a company of MI. (Carruthers had moved his men to the east to plug a gap in the line.) As soon as movement was detected, the Boers advanced in strength from the north. In the centre and west the retirement went well, and the screen held off the Boers. In the east, the MI broke and ran for their lives. Evans called it a stampede. Some rode through the Canadian lines, causing a few men to join in until they were checked by Lieutenant Carruthers and Sergeant Hodgins.[20]

The Boers now turned their attention to the CMR detachment. What followed is rarely seen in real life-a fight to the end against overwhelming odds. The 21 Canadians lay prone in the grass and fought for their lives. Before their ammunition was exhausted and their position overrun, 17 were killed or wounded. The Boers marched the survivors off for about two miles and then stripped them, taking their clothing and equipment. Evans was moved to write:

The splendid stand made by Lieut. Carruthers's party without cover of any kind, and against overwhelming odds, was well worthy of the best traditions of Canada and the whole Empire."

Evans went on to feature the conduct of:

Sergt. Perry, although badly wounded, fought until he was killed. Corporal Wilkinson, shot twice through the arm and body, continued fighting until he was shot through the eye. He then threw the bolt of his rifle into the long grass to render it useless to the enemy. Private Evans, although mortally wounded through the bowels, exhausted his ammunition, secured another bandolier, used it up, and, as the Boers were making their final rush, he broke his rifle rendering it useless. Private Evans died shortly after being brought into camp. Private Minchin, although wounded in six places, fired his last shot when the Boers were only 25 yards off, and threw his bolt into the grass.

At 5:00 the Boer fire suddenly slackened and then ceased. *The Times History* suggested that de la Rey had arrived shortly before and ordered a halt to the attacks. Certainly, to persist in assaults against an entrenched camp was against Boer military practice. From the Boer point of view they had been repulsed nearly everywhere. The only success had been achieved against the "stampeded" MI, chasing from the field those they had not killed or captured. However, this had been followed by the attack on Carruthers's men, which must have impressed the Boers, who rarely stood and fought. The only logical course was to wait for easier game. The besieged column had little respite, however. All ranks set to digging trenches, setting trip wires, and preparing for a night attack. Three men, including Sergeant Lee of A Squadron, attempted to make their way through enemy country to Kitchener's column but were driven back after encountering a large party of enemy. After an anxious night, some enemy appeared on the surrounding ridges in the morning but soon withdrew again.[21]

At 11:00 a.m. on 1 April, in a heavy downpour, Evans read the burial service over the Canadian dead. Their graves were marked with crosses and a common memorial, surmounted by a Maple Leaf, inscribed "To the memory of the Canadian Mounted Rifles who fell in action here on March 31." It was not until 12:30 p.m. (*The Times History* says 1:00 p.m.) that relief arrived from Kitchener's camp 20 miles away at Driekuil. The tardy relief of the column was noted obliquely by Evans, who remarked, "A peculiar circumstance in this engagement was that the party of Mounted Infantry referred to as stampeding made its way to Driekil, [sic] where General Kitchener had made his camp—a distance of 20 miles—and reported to him that our camp had been cut up and captured."[22]

Kitchener's column had reached Driekuil in the morning and begun to prepare a permanent camp. Cookson had sent a number of messengers back with reports that his column had encountered the enemy. None got through. In the afternoon the sound of distant guns alerted Kitchener to Cookson's plight. Kitchener with Lowe's column of 1000 mounted troops and three guns set out to investigate. At Doornlaagte, one-third of the way to Boschbult, the relief column encountered the first fugitives—some drivers and MI—who insisted that Cookson had been overwhelmed. This could not have been before 3:30 at the earliest. During the afternoon more and more fugitives arrived, having a cumulative effect on the commander-in-chief's brother. When the firing ceased, at about 5:00 p.m., he decided that Cookson had indeed been defeated and it was prudent to return to Driekuil. Back in camp he wired to headquarters that Cookson's force was destroyed. He then requested that Rawlinson, who had marched to Rhenoster Spruit that day, come to his assistance. On reflection, he must have decided to investigate further, or a messenger from Cookson had arrived, for he led a relief column forward the next morning, which arrived just after midday.[23]

The battle had been a British defeat. There had been little time to finish trenches before the first attacks, which accounted in part for the relatively high casualties, 33 killed or mortally wounded, 126 wounded, and over 70 missing. Included in this total were 11 Canadians killed or died of wounds, 43 (including one from 10 CFH) wounded, and seven missing. Boschbult or Harts River, as it is known in Canada, was, second only to the first day of Paardeberg, the bloodiest day of the war for Canada. Boer casualties were lighter, although the number was never established. The mobility of the column was seriously impaired by the loss of more than 400 horses and mules. Evans reported Canadian losses as 121 horses and 22 mules. More important than the losses, which could be easily replaced, the British design to clear the western Transvaal was stalemated. There was a positive result, however. General Sir Ian Hamilton, who had been Kitchener's chief of staff for the past 17 months, was placed in charge of operations in the area.[24]

It is difficult to see any merit in the conduct of the battle by either side, other than the characteristic doggedness of the British (and Canadian) soldier. Cookson managed to place most of his troops and his transport in a shooting gallery. The casualties were the result of tactics more fitted to Black Week than to guerilla warfare. As for the Boers, rather than exploiting their superior position, they ventured out to mount wild charge after charge. That their casualties were not higher was the result of poor marksmanship on the part of the defenders. Against this, the Canadians had earned their rightful place in the troops that made up the mobile columns, the elite of the army. This place did not come automatically to mounted troops, as evidenced by the conspicuous absence of regular cavalry from the columns.

It was not until a few days later that the Canadians learned the fate of six of their missing comrades. Corporal Knisley, who had won a DCM at Leliefontein, and Privates Brace, Cline, Day, Minett, and McCall had been cut off in the fighting that saw Carruthers and his men overwhelmed. Seeing that they could not reach the camp, they decided to make their way back to Klerksdorp. After nightfall they cautiously rode east through the night, pausing only to rest their horses and eat the last of their rations. The next day, 1 April, the six tired and wet men continued their ride, successfully beating off an attack by four armed Boers. After dark they broke contact and rode on through persistent rain until exhaustion forced them to rest. The morning would see Boers hot on their trail. After dawn Knisley led his men onto a stony kopje where they built a hasty sangar in the rocks. Soon a party of 50 Boers appeared, following their trail. The Canadians fought for five hours. By then the Boers had closed in to 200 yards, bullets rained down on the kopje top, ammunition was short, and Knisley and Day were dead. The four survivors surrendered. The Boers joined them in a burial service for their dead comrades, and, after stripping them to their underclothes, turned the barefooted men loose. It took two days and rainy nights for the four to walk 60 miles to Klerksdorp. They finally arrived on the 4th, hungry, sore, and with blistered feet. The gallantry of their stand was small consolation for the death of two more Canadians. Evans wrote that "Corporal Knisley's party was composed of several of the best men in the regiment, and he personally had made a splendid record while out in South Africa with the Royal Canadian Dragoons previously; and his death, as well as that of Private Day, is a distinct loss to the regiment."[25]

After returning to Driekuil, the column rested and refitted. During April and May the Canadians took part in a series of drives. While Kitchener's division took part in the drive that commenced on 10 April and saw 127 Boer casualties in an abortive attempt to break through the British line, they played only a supporting role. Next, the British mounted drives to clear the country back to Klerksdorp of the enemy. The tactics were simple, although a great deal depended upon planning and coordination. The drive of 14 April, which covered 37 miles, saw the three columns stretching across 15 miles. The Canadians, with five squadrons in line and one in support, covered a frontage of three miles. The result, about 100 Boers captured, was satisfying. Of the total, 2 CMR had captured 13, nine falling to Lieutenant Ryan's troop.[26]

One of the last major operations of the war, a drive to Vryburg by 10 000 troops, kicked off on 5 May. The Canadians first rode to Kurannafontein, a short distance east of Driekuil. While waiting for the drive to commence, the 2 CMR scouts picked up two prisoners, their cape cart, four horses, and two mules. On 7 May the columns formed into a long line and the formal drive was underway. Private Smith's estimate of a line 190 miles long is exaggerated, but the actual length must have been close to half of that. Groups of Boers could be seen to the front, moving west ahead of the drive. As the long khaki line slowly rode east unopposed, the heat and lack of water became the major enemy. Private Smith wrote, "There was two days wee [sic] were without water exsept [sic] a cup of tea at night and morning / our horses suffered the most as they did not get a drop a lot died [sic]." The line contracted as the flanks of the line squeezed in to the centre, the interval between men being reduced from 25 to 10 yards. While few Boers were picked up during the early stages, 2 CMR collected several hundred head of livestock. The drive ended on the afternoon of 11 May when the line reached Vryburg. Once again the results were satisfying, if not spectacular. One Boer had been killed and 354 captured along with more than 17 000 animals. The writing was on the wall. In six weeks 20 percent of the Boers in the western Transvaal had been taken out of the war.[27]

The regiment was back in Klerksdorp on the 23rd, where, on 31 May, word was received of the end of the war. There was a postscript. Lieutenant Ryan and 25 men, as well as Corporal MacDonald from 10 CFH, formed part of General Walter Kitchener's escort of Imperial, Canadian, Australian and New Zealand troops as he rode through Boer territory, accepting the surrender of commandos. Within weeks of the ceasefire, the third contingent was on its way back to Canada.

The story of Canadian participation was not over. The Canadian government, ambivalent as ever, grudgingly accepted a proposal from the Imperial government to provide 2000 troops. The contingent was recruited in April 1902 and organized into four regiments of Canadian Mounted Rifles, numbered 3rd through 6th. Each regiment had 26 officers, 483 men and 539 horses organized into a headquarters and four squadrons. The fourth contingent fielded 16 squadrons, three more than the other Canadian contingents combined. Unfortunately, the only Canadian mounted units except for the Strathconas that were sensibly organized arrived too late to take part in the war. As each ship arrived in turn, the Canadians found that the war was over and they were to be returned to Canada as soon as possible. It was a sad ending to the saga of the Canadians in South Africa, but sadly indicative of the country's divided approach to the war. The Canadian government, but not the majority of the population, approached the war as an exercise in political opportunism, like building a post office in a swing riding during an election year.

Chapter

16 Epilogue

ONLY ABOUT HALF as many Canadians as Australians served in South Africa. The comparison is even more marked when compared with New Zealand which had a population one-twelfth of Canada's. New Zealand fielded 1800 men in the early months of the war, compared to Canada's 3000. No further contingents were sent until January 1901 when a sixth contingent of 579 was followed by a slightly larger force two months later. The Eighth Contingent, which sailed towards the end of 1901, saw hard service but little fighting. The Ninth and Tenth Contingents, raised early in 1902, saw no action. These last three contingents, each more than 1000 strong, composed more than half of the New Zealanders who went to war. In all, 6495 New Zealanders could claim service in South Africa.

Still, the Canadians had made a name for themselves, in more ways than one. Their fighting record speaks for itself. As well, stories abound about their profanity, their looting and their carousing. Some, if not most, were inflated, but it was, perhaps, fortunate that the camcorder did not exist. What was not inflated was the feeling that grew in all ranks that come the next war, Canadians should fight together in a Canadian division under Canadian command. They did.

We should look objectively at the Canadians' record in the field. That they did well is beyond dispute. Given the state of the army in Canada it was a truly remarkable accomplishment. The credit must be shared. First, the volunteers themselves were drawn from militia regiments, shops, universities, ranches and farms from sea to sea. The nights and weekends spent in cavernous drill halls and the too-short annual camps had prepared the way. The permanent force deserves credit for providing the guidance and the depth of knowledge to pull the volunteers' enthusiasm and inexperience together. Ultimately much of the credit has to go to the commanding officers. William Dillon Otter, nicknamed "Black Bill" and heartily disliked, nevertheless provided the thrust and direction for his battalion. While one could question his malevolent autocracy, war is not a popularity contest, and his methods got results. François Lessard was more popular but less capable. There were a number of occasions were he displayed a less than adequate grasp, including at Leliefontein. Sam Steele was a better commander than Lessard, however, he was a bit of a self-promoter and much of his reputation is based on his version of events. Charles Drury never had a chance to shine, although he was well thought of. Last, and in a class by himself, was Thomas Evans. He was tactically able and a good leader. Evans was not perfect either, though, and his blunder at Leliefontein cost Canadian lives.

The Canadians were fortunate in their British commanders, as can be seen from their subsequent careers. Hutton became a lieutenant general. Ian Hamilton, Smith-Dorrien, and Alderson were senior commanders in the next war. Byng, of the SALH, commanded the Canadian corps, and, as Byng of Vimy, served as governor general.

None of the Canadian Boer War commanders saw active service in the Great War. Evans died in 1908 and Drury in 1913. Lessard, Steele, and Otter all served as generals during World War One, but none saw action. Their subordinates, however, carried on their traditions. Richard Turner, Archibald Macdonnell, "Dinky" Morrison and Henry Burstall were senior commanders in the Canadian corps. Brigadier General Victor Williams of the RCD was the only Canadian general captured during the first war. Other brigadier generals included William Griesbach, J.H. Elmsley, and William King of C Battery. Also among those who died before the next war were Richard Thompson and Russel Hubly of The RCR and Arthur King and Hampton Cockburn of the RCD. The roll of Great War dead who had been Boer War veterans includes far too many familiar names, including William Hart-McHarg, John McCrae, Charles Van Straubenzie, and "Casey" Callaghan. Sam Hughes, of course, fulfilled Hutton's prediction and was the Minister of Defence who led Canada into that war.

The war in South Africa had provided a long-overdue dose of reality to the Canadian defence establishment. While the government remained wedded to the doctrine of the militia myth, training became more realistic, and the need for discipline was recognized, albeit somewhat reluctantly. The army's order of battle was expanded to include engineers, signal corps, army service corps, ordnance corps, and the corps of guides. The foundation for a modern army had been laid.

GLOSSARY OF AFRIKANER TERMS AND ABBREVIATIONS

Term	Meaning	Term	Meaning
Aarde,	earth, ground	*Modder,*	mud
Afgang,	slope	*Mooi,*	pretty
Beek,	brook	*Nek,*	depression between two mountains
Berg,	mountain		
Blaauw,	blue	*Nieuwe,*	new
Bloem,	flower	*Oom,*	uncle
Boer,	farmer	*Outspan,*	to unharness
Boom,	tree		
Boschveld,	open, brushcovered plain	*Pan,*	bed of a dried-up salt marsh
Brock,	marsh, pool	*Poort,*	passage between mountains
Burg,	town	*Rand,*	edge, margin
Burgher,	citizen	*Rooinek,*	term of contempt applied to the British by the Boers
Commando,	military force of any number		
		Ruggens,	barren, hilly country
Daal,	valley	*Schantze,*	heap of stones used to protect a marksman against opposing rifle fire
Donga,	ravine		
Dorp,	village		
Drift,	ford	*Slim,*	cunning, crafty
Fontein,	spring	*Slui,*	ditch
Hout,	wood, timber	*Spruit,*	small river
Inspan,	to harness up	*Stad,*	town
Kaffir,	Native, from Arabic for "infidel"	*Transvaal,*	across the valley
		Trek,	journey
Karroo,	(Hottentot) a "dry place"	*Uitlander,*	outsider or newcomer
Klei,	clay	*Uitspan,*	to unharness, to stop
Kloof,	valley or ravine	*Vaal,*	valley
Kop or *Kopje,*	hill	*Veldt,*	open plain
Kraal,	Native village	*Vlei,*	swamp or marsh
Krantz,	precipice	*Vley,*	prairie-like meadow
Laager,	camp or enclosure for defence; often made of a circle of wagons	*Voortrekker,*	pioneer
		Vrou,	housewife
		ZARP,	South African Republic Police
Loop,	course, channel	*Zuid,*	south

Glossary of Army Terms and Abbreviations

Abbr.	Meaning	Abbr.	Meaning
Argylls	Argyll and Sutherland Highlanders	BDSM	Brigade Division Sergeant Major
ASC	Army Service Corps	Bglr	Bugler
Bdr	Bombardier (a rank used only by the artillery which was equivalent to Lance Corporal at the time)	BL	Breech loading
		Bn	Battalion
		BQMS	Battery Quartermaster Sergeant Major
		BrigGen	Brigadier General

BSM	Battery Sergeant Major		MI	Mounted Infantry
Bty	Battery		MLE	Magazine Lee-Enfield
Capt	Captain		MLM	Magazine Lee-Metford
CinC	Commander in Chief		MR	Mounted Rifles
CIV	City Imperial Volunteers		NWMP	North West Mounted Police
CMR	Canadian Mounted Rifles		OC	Officer Commanding
CO	Commanding Officer		OFS	Orange Free State
Col	Colonel		ORC	Orange River Colony (used after
Colt	British machine-gun			the OFS was absorbed into the
Cow Gun	British heavy artilley			British Empire)
	piece			
Coy	Company		PMO	Principal Medical Officer
Cpl	Corporal		Pom-Pom	British built automatic cannon
CS	Canadian Scouts		Pte	Private
CSgt	Colour Sergeant		QF	Quick firing
DCLI	Duke of Cornwall's Light		RA	Royal Artillery
	Infantry		RAMC	Royal Army Medical Corps
Dgns	Dragoons		RCD	Royal Canadian Dragoons
Dvr	Driver		RCFA	Royal Canadian Field Artillery
			RCR	Royal Canadian Regiment, The
FM	Field Marshall		RCRI	Royal Canadian Regiment of
Gds	Guards			Infantry
Gnr	Gunner		RE	Royal Engineers
Gen	General		RFA	Royal Field Artillery
GOC	General Officer		RHA	Royal Horse Artillery
	Commanding		RQMS	Regimental Quartermaster
HLI	Highland Light Infantry			Sergeant
Imp Yry	Imperial Yeomanry		RSM	Regimental Sergeant Major
Krupp	German built artillery piece		SAC	South African Constabulary
KOSB	King's Own Scottish		SALH	South African Light Horse
	Borderers		Sect	Section
KSLI	King's Shropshire Light		SH	Strathcona's Horse
	Infantry		SM	Sergeant Major
			SQMS	Squadron Quartermaster
LCpl	Lance Corporal			Sergeant
LSgt	Lance Sergeant		Sqn	Squadron
Lt	Lieutenant		SSgt	Staff Sergeant
LtCol	Lieutenant Colonel		SSM	Squadron Sergeant Major
LtGen	Lieutenant General			
Maj	Major		Tp	Troop
Maj Gen	Major General		Tpr	Trooper
Mauser	German built rifle		Tptr	Trumpeter
Maxim	water-cooled machine-gun		12-pdr	British light artillery piece
			15-pdr	British light artillery piece

CHAPTER NOTES

Chapter 1 - Background to the War

1. The attitudes and goals of Transvaal President Paul Kruger, Colonial Secretary Joe Chamberlain, and mining magnate Cecil Rhodes provide an interesting outline of the forces that led to war. See the foreword by Sir John Bourinot in Capt A.T. Mahan's *The War in South Africa*.
2. Hopkins 352-3
3. The Buller enigma is discussed by Keith Surridge in a review of *Buller: A Scapegoat? A Life of Sir Redvers Buller 1839-1908* in "Soldiers of the Queen," *The Journal of the Victorian Military Society*, Issue 79, Dec 1994

Chapter Two - The Players

1. The ranks were vecht-general (fighting general), commandant (roughly equivalent to lieutenant-colonel), field cornet (major), and corporal (lieutenant). *Times History* vol 4, 513, 514; Anglesey 35
2. Lee 37; Kruger 61; Pakenham 104; Pemberton 19; Reitz 21; De Villiers 216; De Wet 9
3. Lee 49-57
4. Boer artillery strength peaked at 152, including 55 guns captured from the British and 37 old smooth-bores, muzzle-loaders, and the like. The maximum British gun strength was 496. Lee 44; *Times History* vol 4, 513; *Times History* vol 6, 469-73; Harding 36, 41; German Great General Staff (hereafter German GGS) *The War In South Africa, The Advance to Pretoria after Paardeberg, the Upper Tugela Campaign, Etc.* 324-5
5. The Boers were not known for their personal courage. The author of the *Handbook of the Boer War*, himself a veteran of the war, wrote "There is scarcely an instance of an individual feat of arms or act of devotion performed by a Burgher." Hart-McHarg 204; *Handbook of the Boer War* 5; German GGS 326-7
6. A few observers noted similarities with another citizens' army, Oliver Cromwell's Roundheads. *Handbook* 1-6
7. There was an exception to the army's lack of experience on active service. Most of the senior British officers who would play key roles in the war had seen considerable action in South Africa and elsewhere. The best description of the British army of the time is Walton's *Scarlet into Khaki*. Farwell's *Queen Victoria's Little Wars* or Featherstone's *Colonial Small Wars 1837-1901* give a hint of the limited number of units that fought in the two decades preceding the South African War. Harder to find but more authoritative is Anthony Baker's *Battle Honours of the British and Commonwealth Armies*. Walton 108
8. After the war a flood of books flagellated the army in a manner that would not be seen until the post-Vietnam era in the United States. *Handbook* 17-25; Fuller, *The Last of the Gentlemen's Wars* 19
9. Walton 40-41; German GGS Oct 1899 to Feb 1900, 251-2
10. In Feb 1900 Roberts' seven cavalry regiments averaged 24 officers and 458 men. While on paper this was over 90% strength, the cavalry often had more men dismounted than mounted. The average daily horse loss through the 32 months of the war was 336! Anglesey devotes two chapters to the subject of horse care and the supply of remounts. Griesbach 265; Anglesey 279-375
11. Colvile 24; Walton 42; Anglesey 98
12. Photos exist of a variety of Maxim carriages with one-, two- and four-horse teams. Lessard noted that the RCD Maxim required at least four horses, which implies that a six-horse team may have been used on occasion. Anderson, a member of the RCD Maxim crew, mentioned six horses. SP35a 98; Letters Pte Anderson 2 and 5 Apr

13. Bethell 201-13
14. Fuller 19
15. German GGS Oct 1899 to Feb 1900, 25-7
16. Both Anderson and Griesbach provide vivid descriptions of MI in action. Letter Pte Anderson 8 May; Griesbach 256-7; German GGS Oct 1899 to Feb 1900, 29
17. As the war progressed some cavalry regiments exchanged their swords, carbines and lances for rifles. German GGS Oct 1899 to Feb 1900, 28
18. Surely the most extreme example of military miserliness was Prime Minister Mackenzie's proposal to the governor general that the U.S. army pacify the Canadian west as an economy measure. A typical example of self-delusion was Denison's credit of victory in the War of 1812 to "the Canadian militia, aided by a few regulars." While the army was known as the Militia, which was administered by the federal Department of Militia and Defence, the term "militia" will be used in its modern context—the land forces reserve of part-time officers and soldiers. NAC: Dufferin Papers reel A 406, no. 251, Dufferin to Kimberley 24 Dec 1873; Denison *Soldiering in Canada* 9; Bercuson 133
19. The army maintained an infantry battalion staffed by men enlisted for full-time service in Manitoba from 1872 to 1877. In 1876 the Canadian government had established the Royal Military College at Kingston to produce officers who were well-educated members of society. The college adopted British routine, uniforms, and procedures, and a curriculum modelled on West Point. Graduates always exceeded the number of commissions available in the permanent force and the North West Mounted Police. As an incentive the British army offered a few commissions to each year's graduates, starting at the top of the class. In 1899 103 ex-cadets were serving British officers while there were only 86 officers, not all RMC graduates, in the entire Canadian permanent force. Stanley 234, 244, 265-7; Hart-McHarg 54; Canadian Almanac 1900
20. Fetherstonaugh *The Royal Canadian Regiment 1883-1933* 49; Stanley 275-7; Mitchell 25-9
21. The NWMP had roughly 500 men on the prairies and 250 in the Yukon. Volunteers for South Africa were only drawn from the former group. Steele 339; Macleod 106; Canadian Almanac 1901; RG 18 A.1 vol 176 no 751, Commissioner NWMP to Comptroller NWMP 17 Dec 1899

Chapter 3 - Mobilizing the First Contingent

1. The governor general represented the British government, not the Crown, until the promulgation of the Statutes of Westminster in 1931. Canada was guided by the colonial secretary in London via the governor general in Government House. Evans 10; Morton, *Otter* 162
2. Edward T.H. Hutton has been a favourite target of Canadian historians because of his quarrels with the Laurier government. His outrage at the inefficiency, political interference, and patronage that plagued the forces was a major contributing factor to the controversy. Other factors included his abrasive personality, his meddling in politics, and his belief that he owed his loyalty to the British, not the Canadian government. Hutton had seen active service in the Zulu War and Egypt, had formed the Mounted Infantry School at Aldershot, and commanded the colonial forces in New South Wales. "It was due to him more than any other man that Mounted Infantry became a recognized branch of the Army and so remained for the next twenty years." A biographical sketch may be found in Volume 4 of *The Annals of the King's Royal Rifle Corps* 371-3; Morton, *Otter* 161
3. His was not the only offer. If all had been accepted, Canada would have provided 4500 troops. Evans 41
4. Laurier claimed the government had no constitutional power to send a contingent, and even if it had, it could not commit the country to the expenditure without consulting Parliament, and therefore the matter had not been considered. This rather lame argument did not sell in English Canada. Evans 13; NLC, reel N 19875, Toronto *Globe* 4 Oct

5. The wire is often cited as a mistake. However, the British were clearly aware of the situation in Canada. 63 Victoria, Sessional Papers (hereafter SP) 20, 20a, A 1900, number 18, number 97

6. This has led to claims that Canada did no more than assist volunteers to travel to South Africa. This was not the opinion of the volunteers, the majority of Canadians and most members of Parliament. Evans 81

7. Morton's biography is well worth reading.

8. RG 9 II A.3 vol 26

9. Morton, *Otter* 167

10. At least one regular was pressed into service. Captain Denison, the quartermaster, ordered Private Charman, his servant, to board the troopship despite pleas that he had promised his wife he would not volunteer for South Africa. Denison, *Memoirs* 56

11. MO 108 11 May 1900

12. SP35a 14

13. SP35a 22-23; Smith, *Passenger Ships of the World, Past and Present*

14. MO 217, 23 Oct 1899 and MO 219, 25 Oct 1899; Hubly 15

15. Otter to his wife 12 Nov

16. RG 9 II A.3 vol 28

17. He was a popular young extrovert who had circulated among the pretty girls out to see the troops off from Ottawa, insisting successfully that "the major had told him to kiss all the girls." The cause of death was listed as "heart failure" but was widely suspected to be delirium tremens. RG 9 II A.3 vol 34; CBC *Ideas* transcript 25 September 1993, 3

18. Fuller, *The Army in My Time* 80-1

19. While it was impossible to do other than limited "squad" drill, the battalion had also practised weapons handling and firing. RG9 II A.3 vol 34; Hart-McHarg 54

Chapter 4 - Mobilizing the Second Contingent

1. SP20 no 83

2. SP20 no 89; SP20a no 105

3. Hutton believed cavalry armed with sword and lances was obsolete and that mounted rifles could outperform the *arme blanche*. His theory would be proven in South Africa, although horsed cavalry would survive in the British army until 1940. RG 9 II B.3 vol 15; Evans 123-6; Marquis 332; Macleod 107, 285; Morton, *Ministers and Generals* 156; Miller, *Minto* 103-7; Steele 338

4. An officer noted that, after inspecting his battery, Roberts expressed surprise that the officers were all trained artillerymen as he had been informed otherwise. SP20a no 109, no 110, no 111; Miller, *Minto* 107; Morton, *Ministers and Generals* 156; Morrison 193

5. Evans 126; Macleod 107

6. MO 25 31 Jan 1900

7. Lessard obituary; Marquis 334; Griesbach 229; Mitchell 30; Nicholson 134, 143

8. Militia field batteries were tested each year by means of an annual competition. In 1899 Hurdman's battery was the winner in the general efficiency category with a score of 417 out of a possible 451.2. MO 25; Ross 19

9. While the available data are incomplete, the approximate average age for each rank in the first and second contingents was lieutenant colonel 48, major 39, captain 33, and lieutenant 29. (The average age of the ex-NWMP lieutenants in 2 CMR was 36.) On the whole Canadian officers seemed to have been older than their British counterparts, and this was the case for other "colonial" contingents as well. However, Stirling credited the success of many colonial contingents to the

maturity of their officers compared with members of the British army. MO 25; Griesbach 229; *Militia List* 1904; Stirling 377

10. The permanent force was not large enough to provide complete troops or sections. For example, A Battery in Kingston provided 33 men to C Battery, 25 to D Battery, and 22 to E Battery. B Battery, which was much smaller than A, could not have made up the shortfall between the above and a section establishment of 54. MO 25; Ross 16

11. Today we would call it the "nothing is too good for our troops" syndrome. SP35a 188

12. SP35a; Marquis 333; Evans 127; Nicholson 147

13. In an effort to prevent discrimination, Ottawa included the caveat that the men must be able to pass as white. As can be seen from Villebrun's picture in the Toronto *Globe*, it was impossible to hide their racial origin. However, the "half breeds" were treated as equals, and Davis was later commissioned in the Canadian Scouts. RG 18 A.1 vol 180 no 776, White to Herchmer 27 Dec 1899; RG 38 1.A vol 25; NLC Reel 19878, Toronto *Globe* 23 June 1900

14. Revolvers were provided to allow the troops to fight mounted at close range. MO 271 28 Dec 1899; SP35a; RG9 II A.3 vol 32; Steele 241; Greenhous 33

15. The 12-pounders were lighter and fired a more effective shell nearly a mile farther than the 9-pounder muzzle loaders they had replaced in 1897. "In "breech loading" (BL) guns the smokeless propellant, the "gun powder," was contained in a cloth bag that was loaded into the chamber separately from the shell. In "quick firing" (QF) guns the propellant was enclosed in a brass case crimped to the base of the shell and the round was loaded in one operation, like a rifle. QF guns were also fitted with a device to control recoil so that the gun carriage would remain in place during firing. While some BL guns were equipped with recoil brakes and spades, Canadian guns lacked these rudimentary devices. The guns had to be manhandled back into position after each round was fired, which slowed the rate of fire. Mitchell 30; Nicholson, *Gunners of Canada* 147; RG 9 II A.3 vol 32, vol 33

16. Boulanger also served in China during the Boxer Rebellion. The postal detachment, led by William R. Ecclestone, who was appointed a temporary captain in the (British) Army Postal Corps, was noted for its good work in both British and Canadian reports, while Ryerson was mentioned in the commander-in-chief's despatches. *South African War Honours and Awards* 58; Army Order 28A, 21 Feb 1900; SP35a; Evans 130

17. Morton 157-61; Miller 109-17; RG 9 II A.3 vol 32

18. The *Polynesian* was a sister ship to the *Sardinian*. Marquis 342

19. Bapty diary

20. RG 9 A.3 vol 33

21. Marquis 337; Miller 91; RG 9 II A.3 vol 33

22. Marquis 347, 50; SP35a;

23. Marquis 347, 488; Nicholson 151

24. Evans 151

25. Members of the unit, unlike other Canadian units, wore high brown "Strathcona Boots." There is a full-page advertisement for Strathcona Boots in *The Quarterly Militia List* of 1 Jan 1904. Ibid; Fraser 24; Wilson 524

26. *SAFF Casualty List*; *South African War Honours and Awards*

27. Fraser 24; D Hist 141.4A2055 (D1)

28. Fraser 24-5; Haycock 79

29. RG 18 A-1 vol 180 no 138

30. The British would not accept Robert Parker, who had been cashiered from the British army, as a lieutenant. He served as a sergeant and was killed in action. RG 9 II B.3 vol 16; Fraser 28

31. The regiment also purchased two horses for Hutton, who promised to reimburse the regiment when the horses were delivered in South Africa. There is no indication that the horses ever reached their destination. RG 38 A-1 vol 180 no 138; Hutton letter 14 Feb; Fraser 24, 31
32. Steele 340
33. Marquis 348; Fraser 32; Wilson 526
34. D Hist 500.009 (D79)
35. While the Canadian government had no intention of sending the battalion overseas, the militia department planned, that if Canada committed troops to suppress the Boxer Rebellion in China, the contingent would include the 3rd Battalion. Stanley 281-2; Evans 148-9; Otter papers CWM

Chapter 5 - Building a Battalion

1. Marquis 92-3; Hubly 38
2. Otter papers; Marquis 94
3. Marquis 98; *War in South Africa* 376
4. Hubly 38; Floyd diary
5. Only one of the four storage areas was secure. As a result, the stores were pilfered. Hart-McHarg 56-8; Hubly 38; Floyd diary; Otter papers
6. Layborn was a 29-year-old regular infantry officer. After being replaced on the rear party Layborn served with Broadwood and French, returning to Canada in 1901.
7. Marquis 104
8. Marquis 104; Hart-McHarg 59; Hubly 40
9. Hart-McHarg 60
10. Hubly 42; Hart-McHarg 60
11. RG 9 II A.3 vol 34, vol 18
12. Marquis 115
13. *SAFF Casualty List* 71; Marquis 118-19
14. Capt and Bvt Maj (Local Lt Col) E.P.C. Giouard was only 31 when he was appointed Director of Railways. The operation of the railways is discussed in the *Times History* vol 6 297-331.
15. *SAFF Casualty List* 65; Marquis 120-3
16. Hubly 44; Hart-McHarg 63; Marquis 127-8; Evans 103
17. The garrison also included a section of field guns and the mounted infantry company of the Royal Munster Fusiliers. RG 9 II A.3 vol 34; Hart-McHarg 64-6; Hubly 46
18. Otter submitted periodic reports to Ottawa and in return was provided with a stream of correspondence, orders, and regulations. Of greater importance, the British pay staff was bloody minded and at various times refused to pay the chaplains, the nurses and a number of others, including some members of the battalion. Otter was especially irked over the case of the nurses for, as he noted to the chief staff officer in Ottawa, the Imperial authorities had wasted no time in putting them to work in a British hospital. The matter dragged on for months between the battalion, Cape Town, Ottawa, and London. The financial authorities finally relented after they were provided with a copy of an Act of Parliament formalizing Ottawa's obligations to assume costs above those agreed upon with the Imperial authorities. Otter report 25 Jan
19. Hart-McHarg 67-9; Hubly 46; Marquis 133-142
20. Casualty reports flowed from the unit through the chain of command to the War Office in London, who passed the report to the Colonial Office. The Colonial Office wired the governor general, who passed the report to the Department of Militia and Defence. The department notified the next of kin by telegram, often within 48 hours of the soldier having become a casualty. Casualties were also published for administrative reasons in Militia Orders. Much had been made of

the generous insurance policy provided to members of the Canadian contingents. However, the insurance company at first refused to honour claims without a Canadian death certificate. Casualty returns and correspondence are found in RG9 II A.3 vol 25, vol 26.

21. Hart-McHarg 73-4; Hubly 52; Marquis 134

22. Hubly 49

23. A few men believed the officers had either appropriated their rations or diverted the money to their own purposes. They vented their feelings in letters to their MPs, relatives, or newspapers, and weeks later Otter was called to account for the expenditures. The charges were easily disproven. Hart-McHarg 75; Hubly 51; Marquis 147-52

24. The account of the raid is based on several contemporary sources including Hart-McHarg, Denison, Marquis and the *Times History*. A number of popular histories also published accounts, one of which states that Lt Col P.R. Ricardo, commanding the Queenslanders, had served in the Canadian Militia. Lt Col T.D. Pilcher of the Bedfordshire Regiment had some 20 years service at the time, including active service in West Africa 1897-8. Denison and Maj Charles Dobell accompanied Pilcher as staff officers. Dobell, an RMC graduate, was an officer in the Royal Welsh Fusiliers, not, as some sources claimed, The RCR. In the Great War Brig-Gen Dobell commanded the Cameroons Expeditionary Force in 1914-16.

25. On 16 Jan Pte A.E. Cole of B Company accidently shot himself while preparing to go on guard. He was evacuated to England just in time to be presented to Queen Victoria, who visited his hospital after Paardeberg. When she asked where had he been wounded, he blurted out "during the raid on Sunnyside." Although he is sometimes still listed as a casualty at Sunnyside, both the *South African Field Force Casualty List* and his records in the National Archives agree that he was accidentally wounded on 16 Jan. Private Floyd of B Company wrote in his diary on the same day that "one man shot himself through the foot." RG 32 I.A vol 20; Floyd diary

26. We cannot criticize Otter for not mounting a raid on Douglas earlier. It required the arrival of the Cornwalls and the Queensland Mounted Infantry to make the raid a viable proposition. While Pilcher was striking at the rebels, Belmont was still defended by seven rifle companies. For Otter to have mounted an equivalent raid while he was in command would have left only three companies at Belmont, an unacceptable risk. Hart-McHarg 81-7; Marquis 152-179; Otter papers

27. The Australian infantry companies on the L of C were converted to MI in Jan. The order should not be misinterpreted as an attempt to break up the first contingent. See Stirling's *The Colonials in South Africa*. Otter to CSO 22 Jan 1900.

28. Denison had volunteered to serve on Roberts' staff, without apparently informing Otter. Denison 57

29. Otter may have been justified in his assessment of Pilcher who was described by a fellow officer as one of the "worst men in South Africa." Anglesey 173

30. Marquis 207, 213; *SAFF Casualty List* 98

31. Brevet Colonel Horace Lockwood Smith-Dorrien, DSO was promoted major general on 11 Feb. He was 41 years old and had seen active service in the Zulu War, the Egyptian and Sudan campaigns of 1882, 1884, and 1885-6, the 1895 Chitral Relief Force, and the Tirah Campaign of 1896-7 in India and the Nile Expedition of 1898.

Chapter 6 - Paardeberg

1. Sources vary on the size of Roberts' army. I have used the figures cited in *The Times History*. Forty-seven year old Major General Sir Henry Colvile was appointed to command 9th Division. He had seen active service in Egypt, the Sudan, India, and Uganda. Colvile had commanded the Guards Brigade prior to being appointed general officer commanding 9th Division. *Times History* vol 3 338-42, 375-8

2. Even the tents required to shelter one battalion required several wagons. The RCR transport before the reorganization included seven wagons, a water cart, ten horses, and 80 mules. *The Times History* advanced a well-reasoned argument that the existing system would have worked. The argument, however, failed to consider Roberts' aim to free the army from the impedementia of large unit baggage trains. The author of the pro-Boer *The Transvaal Outlook* proved, at least to his own satisfaction, in a work completed in Feb 1900 that the British would be unable to leave the railways and faced imminent defeat. *Times History* vol 6 385-90; Stickney 92-5

3. Colvile 23-4; Hart-McHarg 94

4. Hart-McHarg 95; *War in South Africa* 530-1; *Naval Brigades during the South African War* 57-8

5. A number of Canadians were serving with the cavalry division. Lt Colonel Lessard, Capt Forester and their grooms and batmen received the "Relief of Kimberley" bar to their South Africa medals as did Lt Molyneux, late of E Company, and Lt Layborn and his batman late of the rear party. Otter originally believed that the seven men left at Waterval Drift had been captured. However, the men were both safe and fit enough to fight. The Gordons' history related that a "nasty-looking" attempt to seize the drift was foiled by a handful of Canadians. Gardyne 114

6. Pte Bill Warren of C Company found a dead Boer in a bedroom and a frightened woman and her newborn baby in another room of a house he was searching. In 1918 in England he was introduced to a young South African from Jacobsdal. Furthermore, the young man added, on the day he was born, the British had attacked the town and killed his father. Later, a soldier had searched the house just after he was born, badly frightening his mother. After drawing a sketch of the house to establish his *bona fides*, Warren told the lad to tell his mother that she needn't have worried about being killed. Colvile 27; Kingsley Brown 112; *The Canadian Military Journal*, Easter 1952, *15*

7. Colvile 31; Harding 531

8. Smith-Dorrien 150-1; Hart-McHarg 106; Gardyne 124-5

9. Smith-Dorrien 150; Otter papers

10. Some accounts state Findlay fell near where Captain Arnold was mortally wounded. Arnold and/or Scott may have been hit at about the same time or even before Findlay. Both A Company stretcher-bearers were wounded on 18 Feb, probably in an attempt to rescue Arnold. Hart-McHarg 106-10; Smith-Dorrien 152; Tweddell diary

11. Aldworth had obtained permission to feed his men before crossing the river, not an indication of a deranged or overwrought officer. As for the heated discussion between Otter and Aldworth, both were under considerable stress at the time. Otter papers; Mason papers; Thompson papers; Tweddell diary; Hart-McHarg 111; Colvile 40; Labat 144; Toronto *Globe* 7 Apr 1900

12. Pte Gordon Corbould of A Company had been unable to continue the march at Wedgraal Drift. After helping beat off De Wet's attack, he joined the MI in the pursuit of Cronje and arrived at Paardeberg on the 17th. He rejoined the battalion on the 19th. Gamble letter 20 Apr

13. Smith-Dorrien 155

14. Ibid 158-9

15. Otter reported that Maj Buchan was the last man to return to the trenches, after failing to halt the retreat. Both Stairs and Macdonnell received the DSO. Smith-Dorrien 159-60; Hart-McHarg 126-9; Hubly 77-8; Tweddell diary; Thompson papers

16. The citation on a scroll dated 24 Dec 1908 presented to the Thompson family by the Department of Militia and Defence states that Thompson was awarded the scarf for his actions on the 18th and 27th. In July 1901 Otter submitted a recommendation for the award of the Victoria Cross to Thompson, citing the award of the Queen's Scarf as justification. The Imperial authorities rejected the application as the award of the scarf in itself did not justify the award of the VC. It seems likely that an application citing his bravery on either the 18th or the 27th submitted at the time of Cronje's surrender would have been successful as both VCs won at Paardeberg were awarded

for rescuing wounded men under fire. The medical corporal's fate is a mystery. Cpl Cawdron, also of D Company, wrote that the corporal went forward with Thompson to succour the wounded man, who died as they lifted him up. No casualties were reported by medical units on 27 Feb. Gardyne 433; Thompson pers file; Thompson papers; *Honours and Awards* 85, 106, 118; Labat 153; *Ideas* 8

17. Otter papers; RCRI diary; Gardyne 133-5; Smith-Dorrien 160; Conan Doyle 253; Pemberton 92, 105

18. After the event E Company was told the retreat was planned and cautioned not to discuss the circumstances. Over a year later Capt Rogers of D Company, perhaps diplomatically, used the phrase "ordered to retire" in a letter to Otter. Otter papers; RCR staff diary; Thompson pers file; Tweddell diary; Marquis 284; McCormick MS; *Ideas* 8; Kingsley Brown 115

19. The prisoners included Cronje, Maj Albrecht, three other officers of the Free State Artillery, 12 Commandants, and 21 Field Cornets. The guns were three Krupp 7.5-cm field guns, an old pattern 12-pdr, and a damaged Vickers-Maxim 3.7-cm pom-pom. Hart-McHarg 131

20. Harding 466, 468-9

Chapter 7 - Bloemfontein

1. Colvile 53; Smith-Dorrien 164-9

2. Hart-McHarg 143-7; Hubly 84

3. Roberts had issued an order threatening looters with death. Belyea's sentence for what was a minor transgression in civilian life raised a storm in Canada. After Otter pointed out what might have happened, official Ottawa agreed the punishment was quite appropriate. Incidentally, Capt S.M. Rogers, who commanded D Company, told his men, "Now listen, boys, it wasn't for stealing the chicken that [Belyea] was going to be hung, it was for getting caught at it, so watch yourself." RG 9 II A.3 vol 34; Colvile 28; Otter papers; *Ideas* 11

4. It has been suggested that the Canadians suffered unduly from disease compared with the regulars because of their lack of discipline. However, the casualty returns show that, of the 125 soldiers in 19th Brigade who died of disease, 24 were Canadian. During this period The RCR ranked in the lowest third of the South African Field Force in death from disease, while the four Guards battalions in Roberts' army averaged nearly twice as many deaths from disease as the Canadians. Hart-McHarg 152, 157; Prescott 36; SAFF *Casualty List*

5. Ernest Pullen left Toronto on 6 Feb, travelled to South Africa at his own expense, and presented himself to Otter on 22 Mar and was sworn in the next day. He was the first of seven Canadians who joined the battalion in South Africa. RG 9 II A.3 vol 28, vol 32, vol 34; RG 9 II B.3 vol 16; Pullen diary

6. At least two Canadians fought at Sannah's Post. Capt Herbert Carrington Smith, an RMC graduate who had fought at Omdurman in 1898 was wounded while Lt Charlie Ross, who had been Otter's chief scout in the North West Rebellion, was awarded the DSO. Both were serving in Roberts' Horse. Hutton to Minto 23 Apr

7. Smith-Dorrien 181

8. Hart-McHarg 166; Pullen diary

9. Smith-Dorrien 180; Pullen diary

10. Hart-McHarg 166; Smith-Dorrien 181-2

11. Smith-Dorrien's memoirs, usually polite and gentlemanly in tone, make it clear that he considered Colvile deficient in these qualities. Smith-Dorrien 182; Pullen diary

12. Churchill 497; Smith-Dorrien 183-4; Hart-McHarg 171-2; Pullen diary; Marquis 378; Evans 170

13. Hart-McHarg 171-2; Smith-Dorrien 184

14. Henry Burstall was a 29-year-old permanent force artillery officer who had also commanded a company in the Yukon Field Force. Smith-Dorrien 185-6

15. Otter diary; Hart-McHarg 176; Smith-Dorrien 184, 186; Hubly 89; Evans 170-1; Marquis 383; *Ideas* 10

16. Israel's Poort was not a victory. The aim was to trap the Boers retreating from the siege of Wepener. The Boers had gained a day by their defence of Israel's Poort.

17. Pullen diary

18. Smith-Dorrien 188; Hart-McHarg 174; Pullen diary; Churchill 500

19. Buchan report; Smith-Dorrien 188-190; Churchill 500-3; Hart-McHarg 174-6; Pullen diary

20. Churchill 500

21. Ibid 504; Hart-McHarg 177

22. Smith-Dorrien 194-5; Churchill 507; Hart-McHarg 181; Pullen diary; Marquis 388-91

Chapter 8 - Chasing Shadows in the Dust

1. Charles Drury was a 44-year-old native of Saint John, NB who had served with A Battery in the North West Rebellion. Henri Panet was a 30-year-old permanent force RMC graduate. RCFA staff diary; Bapty diary; Morrison 48

2. RCFA staff diary; Morrison 48; Nicholson 134, 142

3. There were two Gunner Williams in D Battery. The accounts do not provide a first name or initials. RCFA staff diary; Morrison 51

4. John McCrae was a 27 year-old-native of Guelph, Ontario. He had graduated from the University of Toronto Medical School in 1898 and interned at Johns Hopkins in Baltimore. He postponed a fellowship at McGill to serve in South Africa. Morrison 52-4; Prescott 17, 25, 31

5. RCFA staff diary

6. Griesbach 229; Mcleod 106

7. Herchmer letter in 2 CMR file RG9 II A.3 vol 34 and RCMP file RG 18 vol 180 no 776; Dynes 9; Phillips 15; Reynolds 61-3

8. Walter Bapty was 15 years old. After his service in D Battery he transferred to the Canadian Scouts. Bapty returned to Canada in Aug 1901, having completed nearly 18 months on active service before his 17th birthday. RCFA staff diary; Nicholson, *Gunners of Canada* 52-4; Bapty diary

9. Edward Whipple Bancroft (Dinky) Morrison was 32 years old and a journalist by profession. His nickname reflects his height, or rather the lack of the same. Morrison 60; Nicholson, *Gunners of Canada* 150; Prescott 34

10. Herchmer letter; Bapty diary; Mitchell 31

11. RCFA staff diary; Bapty diary, Marquis 352-3

12. Morrison 75; RCFA staff diary

13. Herchmer letter; CMR staff diary

14. Morrison 95

15. Morrison 93, 99

16. Ibid 82; *Ideas* 16

17. Archibald Cameron Macdonnell was born in Windsor, Ontario, in 1864. He graduated from RMC in 1886. Originally a member of the permanent force, he had transferred to the NWMP. MG 30 E20 vol 1; Prescott 35

18. Morrison 90-1; *Ideas* 16; *SAFF Casualty List* 21 Mar to 31 Jul 1900 p x.i; Marquis 358; SP 35a 140

19. RCFA staff diary; E Bty staff diary

20. Haycock 78

21. Ibid 85-7

22. Hughes visited Victoria Roads and informally inspected the camp on 23 Apr. RCFA staff diary; Right Section D Bty report
23. Sir Charles Warren gained dubious fame as the commissioner of Metropolitan Police who bungled the Jack the Ripper case. More recently he had been outgeneraled by the Boers in Natal. However, Warren had skilfully put down a Boer insurrection in Griqualand and Bechuanaland in 1884-5 and knew the country well. Haycock 88
24. G. Hunter Ogilvie had turned 40 years old on the Karroo. He graduated from RMC in 1882 and had seen active service in the North West Rebellion. E Bty staff diary
25. Ibid
26. Ibid
27. Haycock 90; *Honours and Awards* 21
28. Haycock 92-4
29. General Hutton, no fan of Canadian politicians at the best of times, questioned Hughes' sanity and felt that Sam had "lowered the opinion generally held of Canadian officers." While both statements are open to question, it was fortunate that Hughes had not been appointed to a command position in any of the Canadian contingents. Hutton also predicted that Hughes would become the minister of militia and defence. Hutton letter to Minto
30. RCFA staff diary; Morrison 47; Prescott 33

Chapter 9 - The Relief of Mafeking

1. C Bty diary; Mitchell 30; Marquis 371
2. C Bty diary; Evans 140; Nicholson 150; Mitchell 30
3. Evans 138; Kruger 292; Anglesey 173-4
4. C Bty diary; SP35a 126; *12-Pounder Handbook*
5. Hudon quoted ranges and fuse settings for a reason other than a gunner's fascination with the trivia of his craft. The maximum range on the sights of the 12-pdr was 5200 yards, although with practice Canadian detachments were able to accurately shoot several hundred yards further. The only shell available was shrapnel, a hollow round packed with lead balls, designed to burst in the air and spray the balls down on the enemy. However, the maximum setting on the fuse was for a range of 3700 yards. Beyond this range the fuse could only function on impact with the ground which reduced the effectiveness of the round considerably. The long range "blue fuse" would soon enter service, but there are no indications it was available at Mafeking. SP35a 126-7
6. Morrison 296-7

Chapter 10 - We're Marching to Pretoria

1. There also were a few thousand in Griqualand opposing Warren and in the northern Cape Colony besieging Mafeking. *Times History* vol 4, 94-5; *German GGS*, Mar 1900 to Sept 1900, 296-7
2. *Times History* vol 4, 86-8; *German GGS* 296
3. Evans 134
4. The delay proved to be a blessing in disguise. A Squadron was concentrated at Stanley Barracks on the lakeshore in Toronto, while the two western troops of B Squadron had begun the long rail voyage to Halifax. The authorities decided to concentrate B Squadron in Halifax. Here Major Victor Williams, the 33-year-old squadron commander and son of the commanding officer of the Midland Battalion in the North West Rebellion, began to turn his volunteers into a squadron. He was an RMC graduate who had originally been commissioned in the NWMP but exchanged into the army with Archibald Macdonnell in 1889. In both cities, which enjoy mild winters by Canadian standards, mounted infantry tactics and drills were practiced by fours, sections, troops, and finally as a complete

squadron. Both squadrons made good progress and were soon well drilled as mounted infantry, although the test of battle would strip away the veneer of well-executed drills to reveal deficiencies in tactics.

5. Turner diary; Hutton to Minto 23 Sept 1900

6. Hutton had attempted unsuccessfully to have Drury's gunners moved forward from the lines of communications to provide the artillery for his brigade and protested when the Strathconas were diverted. It is unfortunate that he was unsuccessful for a number of reasons, including, of course, that it would have made the historian's task much easier. The antipathy towards Hutton felt by politicians, the press, the militia, assorted nationalists, and Liberal horse traders has been sustained by Canadian historians who ignore his military accomplishments. In spite of more than his share of arrogance and ego, Hutton was an experienced mounted infantryman and a more than adequate general. Charlie Ross was born in Australia and raised in California. He had served as a scout for the U.S. Army before enlisting in the NWMP. Ross had been Otter's chief scout with the Battleford Column in the North West Rebellion. He later ranched in the Lethbridge area. With the outbreak of war, he travelled to South Africa and won a commission in Roberts' Horse. Hutton to Minto April 14; *Times History* vol 4, 504

7. SP35a Report C 81-2

8. Charles Van Straubenzie was a 23-year-old regular. Casualties to horses in action were much higher than those to men. From the front the only exposed portions of a rider were parts of the legs, head, upper body, and arms, especially if the rider was "scrunched down" in the saddle. Turner diary; Hilder ms; Despatch by R.E. Finn, special correspondent for the Montreal *Herald* published 30 Apr, 1900; Evans 135-7; Marquis 371, 373-4

9. Fischer's Farm was a convalescent depot for sick and injured horses. Marquis 374; Anglesey 166

10. The only remaining senior officer, Major Joseph Howe, did not enjoy Hutton's confidence. He also, apparently, was an object of derision of some of the men of the CMR. SP35a Report D 105; Hutton to Minto 14 Apr and 14 May; Griesbach 65-6

11. The despatch plumbed new depths of fatuousness. Considering the strength of the battalion at the time, the number of reinforcements who were able to continue the march does not suffer by comparison.

12. SAFF Casualty List 150; Smith-Dorrien 196-201; Churchill 513-59; Hart-McHarg 189-191

13. Smith-Dorrien 203-4; Pullen diary; Hart-McHarg 199; Marquis 432-4; De Wet 119

14. Eugene Fiset was the junior of the two medical officers with the battalion. The other doctor had developed a taste for more sedentary activities and missed Paardeberg and much of the subsequent mobile operations. De Wet 117-18

15. Smith-Dorrien 204; Pullen diary; Hart-McHarg 201; Marquis 438-9

16. SP35a Report C 82-3; Hutton to Minto 14 May

17. Lessard's report claimed credit for forcing the Boers to retreat. However, *The Times History* indicates that the 3rd MI Corps had crossed the river and outflanked the Boers, forcing their retirement. Neither of the wounded officers appear in either the official casualty report or the regimental report. However, their names are included in a despatch by John Ewan. SP35a Report C 83; *Times History* vol 4, 108-9; undated despatch by John A. Ewan

18. SP35a Report D 105; Hutton to Minto 14 May

19. *The Times History* accused Roberts of excessive caution on this and a number of other occasions. Hutton to Minto 14 May; *Times History* vol 4, 110-1

20. SP35a Report C 83; Hutton to Minto 14 May

21. The limiting factor often was the condition of the army's horses. Not only were the horses often both severely overloaded and malnourished, but many units, especially the regular British cavalry, were ignorant of the most basic principles of animal care. At the same time, the army was often short

of rations and looting, which had been specifically prohibited by Lord Roberts, was condoned. The Canadians, especially the CMR, were generally acknowledged to be "the most accomplished looter[s] in the world." This assessment is supported by private correspondence and diaries. Letter Pte Anderson 8 May; Griesbach 263-4; Abbott 13

22. Hutton to Minto 14 May

23. Turner diary; SP35a Report C 8, Report D 105; *Times History* vol 4, 129

24. Major Sanders later suggested Lt. J.A. Devine, the medical officer, whom he accused of cowardice, had engineered the whole thing, and a deputation of officers had taken a petition to Hutton. However, Sanders had not been with the battalion during the advance, so he could not have made any first-hand knowledge of cowardice. Devine won the DSO on a second tour in South Africa in 1902, not usually an indication of cowardice. As medical officers do not lead troops in action, Miller's suggestion that the MO was the cowardly troop leader, referred to by Griesbach is unsupportable. Allegations of unscrupulous manoeuvering by some of the officers appeared nearly half a century after the event in Griesbach's memoirs. However, Hutton wrote that Evans, the only non-medical officer consulted, had been very reluctant to discuss Herchmer's condition with him. John Ewán, the correspondent for the Toronto *Globe*, reported that Hutton, whom he described as having all the tact of a bull in a china shop, had not been prepared to reinstate Herchmer and had handled the situation badly. There are no indications in Hutton's correspondence with Minto that the decision was based on other than medical grounds, although he may not have told the whole story. The use of a medical board to relieve an officer is not unknown. Whatever his reasons, if Hutton concluded that Herchmer was not fit to command, he was duty bound to act. Hutton to Minto 2 Jun, 20 Jul, 20 Oct; Griesbach 258-9, 268; correspondence Herchmer/Sanders 29 Oct, 17 Nov 1911 cited in Miller 234; Toronto *Globe* 30 Jun 1900

25. SP35a Report C 84; CMR staff diary

26. The RCD advanced 5000 yards under heavy fire without loss. An Australian who fought in the battle wrote that a Canadian regiment feigned withdrawal from the ridge to lure the Boers into an ambush. The feat is not mentioned in Canadian accounts. CMR and RCD staff diaries; Letter Gat Howard 30 Jul; Bartlett 40-3

27. Hart-McHarg 205-7

28. Smith-Dorrien 208-10; Pullen diary; Hart-McHarg 209-10; Churchill 539-43; *Times History* vol 4, 144-7

29. Hart-McHarg 213

30. SP35a Report C 85; Hutton to Minto 2 Jun

31. CMR staff diary; *Times History* vol 4, 155; Griesbach 272

32. RCD staff diary; Hilder ms

33. Hart-McHarg 223

34. McCormick ms

35. SP35a Report A 20-1, 36

Chapter 11 - After Pretoria

1. SP35a 87-8, 107; Griesbach 273-4; *Times History* vol 4, 260, 278

2. *Times History* vol 4, 271-2

3. De Wet's attack caught two RCR officers and their servants en route back to the battalion. Lt J.A. Blanchard was severely wounded and died on 15 June. The Boers held Lt A.H. Macdonnell and his servant prisoner for several weeks. Blanchard was the second and last RCR officer to die in South Africa. Both were from A Company. SP35a 20-1; Hart-McHarg 227-30; Smith-Dorrien 213; De Wet 130-4; *Times History* vol 4, 264-5, 272

4. Smith-Dorrien 215

5. An unpublished biography states Macdonnell's lanyard had caught on a rock and dragged his pistol from its holster and the weapon fired when the hammer struck a rock. Pte Hilder of the RCD reported Macdonnell had dropped his pistol while mounting his horse. Pte Anderson wrote "Capt Mcdonald [sic] shot himself through the stomach with his revolver purely accidental." Hutton reported Macdonnell "was badly wounded during the action while building a Sangar for the protection of one of his posts," while Evans reported Macdonnell was wounded by his own revolver as he was assisting men to cover. RCD and CMR staff diaries; Hutton to Minto 20 Jun; SP35a 114-5; Pte Anderson Letter 19 June; Hilder ms

6. SP35a 107

7. *SAFF Casualty List* 21 Mar-31 Jul 1900 101-3, 137-8; SP35a 114-15; De Wet 130-4, 150

8. SP35a 107, 114-115; CMR staff diary; Evans 200-5

9. SP35a 21-2; Hart-McHarg 229

10. For the first time since Belmont, except for a short time at Bloemfontein, officers and men slept with more than a lone, lousy blanket between them and the sky. Otter also, in an about face, allowed the battalion a canteen. SP35a 21-2

11. Ibid 22

12. By comparison, the Shropshires numbered 680 and the Gordons 597. SP35a 22; Hart-McHarg 229; McCormick ms, Smith-Dorrien 218n

13. Administration was not Roberts' forte and the high command allowed the pillaging to get out of hand. Armies usually address short-term problems by robbing field units of one or two men at a time. Soon, after a succession of one or two men have been siphoned off, the field units are in very dire straits.

14. Young, said to be the shortest man in B Squadron, had seen active service in Afghanistan and the North West Rebellion. He proved on this and other occasions that courage and ability are not measured vertically. SP35a 87; Turner diary; Hutton to Minto 20 Jun; *Times History* vol 4, 345

15. RCD staff diary

16. In his report prepared en route to Canada Lessard wrote that Captain Nelles and seven men were wounded. However, appendix C2 to this report lists Nelles and eight men wounded on 7 July. The *SAFF Casualty List* includes Nelles and six men, one of whom is not on Lessard's list, but omits three other names. A member of the regiment died of disease at Bloemfontein two days later. The RCD suffered one more casualty during this period. On the 8th an unexploded shell struck Lt Young a glancing blow on the head, resulting in his evacuation to England. Young later returned to South Africa to serve with the Army Service Corps. RCD staff diary; Turner diary; Hutton to Minto 19 Jul; SP35a 88, 103; *SAFF Casualty List*

17. Hutton to Minto; Letter Pte Anderson 5 Aug

18. SP35a 22-3; *Times History* vol 4, 389

19. *Times History* vol 4, 395-6

20. Borden's death unleashed a wave of mourning in Canada, and Roberts went so far as to suggest that Borden should have been nominated for the VC for the action in which Turner had won the DSO in May. Dr Miller stretches credibility by attributing the death of the two officers to Hutton's failure to release more troops from his central reserve. Hutton's left and right flanks had been severely pressed, his centre was lightly held, and he had a relatively small reserve. After all is said and done, the important thing was that the counterstroke succeeded, not that a prominent politician's son died. Viljoen 108-9; *SAFF Casualty List* 21 Mar-31 Jul 1900 133, 137; Turner diary; Hutton to Minto 19 July; SP35a 88-9, 104-5; *Times History* vol 4, 395-7; Miller 248

21. After having been relieved at his own request at Kroonstad, Maj Joseph Howe restored his reputation commanding mounted infantry under "Fighting Mac" in the Wittenberg operation. This was not a sign of what Hutton had called "funk" when he had reported on Howe's performance in

South Africa. SP35a 23; Hutton to Minto 30 Oct; Howe application for award of Wittenbergen clasp 30 May, 1902

22. SP35a 24
23. Otter reported the crossing of the Vaal was "very bad." While the bottom was slippery, Lt Winter described the crossing as "fun". It is unlikely Otter was referring to the pompous British major who suffered a dunking in full sight of the greatly amused Canadians or the plight of the floundering players in a British battalion's brass band. SP35a 24; Hart-McHarg 234; McCormick ms; Winter, CDQ 484
24. SP35a 24-5
25. SP35a 25; Hart-McHarg 236-9
26. SP35a 27; Hart-McHarg 238
27. According to Hart-McHarg, who was at Eerste Fabriken, the only officers present were one medical officer, the adjutant, the quartermaster, and three company officers, and two of the last were not consulted. If this is true, four, or at the most six, officers rubber-stamped Otter's decision. SP35a 27-8; Hart-McHarg 243-4, 248; Smith-Dorrien 247-50
28. SP35a 28; Hart-McHarg 244
29. SP35a 28-9; Hart-McHarg 244-5
30. While this may have been true in the case of the reinforcements, the permanent force members were serving under the same terms as the other volunteers. SP35a 28-9; Hart-McHarg 245-7
31. SP35a 26-7, 30; Hart-McHarg 249-61

Chapter 12 - Their Finest Hours

1. RCFA diary
2. CMR diary; Griesbach 288, 298; SAFF *Casualty List* 1 Aug-31 Dec 1900, 79
3. CMR diary
4. By contrast, Hutton (and perhaps Evans) did not have a great deal of confidence in the CMR machine gun section. Hutton described its officer as an unmitigated scoundrel for his habit of leaving unpaid bills along the trail. The errant lieutenant later took command of the D Squadron troop at Aasvogel Krantz, until Evans relieved him in response to a plea from the troop NCOs. CMR diary; Hutton to Minto 30 Oct
5. Sanders, Lt Moodie, and Pte Johnson were wounded while the prisoners were soon released. CMR diary 5 Sept, 10-12; Morrison 219-20
6. CMR diary
7. The Boers, in their ignorance of war, did not realize the implications of wearing British uniforms. Morrison puts Villamon's death in Nov but his description matches an incident logged in the CMR diary on 15 Oct. RCD diary; Turner diary; SP35a 93; Morrison 213-4, 304
8. RCD diary; SP35a 92
9. The action was the first time that Morrison's left section took to the field with the RCD. The diminutive militiaman (and editor of the Ottawa *Citizen*) and his eastern Ontarians were delighted to be united with the dragoons. Hutton described Morrison as "a regular fire eater," and Alderson attempted to persuade him to extend his service in South Africa. Hutton to Minto 30 Oct; Morrison 288
10. RCD diary; SP35a 92; Morrison 225-7
11. The lone Canadian casualty, Pte McCarthy, was a machine gunner. The events do not reflect well on Lessard. First, he did not seem to have any plan except to look for the enemy. Second, it was a mistake to send the field gun back unescorted, in fact, he should have kept the gun with him to help cover his withdrawal. Last, he lost contact with Howard at a key time. It is hard to avoid the

conclusion that he did not have a tight grip on the action. Morrison 229-31; *SAFF Casualty List* 1 Aug-31 Dec, 1900 79

12. SP35a 92; Morrison 236
13. Smith-Dorrien 252; Morrison 249-50
14. Smith-Dorrien 252; SP35a 94-5; Morrison 249-51
15. SP35a 93; Morrison 251-2, 254-5
16. CMR diary
17. Smith-Dorrien 253-4
18. Morrison reported the pom-pom section had stopped to water its horses. RCD diary; SP35a 93; Smith-Dorrien 254; Morrison 252
19. Ibid, 254
20. SP35a 95; *SAFF Casualty List* 1 Aug-31 Dec 1900 2, 19, 59, 65, 79; Morrison 255-6
21. D Bty diary
22. Smith-Dorrien 255-6; Morrison 259
23. Lessard puts the baggage train in the rearguard. However, a rearguard, responsible for keeping the enemy away from the column, would not be encumbered with the baggage train. SP35a 96; Morrison 259
24. Lessard said 3:00 in his official report, but Smith-Dorrien, Evans and Morrison agree on 3:30. CMR diary; SP35a; Smith-Dorrien 256; Morrison 259-60
25. CMR diary
26. Smith-Dorrien 256; SP35a 94; Morrison 260-1
27. RCD diary; CMR diary; SP35a 94; *SAFF Casualty List* 1 Aug-31 Dec 1900 19, 37, 59, 79; Smith-Dorrien 256-7; Morrison 262-3; Robertson 184
28. CMR diary; Smith-Dorrien 256; Morrison 263
29. It appears each troop was divided into two "troops" as Turner wrote of his two troops, and Lessard referred to Cockburn's two troops. Writing nearly five decades later a veteran referred to six half troops. The alternative is four troops as Turner also mentions a troop commanded by Sgt Fuller in addition to his own "two troops." The numbers of Dragoons engaged at any one time supports the first option. Lessard's plan is unclear because he repeated Smith-Dorrien's report in the RCD diary rather than prepare his own summary. RCD diary, statement by Cpl P.R. Price; SP35a 95; Morrison 265, 271; Turner diary; Robertson 189
30. *Times History* vol 4, 513; Robertson 186, 192
31. Robertson 187
32. Ibid 188; Morrison 265
33. I have accepted the Boer figures quoted by Robertson rather than the much higher British and Canadian estimates. CMR diary; Smith-Dorrien 257; Morrison 265; Robertson 188-9
34. Morrison 265-6; *12 Pounder Handbook* 70-5
35. CMR diary; Morrison 266-7; Turner diary; Robertson 190-1
36. Morrison 267-8; Robertson 192
37. RCD diary, statement by Cpl Price
38. CMR diary; Turner diary; Morrison 269-70; Nicholson, *Gunners of Canada* 157
39. RCD diary; D Bty diary; Robertson 196-7; Greenhous 131; Nicholson, *Gunners of Canada* 157
40. At a critical stage of the battle Morrison had told the gun detachment that "we could not go to Canada without the gun." The gunners told him, in no uncertain terms, that they would either save the gun or stay with it. Turner diary; D Bty Left Sect report; Morrison 269
41. CMR diary; Morrison 270-1; Smith-Dorrien 258
42. RCD diary; Greenhous 131

43. Smith-Dorrien 258-9
44. Morrison 274-5
45. The Lancers had left their lances in camp and would soon exchange their carbines for rifles. CMR diary; Smith-Dorrien 260-1; Morrison 276-7
46. Smith-Dorrien 261-6; Morrison 280
47. Smith-Dorrien 262; Morrison 282-3
48. The Canadians joined the Australians in breaking out of camp and going on a colossal tear in Cape Town the night before sailing, a happening conspicuous by its absence from the official reports. Morrison 290, 307

Chapter 13 - The Queen's Cowboys

1. Steele's claim that western horses had difficulty adjusting to the damp air in eastern Canada and on board the ships seems credible, but there is an anomaly. The regiment had spent a month in Ottawa where 10% of the horses had caught and recovered from colds. A team of veterinarians had inspected the animals in Halifax. Several horses were hospitalized, and one was left behind suffering from puerpera, an ailment caused by failure to discharge the afterbirth. The first horse to die of pneumonia, moreover, had been purchased in Montreal. While the CMR had lost only nine of their western horses, or 2%, the SH lost 176 or 27% during the voyage. This figure appears in Steele's report dated 23 Mar 1901, although he reported the losses at 162 in a wire to Lord Strathcona and elsewhere as 173. The average loss of horses and mules at sea during the war was 3.5%. As for the glanders, Steele's explanation that infected horses had previously been quartered at Green Point seems plausible as the symptoms of glanders normally appear ten days to two weeks after infection, except that the first case was reported on 18 Apr, not the 21st, seven days after the regiment moved to Green Point. It is still possible the disease was contracted at Green Point. It is also possible that contaminated fodder was brought on board in Canada. Steele to Strathcona 11 and 18 Apr; Report by Vet-Lt. George Stevenson to Steele; SP35a 161-2; Anglesey 301-2
2. Hutton still included the Strathconas in his plans after this date. Army Order 60, 7 Apr; Hutton to Minto 14 Apr; Orders High Commissioner to Steele 29 May; SP35a 162; Steele 342-4
3. Staff diary; Steele to Strathcona 4, 7, and 12 Jun; SP35a 162; Steele 343-4
4. Other Boers and most British, including the CinC, did not share this view of the difficulties facing Sir Redvers. Both because of his size and the pace of his advance, he was labelled with nicknames such as "Sitting Bull" and "Trek Ox." *Times History* vol 4, 509-11; Anglesey 185-8; Charles Dudley. "The Boer View of Buller: New Evidence", *The Army Quarterly and Defence Journal* vol 114, no 3, July 1981
5. Staff diary; Steele to Strathcona 26 Jul; Steele 345
6. Staff diary; Steele to Strathcona 3 Jul; Viljoen 107
7. Staff diary; Steele to Strathcona, 6 Jul, 4 Aug; SP35a 178; *Ideas* 19
8. Staff diary; Steele to Strathcona 6 Jul; SP35a 163, 178
9. Other than Richardson's gallantry there was little to commend the affair. Intent on luring the Boers into an ambush, Adamson had fallen for one of the oldest tricks in the book. As a result three men were wounded, and two others were captured. The draft had suffered 10% casualties before it joined the regiment on 17 July. Staff diary; Steele to Strathcona 20 Jul; SP35a 179; SAFF *Casualty List* 21 Mar to 31 Jul, 1900 180; Evans 163-4; Fraser 35-6; Miller 318-9
10. Staff diary; Steele to Strathcona 16 Jul and 5 Aug; SP35a 163; SAFF *Casualty List* 130 21 Mar to 31 Jul, 1900; Anglesey 189; *Ideas* 17
11. Steele 347-8
12. Staff diary; Steele to Strathcona 16 Aug

13. Staff diary; SP35a 166; *Natal Field Force Casualty Roll* 231; McCormick ms; Steele 357; Witton 35-7, 83; Miller 323-4
14. Staff diary; *Times History* vol 4, 448-56; Viljoen 114-6
15. Staff diary
16. Staff diary; Report, Leckie to Steele 31 Aug
17. Staff diary; SP35a 163; *Times History* Vol 4, 460-1
18. *The Times History* puts the events one day later than the regimental staff diary. Staff diary; *Times History* vol 4, 462-3
19. A 6-inch gun was too large to be moved fully assembled. The derrick was used to mount and dismount the barrel from the carriage. Without these accessories the gun was so much dead weight. Staff diary; *Times History* vol 4, 465-9; Wilson, vol 1, 186
20. While Steele vehemently denied that his regiment looted, he had too much experience as a policeman and soldier not to know this was untrue. Like the rest of the army, the Strathconas would loot whenever the opportunity presented itself. Moreover, B Squadron of the regiment had operated an abandoned goldmine until the provost marshal shut it down. Staff diary; Steele 350-1; Miller 334-5
21. Staff diary; SP35a 169; *Times History* vol 4, 480-1
22. The quotation is taken from the staff diary. It differs in small details from the quotation in the sessional paper. Staff diary; SP35a 169; *Honours and Awards* 31
23. Staff diary; Steele 352
24. Another version had the men collecting kegs of rum at gun point and then shooting their revolvers to make the provost marshall dance. In a letter dated 14 Oct Lt Morrison of D Battery related an incident at Machadodorp where some Strathconas shot out the provost marshal's lantern. He also wrote that the regiment had painted Pretoria "a delicate heliotrope" and that a common British caution was to threaten to toss someone into a "den of Strathcona's Horse." Staff diary; Morrison 241-2, 305; Miller 338-9; *Ideas* 21
25. The ration scale could not sustain large horses. Staff diary; Anglesey 346, 351
26. Staff diary; Steele 352-3; De Wet 213-5; Kruger 380
27. Staff diary; SP35a 170-1; Steele 353-5; Miller 342-6
28. Staff diary; SP35a 171; De Wet 230; Kruger 392-3; Miller 346-7
29. De Wet failed to mention that his attempt to cross at Commissiedrift was foiled by its small garrison. Staff diary; De Wet 231-3; Kruger 395; Miller 350-1
30. SP35a; Steele 355-7; Hart-McHarg 251; Miller 350-9

Chapter 14 - Other Canadians

1. How many Canadians served outside Canadian units? In an effort to answer the question, I did a gross error check. First I established the casualty rate for the war by dividing the total deaths from all causes (21 942) by the number of men who served in imperial and colonial units (448 165) to arrive at a figure of 4.9 percent. I applied this figure to the number of Canadians who died serving outside the Canadian contingents. My count of Canadian dead includes 90 in the above category. From this method, which is a bit of an educated guess, it seems about 2000 could have served. I have identified about 300 by name and unit, not including members of the South African Constabulary. If this is the case, for every three Canadians who served in the contingents, at least one served in some other unit.
2. Walton 195; *Honours and Awards* 90
3. *Canadian Almanac,* 1900 p 148; Smith letter
4. Kruger 468; DHist 000.9 (D101)

5. Fuller, *The Last of The Gentlemens' Wars* 162, 167, 201-9
6. RG 9 II A.3 vol 22
7. Bapty 29-30; Morrison 287-8
8. Gat Howard's reputation has overshadowed that of Ross, perhaps unfairly. At times he has been confused with Sir Charles Ross, the Ross rifle Ross, who also served in South Africa. Ross was suspected of pocketing the fines he levied for minor transgressions and was later accused of selling captured cattle to the British. RG 9 II A.1 vol 340 docket 20142
9. Moeller 153
10. Smith-Dorrien 276-7; Moeller 162; Bapty 32
11. Capt C.H.L. Beatty, the ADC rode "back to fetch assistance through close and heavy fire; his horse was killed, hit three times." Howard apparently believed that he would not die by a bullet. Settle 524; Pakenham 571; Moeller 166-7; *SAFF Casualty List* Jan-Jun 1901 96-7; *Honours and Awards* 6
12. Hilder ms; DHist memo 6 Mar 56; Pakenham 578

Chapter 15 - The Third and Fourth Contingents

1. SP35a 30
2. Adami 19-20; *Honours and Awards* 21
3. SP35a Suppl 1902 55; Nicholson, *Seventy Years of Service* 51
4. SP35a Suppl 1902 31, 55-6
5. SP35a Suppl 1902 31
6. Pakenham 522-4; Gardyne 449
7. Gardyne 461-2
8. SP35a Suppl 1902 31; *Times History* vol 5, 513-4; De Wet 321
9. SP35a Suppl 1902 56-9
10. *Times History* vol 5, 515
11. SP35a Suppl 1902 34
12. SP35a Suppl 1902 41
13. SP35a Suppl 1902 34
14. *Times History* vol 5, 516-17
15. *Times History* vol 5, 518-19
16. SP35a Suppl 1902 34; *Times History* vol 5, 519
17. SP35a Suppl 1902 35; *Times History* vol 5, 519-20
18. SP35a Suppl 1902 35; *Times History* vol 5, 520
19. SP35a Suppl 1902 35; *Times History* vol 5, 520-1
20. SP35a Suppl 1902 35; *Times History* vol 5, 521-2; CWM Accession 19810845-002 Letter Pte Alex Smith to his mother, 24 May 1902; Letter Pte Harry Ballard to his mother, nd
21. SP35a Suppl 1902 35-6; *Times History* vol 5, 523; Ballard letter
22. SP35a Suppl 1902 36-7; *Times History* vol 5, 524
23. *Times History* vol 5, 523-4
24. SP35a Suppl 1902 36; *Times History* vol 5, 523-4; *SAFF Casualty List 1 Jan 1902 to 31 Mar 1902*
25. SP35a Suppl 1902 37-8; Letter Pte A.J. Brace to Daniel C. Day, nd
26. SP35a Suppl 1902 38; Anglesey 272-5
27. SP35a Suppl 1902 38-9; CWM, Pte Alex Smith to his mother 26 May 1902

BIBLIOGRAPHY

Official Publications

Canada. Department of Militia and Defence. "Further Supplementary Report; Organization, Equipment, Despatch and Service of Canadian Contingents during the War in South Africa, 1899-1902." (Sessional Paper, no 35a.) Ottawa: King's Printer, 1903

_____. "Supplementary Report; Organization, Equipment, Despatch and Service of the Canadian Contingents in South Africa, 1899-1900." (Sessional Paper, no. 35a.) Ottawa: Queen's Printer, 1901

Canada. Parliament. "Copies of Orders in Council, General Orders, Appointments to Office and Militia Orders Affecting the Contingents, in Connection with the Despatch of the Colonial Military Force to South Africa." (Sessional Paper no. 49) Ottawa: Queen's Printer, 1900

_____. "Correspondence Relating to the Despatch of Colonial Military Contingents to South Africa." (Sessional Paper, no. 20, 20a.) Ottawa: Queen's Printer, 1900

Great Britain. War Office. "Regulations for Mounted Infantry" London: HMSO, 1884

_____. "Handbook for the 12-Pr. B.L. 6 CWT. Gun (Marks I-IV and IVa). and Carriages, Marks I*, I**, and II. (Horse Artillery)" London: HMSO, 1905

National Archives of Canada

Official Files

Department of Militia and Defence: RG9 II A.3. Vols 16-35(Departmental correspondence including unit diaries, orders, casualty returns, applications for service); RG 9 II B.3. Vols 15-18 (Militia Orders); RG 24 A.1 and RG 38 1.A. series (service files). Royal Canadian Mounted Police: RG 18 A.1 Vols 176, 180, 187, 202, and 221.

Personal Papers

MG 27 II B-1: Minto Papers Vol 16 (letters from Hutton)

MG 29 Series: E 25 (W.A. Hare); E 85 (Floyd)

MG 30 Series: E 20 (Macdonnell A.C.); E 83 (Leckie); E 84 (Leckie); E 112 (Thompson); E 166 (Strathcona's Horse); E 242(Otter); E 249 (Stewart); E 339 (Hilder); E 356 (Best); E 357(Rooke); E 377 (Vaux); E 397 (Mason); MG 30: E 536 (Morrison-Bell)

MG 55: MG 55/29 no 103 (Howard)

Canadian War Museum

19790733-001 Gamble, Clark N. Letters

19860230-003 Hare, William Archibald. Diary

19870194-008 Pullen, Ernest Fleetwood. Diary

19810845-002 Smith, Alex. Letters

Published Works: Pre-1914

Abbott, J.H.M. *Tommy Cornstalk*. London: Longmans, Green, 1902

Amery, L.S. gen ed. *The Times History of the War in South Africa*, 6 vols. London: Sampson, Low, Marston, various dates

Andrew, Bt-Major A.W. *Cavalry Tactics of Today*. Bombay: Thacker, 1903

Anon. *Handbook of the Boer War*. London: Gale and Polden, 1910

Baden-Powell, Major R.F.S. *War in Practice*. London: Isbister, 1903

Bethell, Colonel H.A. *Modern Guns and Gunnery*, 3rd ed. Woolwich: F.J. Cattermole, 1910

Brown, Harold and E. Sharpe Grew, *War with the Boers*, 5 vols. London: H. Virtue, n.d.

Brown, Stanley McKeown. *With the Royal Canadians*. Toronto: Publishers' Syndicate, 1900

Brunker, Lieut.-Colonel H.M.E. *Hints for Working Out Tactical Problems*, 5th ed. Portsmouth: n.p., 1905

Callwell, Colonel C.E., CB. *The Tactics of Today*. Edinburgh: William Blackwood, 1909

Canadian Almanac, The. For the years 1900, 1901, 1902 and 1903. Toronto: Copp, Clark, 1899, 1900, 1901 and 1902

Canadians in Khaki: South Africa, 1899-1900-Nominal Rolls of the Officers, Non-commissioned Officers & Men of the Canadian Contingents and Strathcona's Horse with Casualties to Date and also R.M.C. Graduates with the Army in South Africa. Montreal: Herald Publishing, 1900

Chambers, Capt. Ernest J. *The Governor-General's Body Guard*. Toronto: E.L. Ruddy, 1902

Childers, Erskine. *In the Ranks of the C.I.V.* London: Smith, Elder, 1901

Colvile, Maj Gen Sir H.E., KCMG, CB *The Work of the Ninth Division*. London: Edward Arnold, 1901

Danes, Richard. *Cassell's History of the Boer War*. London: Cassell, 1901

Creswicke, Louis. *South African and the Transvaal War*, 7 vols. Edinburgh: T.C. & E.C. Jack, 1900-2

Denison, Lt Col George T. *Soldiering in Canada*. Toronto: George M. Morang, 1900

De Wet, Christiaan. *Three Years War*. Westminster: Thomas Constable, 1902

Doyle, Arthur Conan. *The Great Boer War*, rev and enlarged ed. New York: McClure Phillips, 1902

Evans, W. Sanford. *The Canadian Contingents and Canadian Imperialism: a Story and a Study*. Toronto: Publishers' Syndicate, 1901

Everett, Marshall, and H.I. Cleveland. *Thrilling Experiences of the War in South Africa*. Chicago: Educational Company, 1900

German Great General Staff, trans Col W.H.H. Waters, RA, CVO. *The War in South Africa (October 1899 to February 1900)*. London: John Murray, 1904

_____.trans Colonel Hubert Du Cane, RA, MVO. *The War in South Africa (March 1900 to September 1900)*. London: John Murray, 1906

Gwynne, H.A. *The Army on Itself*. London: Frederick Wanne, 1903

Harding, William. *War in South Africa and the Dark Continent from Savagery to Civilization.* Chicago: W.L. Barber, 1902

Hart-McHarg, William. *From Quebec to Pretoria with the Royal Canadian Regiment.* Toronto: W. Briggs, 1902

Hopkins, J. Castell. *South Africa and the Boer-British War; comprising a history of South Africa and its people, including the war of 1899 and 1900.* n.p: n.p, 1900

Hubly, Russell C. *"G" Company. or Every-day Life of the R.C.R., being a Descriptive Account of Typical Events in the Life of the First Canadian Contingent in South Africa.* St John, NB: J. & A. McMillan, 1901

Labat, Gaston P. *Le Livre D'Or (The Golden Book).* Montreal: n.p., 1901

Mackinnon, Maj Gen W.H. *The Journal of the C.I.V. in South Africa.* London: John Murray, 1901

Macleod, Mrs. *For the Flag or Lays and Incidents of the South African War.* Charlottetown: Archibald Irwin, 1901

Mahan, Captain A.T. *The South African War.* New York: Peter Fenelon Collier, 1900

Marquis, T.G. *Canada's Sons on Kopje and Veldt.* Toronto: Canada's Sons Publishing, 1900

Maydon, J.G. *French's Cavalry Campaign.* London: C. Arthur Pearson, 1902

Moeller, Lt B. *Two Years at the Front with the Mounted Infantry.* London: Grant Richards, 1903

Morrison, E.W.B. *With the Guns in South Africa.* Hamilton, Ont.: Spectator Printing, 1901

Otter, Lt Col W.D. *The Guide,* 2nd ed. Toronto: Copp, Clark. 1885

Ridpath, John Clark, LLD, Edward S. Ellis, John A. Cooper, and J.H. Aiken. *The Story of South Africa.* Guelph: World Publishing, n.d.

Settle, J.H. *Anecdotes of Soldiers in Peace and War.* London: Methuen, 1905

Stickney, Albert. *The Transvaal Outlook.* New York: Dodd, Mead, 1900

Stirling, John. *The Colonials in South Africa, 1899-1902: Their Record Based on the Despatches.* Edinburgh: Blackwood, 1907

"Ubique." *Modern Warfare.* London: Thomas Nelson, 1903

Viljoen, Gen Ben. *My Reminiscences of the Anglo-Boer War,* pop ed. London: Hood, Douglas, and Howard, 1903

Wilson, H.W. *With the Flag to Pretoria,* 2 vols. London: Harmsworth Brothers, 1900, 1901

Witton, Lt George. *Scapegoats of the Empire.* n.d., n.p.

Published Works: 1914 and Later

Adami, J. George, MD, FRS. *War Story of the Canadian Army Medical Corps,* vol 1. London: Rolls House Publishing, n.d.

Anglesey, The Marquis of. *A History of British Cavalry, vol 4: 1898-1913.* London: Leo Cooper, 1986

Anon. *The Regimental History of the Governor General's Foot Guards.* Ottawa: n.p., 1948

_____. *Naval Brigades in the South African War 1899-1900*. n.p., n.d. Reprinted by the London Stamp Exchange, n.d.

_____. *Draft History of the Fort Garry Horse*. 1925

_____. "Lillefontein" [sic] in "The Springbok" *Quarterly of the Royal Canadian Dragoons*, Summer 1946

Baker, Anthony. *Battles and Campaigns of the British and Commonwealth Armies*. Shepperton: Ian Allan, 1986

Bapty, Walter. *Memoirs*. Toronto: privately published, 1958

Bartlett, Norman. *Australia at Arms*. Canberra: Australian War Memorial, 1962

Beattie, Kim. *48th Highlanders of Canada, 1891-1928*. Toronto: 48th Highlanders of Canada, 1932

Bell, Ken. *Royal Canadian Military Institute: 100 years 1890-1990*. Toronto: n.p., 1990

Bercuson, David J., and J.L. Granatstein. *Dictionary of Canadian Military History*. Toronto: Oxford University Press, 1992

Birch, James H., Jr, and Henry Davenport Northop. *History of the War in South Africa*. London, Ont: McDermid and Logan, n.d.

Bond, Brian. "Doctrine and Training in the British Cavalry, 1870-1914", in *The Theory and Practice of War*. London: Cassell, 1965

Boss, Lt Col W. *The Stormont, Dundas and Glengarry Highlanders 1783-1951*. Ottawa: n.p., 1952

Brown, Kingsley Sr, Kingsley Brown, Jr and Brereton Greenhous. *Semper Paratus: The History of the Royal Hamilton Light Infantry (Wentworth Regiment) 1862-1977*. Hamilton: The RHLI Historical Association, 1977

Bull, Stewart H. *Queen's York Rangers*. Erin: Boston Mills Press, 1984

Chappell, Mike. *The Canadian Army at War*, 2nd printing. London: Osprey, 1985

Churchill, Winston S. *Frontiers and Wars*. London: Eyre & Spottiswoode, 1962

Crook, Maj E.D., and Maj J. K. Marteinson. *A Pictorial History of the 8th Canadian Hussars (Princess Louise's)*. n.p., 8th Canadian Hussars Regimental Association, 1973

Curchin, Capt Leonard A., and Lt Brian A. Sim. *The Elgins*. St Thomas: privately printed, 1977

De Villiers, Marq. *White Tribe Dreaming*. Toronto: Macmillan, 1987

Denison, Brig Gen S.A., CMG. *Memoirs*. Toronto: T.H. Best, 1927

Dooner, Mildred G. *The Last Post*. London: n.p., 1903, reprinted J.B. Hayward, Polstead, Suffolk, 1980

Duguid, A. Fortescue. *History of the Canadian Grenadier Guards 1760-1964*. Montreal: n.p., 1965

Dynes, Robert J. *The Lee: British Service Rifle from 1898 to 1950*. Bloomfield: Museum Restoration Service, 1979

Farwell, Byron. *The Great Anglo-Boer War*. New York: W.W. Norton, 1990

_____. *Eminent Victorian Soldiers*. New York: W.W. Norton, 1988

Bibliography

_____. *Mr Kipling's Army*. New York: W.W. Norton, 1981

Fetherstonaugh, R.C. *A Short History of the Royal Canadian Dragoons*. Toronto: Southam Press, 1932

_____, with G.R. Stevens. *The Royal Canadian Regiment*, vol 1. Montreal: Gazette Printing, 1936

Fraser, W.B. *Always a Strathcona*. Calgary: Comprint, 1976

Fuller, J.F.C. *The Army in My Time*. London: Rich and Cowan, 1935

_____. *The Last of the Gentlemen's Wars*. London: Faber and Faber, 1936

Gardyne, Lt Col A.D. Greenhill. *The Life of a Regiment: The History of the Gordon Highlanders, vol 3, From 1898 to 1914*. London: Leo Cooper, 1972

Goodspeed, Maj D.J. *Battle Royal, A History of The Royal Regiment of Canada 1862-1962*. Toronto: The Royal Regiment of Canada Association, 1962

Gordon, Maj Lawrence L. *British Battles and Medals*. Aldershot: Gale and Polden, 1950

Gouin, Jacques, and Lucien Brault. *Legacy of Honour*. Toronto: Methuen, 1985

Greenhous, Brereton. *Dragoon: the Centennial History of the Royal Canadian Dragoons, 1883-1983*. Ottawa: Guild of the Royal Canadian Dragoons, 1983

Grey, Jeffrey. *A Military History of Australia*. Cambridge: Cambridge University Press, 1990

Griesbach, W.A. *I Remember*. Toronto: Ryerson Press, 1946

Griess, Thomas E. "A Case Study in Counterinsurgency: Kitchener and the Boers," in *New Dimensions in Military History*. San Rafael: Presidio Press, 1975

Gwyn, Sandra. *The Private Capital*. Toronto: McClelland and Stewart, 1984

Hall, D.O.W. *The New Zealanders in South Africa 1899-1902*. Wellington: War History Branch, Department of Internal Affairs, 1949

Harding, William. *War in South African and the Dark Continent*. Chicago: H.L. Barber, n.d.

Hare, Maj Gen Sir Steuart. *The Annals of the King's Royal Rifle Corps*, vol 4. London: John Murray, 1929

Haycock, Ronald G. *Sam Hughes*. Waterloo, Ont: Wilfrid Laurier University Press, 1986

Hutchinson, Col Paul P. *Canada's Black Watch*. Montreal: The Black Watch (R.H.R.) of Canada, 1965

Jackson, Lt Col H.M. *The Royal Regiment of Artillery, Ottawa, 1855-1952*. Ottawa: n.p., 1952

Judd, Denis. *The Boer War*. London: Hart-Davis, MacGibbon, 1977

Kruger, Rayne. *Goodbye Dolly Gray*. London: Pan, 1983

Lee, Emanoel. *To the Bitter End*. Hammondsworth: Penguin, 1986

Macleod, R.C. *The North-West Mounted Police and Law Enforcement*. Toronto: University of Toronto Press, 1976

McCormick, A.S. *The "Royal Canadians" in South Africa, 1899-1902*. n.p., n.d.

Miller, Carman. *The Canadian Career of the Fourth Earl of Minto*. Waterloo, Ont: Wilfrid Laurier University Press, 1980

_____. *Painting the Map Red, Canada and the South African War 1899-1902*. Montreal: McGill-Queen's University Press, 1993

Miller, Sarah Gertrude. *The People of South Africa,* 2nd ed. London: Constable, 1953

Mitchell, D.G., W. Simcock, and B.A. Reid. *RCHA-Right of the Line.* Ottawa: RCHA History Committee, 1986

Morton, Desmond. *The Canadian General, Sir William Otter.* (Canadian War Museum Historical Publication Number 9.) Toronto: Hakkert, 1974

_____. *Ministers and Generals: Politics and the Canadian Militia, 1868-1904.* Toronto: University of Toronto Press, 1970

Nicholson, G.W.L. *Seventy Years of Service.* Ottawa: Borealis, 1977

_____. *Canada's Nursing Sisters.* Toronto: Samuel Stevens Hakkert, 1975

_____. *The Gunners of Canada: the History of the Royal Regiment of Canadian Artillery,* vol 1. Toronto: McClelland and Stewart, 1967

Pakenham, Thomas. *The Boer War.* New York: Random House, 1979

Pemberton, W. Baring. *Battles of the Boer War.* London: Pan Books, 1972

Phillips, R., and S.J. Kirby. *Small Arms of the Mounted Police.* Ottawa: Museum Restoration Service, 1965

Prescott, John F. *In Flanders Fields, The Story of John McCrae.* Erin: Boston Mills Press, 1985

Reitz, Deneys. *Commando.* London: Faber and Faber, 1968

Reynolds, Maj E.G.B. *The Lee-Enfield Rifle.* London: Herbert Jenkins, 1960

Robertson, Hugh. *The Royal Canadian Dragoons and the Anglo-Boer War, 1900.* 1982. MA Thesis, University of Ottawa

Roncetti, Gary A., CD, and Edward E.Denby. *The Canadians: Those who served in South Africa, 1899-1902.* privately printed

Ross, David, and Robin May. *The Royal Canadian Mounted Police 1873-1987.* London: Osprey, 1988

Schragg, Captain Lex. *History of the Ontario Regiment, 1866-1951.* n.p., 1951

Sixsmith, Maj Gen E.K.G. *British Generalship in the Twentieth Century.* London: Arms and Armour Press, 1970

Smith, Eugene W. *Passenger Ships of the World, Past and Present.* Boston: George H. Dean Company, 1963

Smith-Dorrien, Gen Sir Horace. *Memoirs of Forty-Eight Years Service.* London: John Murray, 1925

South African War Honours and Awards 1899-1902. (reprint of 1902 edition) London: Arms and Armour Press, 1971

South Africa Field Force Casualty List 1899-1902. (reprint) Oaklands, 1972

South African War Casualty Roll: The Natal Field Force, 20th Oct 1899-26th Oct 1900. (reprint) Polstead: J.B. Hayward, 1980

Stanley, George F.G. *Canada's Soldiers, 1604-1954: the Military History of an Unmilitary People.* Toronto: Macmillan, 1954.

Steele, Samuel B. *Forty Years in Canada.* Toronto: McGraw-Hill Ryerson, reissued 1972

Bibliography

Stone, Jay, and Erwin A. Schmidl. *The Boer War and Military Reforms*. New York: University Press of America, 1988

Tascona, Bruce. *XII Manitoba Dragoons: A Tribute*. n.p., n.d.

Upper Canada Historical Arms Society. *The Military Arms of Canada*. Bloomfield: Museum Restoration Service, 5th printing, 1986

Walton, Colonel Peter S., *Scarlet into Khaki*. London: Greenhill Books, 1988 (reprint with additions of: Grierson, James Moncrieff, *The British Army*, by a Lt Col in the British Army. London: Sampson Low, Marston, 1899)

Whitton, Lt Col Frederick Ernest, CMG. *The History of the Prince of Wales's Leinster Regiment (Royal Canadians)*. Aldershot: Gale & Polden, 1924

Williams, Jeffery. *Byng of Vimy, General and Governor General*. London: Leo Cooper, 1983

Winter, Brig Gen C.F. "Some Recollections of Service with the Imperials," *Canadian Defence Quarterly*, vol 4, no 4, July 1927

Miscellaneous

Anderson, William E. Letters (courtesy RCD Archives)

Canadian Broadcasting Corporation. "Patriots, Scalawags and Saturday-night Soldiers," Ideas 25, 26 Sep 1991

Howard, Arthur L. Letters (courtesy RCD Archives)

Smith, Herbert Carrington. Letters (courtesy R. Guy Carrington Smith)

Tweddell, W. Diary (courtesy RCR Museum)

Index